3c

½ Ingram 50⁰⁰

Immigration, Assimilation, and Border Security

Yoku Shaw-Taylor

GOVERNMENT INSTITUTES
an imprint of
THE SCARECROW PRESS, INC.
Lanham • Toronto • Plymouth, UK
2012

325.73 SHA

Government Institutes

Published by Government Institutes
An imprint of The Scarecrow Press, Inc.
A wholly owned subsidiary of The Rowman & Littlefield Publishing Group, Inc.
4501 Forbes Boulevard, Suite 200, Lanham, Maryland 20706
www.govinstpress.com

Estover Road, Plymouth PL6 7PY, United Kingdom

British Library Cataloguing in Publication Information Available

Library of Congress Cataloging-in-Publication Data
Shaw-Taylor, Yoku.
  Immigration, assimilation, and border security / Yoku Shaw-Taylor.
     p. cm.
  Includes index.
  ISBN 978-1-60590-719-2 (cloth : alk. paper) —
  ISBN 978-1-60590-720-8 (electronic)
  1. Border security—United States. 2. United States—Emigration and immigration—History. 3. United States—Emigration and immigration—Government policy.
  4. Immigration enforcement—United States. I. Title.
  JV6483.S537 2011
  325.73—dc23   2011044810

∞™ The paper used in this publication meets the minimum requirements of American National Standard for Information Sciences—Permanence of Paper for Printed Library Materials, ANSI/NISO Z39.48-1992.

Printed in the United States of America

Contents

Acknowledgments

I am grateful to Crystal D. Williams and Zack A. Wilske of the United States Citizenship and Immigration Service History Office and Library for access to historical and current immigration statistics. I am grateful to Linda B. Cullen, Mark Hempstead, and Tamara L. B. Wilson of the Customs and Border Protection Information Resources Center for assistance with locating historical documents on the Customs Service. I am grateful to James Tourtellote, Gerald L. Nino, Charles Csavossy, and Greg Gorman of the Customs and Border Protection Division of Communications for use of photos from the border. I thank *Frontline Magazine* for use of archived frontline photos of Customs operations. I thank Jolene Milot Lorch, curator of the History Division of Customs and Border Protection, and the Virginia Department of Historic Resources State Historic Preservation Office for information on historic Customs houses. I thank Don Philpott, my acquisitions editor, for encouragement, feedback on early drafts and assistance with locating sources. I thank Blair Andrews, associate editor, for reviewing the manuscript. I am indebted to my dear wife and best friend, Elaine, for reading and editing the manuscript and for suggestions that improved the book. I thank my daughters, Anaya and Egjayba, for being patient troupers over the past year as I devoted long hours to researching and writing.

Introduction

The Science of Border Security, the Science of Society

The science of securing the border is based on more than two hundred years of regulatory operations and enforcement actions to deter and detect noncompliance of travel and trade laws at the border. From its inception, the U.S. Customs Service has been tasked with the formidable responsibility of developing and perfecting the activities of border security, first under the auspices of the Department of the Treasury, and now under the Department of Homeland Security (DHS). Over the years, the service has evolved and produced a body of organized knowledge and practices that explain the prevalence and incidence of border events and predict patterns of trade and travel. The scope of operations is defined by the large expanse of the land and maritime border of the United States of America. There was formal realization that the service faced considerable challenges in securing the border many years after its creation. In 1853, then–secretary of the treasury James Guthrie wrote that:

> The border line is so extensive as to make it utterly impossible to cover the whole or even all the points on it favorable to the illicit introduction of merchandise; . . . so far as it has been tried, the expense appears hardly to have been compensated for by the advantages. The persons employed, being generally employed in other business and giving but limited and incidental attention to the safety of the revenue.[1]

As early as 1791, collectors, inspectors and surveyors of the service (as they were called then) were conducting enforcement actions along the border. The officers of the service had to intercept smugglers and collect revenue even as the basic administrative structure was being established. A seizure report filed in 1791 from Boston described actions taken against a vessel from the Bahamas Islands that had reached shore at Tarpaulin Cove with bags of cotton:

> The same vessel came into this port and entered without reserve. The surveyor, afterwards mentioned to the master the hint we had received. At first, he absolutely denied that fact but afterwards, finding us possessed of certain facts, he acknowledged his error. Hereon we brought action against him and his mate for one thousand dollars as directed by the statute.[2]

During those early years, operational guidance came from the executive leadership at the Department of the Treasury in the form of circulars that gave instructions on how to intercept noncompliance of customs laws and how to conduct inspections. The administrative mandates and instructions below come from a letter in 1829 from then–secretary of the treasury Samuel Ingham to all districts:

> Your attention is especially required to a strict examination of the packages shipped coastwise, and also of the evidence produced to show that the duties have been paid on such packages, and particularly those which may be shipped or otherwise transported from ports or places near the line between the United States and the British Possession in North America. . . . You will communicate to this Department, from time to time, any information in relation to actual or contemplated violations of the Revenue Laws, that may come to your knowledge not only within your district but at any other place.[3]

The Bureau of Customs and Border Protection (CBP) continues to make significant contributions to the security of our nation—the tasks of CBP officers at the borders require vigilance and diligence. These operational mandates have perhaps not changed substantively from the early years when the Customs Service was created. Present-day CBP officers describe incidents at the border and how they hone their skills in identifying fraud, counterfeit and false personas presenting at the ports. The important tasks of collecting duties and facilitating trade and travel go hand in hand with intercepting counterfeit goods and false personas. Officers must be well versed in the codes and regulations contained in the Harmonized Tariff Schedule of the United States that govern their many intersecting activities and operations. The schedule is published every year and catalogues all trade agreements and rules based on an international classification system encompassing schedules for more than two hundred countries. In the field, the officers also conduct analyses and inspections of cargo shipments to appraise and determine the value of goods and certify the correct amount of duties to be paid. While 100 percent inspections are an operational impossibility, present-day officers must be diligent about identifying shipments and people who have to be examined or questioned further.

Officers receive extensive training in detection techniques, interrogations and enforcement and become knowledgeable about counterterrorism, critical incident management, when to use force, contraband interdiction, tactical team missions, search and rescue, and apprehension operations. CBP analysts utilize time-series methods to identify associations between seizures and seasonality patterns, and to track patterns of performance at the field offices. The science of border security explains how we defend and deter threats at the border through screenings, inspections, reporting and application of new methods in detection. This requires a trained workforce; advance knowledge of people and goods that come through the border post; effective inspections that require flexibility and streamlining; focused awareness of capabilities and vulnerabilities; improved controls for effective performance of activities; and finally, successful implementation and application of knowledge and emergent technologies.[4]

To understand the reasons behind present-day border operations, we must understand our society and its social facts. This science of society explains our American experience and the context of CBP's operations. It is also a kind of sense making, or simply, how we make sense of the routines of our lives within the multicultural and plural American space where our differences challenge us to overcome simplified conceptions and images of one another. We must overlay the science of border security with the science of society—and the particular impact of immigration in our American homeland. This is the nexus of border security and immigration.

The immigrant history of our American society is the context within which border security is organized. This refers to how immigration has shaped our American identity and our understanding of the fundamental ideas about society in general—how we learn to think and behave in patterns that are recognizable to others within our society (culture) and how we learn to recognize signifiers of capacity and influence (power). It is how groups or societies become functional through coordinated and integrated activities or not, as a matter of degree (social structure). We find out about how we achieve solidarity through our shared experiences and how we become socialized to conform in our actions and interactions, if not always in our thinking. Conformity is not uniform; there are always deviations from what is acceptable and there are varying degrees of deviance. These foundational ideas are social facts:

> Social facts are enduring properties of social life that shape or constrain the actions individuals take. Because they are properties of social life, they cannot be located in the isolated individual but instead appear as external even though individuals participate in them. . . . Although social facts are relatively stable

and enduring, they are never completely fixed. . . . Human beings can change
their world and the way they live. As a result, sociologists are always confronted
with new phenomena to describe and explain.[5]

Social facts help us understand the American experience and its impact
on border security—particularly, how specific laws have moderated the flow
of immigration, how our culture assimilates new immigrants and how our
norms, values, beliefs and concerns about security influence targeting operations at the border to reduce threats and vulnerabilities to our homeland.
This science of society explains the correlation between immigration and
prejudice and stereotype, as well as the relationships among the many and
different ethnic and racial groups that constitute our American character, and
it gives us insights about admissibility of new immigrants and their eventual
transformation into Americans.

The immigrant experience in America is the ethos of assimilation and how
we have become a great nation of one people based on our norms, values and
beliefs. It is this that the science of society explains.

This book discusses what we know about ensuring our security—at the
border and then within the homeland—and what we know about the production of our American reality based on our vibrant natural history of immigration and assimilation and its unfortunate corollary of prejudice. Chapter 1
describes the movement of people and goods and its connectedness to our
human terrain. Chapter 2 tracks the history of CBP and its component inspection responsibilities including customs, immigration and agriculture. Chapter
3 provides the required narrative of our past with discussions of current issues
including immigration reform, undocumented immigration and the so-called
new Americans. Chapter 4 discusses the socializing routines of assimilation and the creation of our identities; we become an inclusive, ecumenical
America based on the variations in our identities. Chapter 5 is the participant
observer's notes. This chapter is based on reconstructions of conversations
describing the scope and complications of operations at the border. The
concluding chapter takes us beyond the border into the homeland. By way
of closure, chapter 6 discusses security engagements beyond the border and
making sense of our vulnerabilities, so we can predict the evolving threats we
face. There are two appendices that add value: the first appendix catalogues
immigration laws to show the progression and evolution of our policies
regarding immigration since 1790. The second appendix contains reference
tables depicting the patterns of immigrant settlement by state, scope of immigration inspections and enforcement actions.

NOTES

1. U.S. Customs Service. 1988. A history of enforcement in the United States Customs Service 1789–1875. Historical Study No. 6. Washington, DC: U.S. Department of Treasury, p. 29.

2. Ibid., p. 36.

3. Ibid., p. 61.

4. U.S. Customs and Border Protection. 2006. Securing America's borders at ports of entry: Office of Field Operations strategic plan fy 2007–2011. Washington, DC: U.S. Customs and Border Protection.

5. Craig Calhoun, Donald Light, and Suzanne Keller. 1997. Sociology, 7th ed. New York: McGraw-Hill, p. 16.

Chapter 1

To Protect the Border,
to Facilitate Travel and Trade

Within a span of forty-five seconds to one minute, an encounter between a traveler and a CBP officer at the ports of entry (POE) will involve two powerful interaction dimensions; the social exchange will represent linked processes to (1) facilitate trade and travel and (2) contain vulnerabilities and deter threats. The social encounter will also encapsulate the natural history of (3) assimilation and resocialization of the core values, norms and beliefs expressed in our policies toward new immigrants and our national mood about threats within the homeland and (4) how attitudes and actions diminish or elevate the incidence of prejudice and stereotype that manifest as discrimination and group profiling. These linked dimensions of that representative and signal social encounter are shown in figure 1.1.

TRADE AND TRAVEL

The Bureau of Customs and Border Protection plays a vital role in the free-market economy of the United States. The bureau (1) collects duty payments on legitimate trade and commerce, (2) facilitates flow of lawful immigrants and nonimmigrants or all travelers across the northern and southwestern borders and (3) secures the border from threats to travelers and the public. In 2009, $1.5 trillion in goods and services flowed through the POEs, generating about $34 billion in customs value in the form of duty payments. Each year an average volume of over $1 trillion of exports and imports flows through some of these POEs. There are almost 80,000 shipments of goods and 5,500 cargo containers processed each day.[1] The majority of cargo is conveyed by trucks and vessels; the rest is carried by railcars and aircraft. International

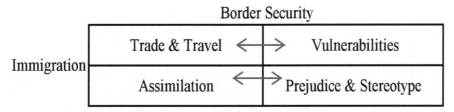

Figure 1.1. The intersection of border security and immigration.

trade is what makes the U.S. economy tick, and CBP plays a necessary role in processing these goods and maintaining the system that allows for an open marketplace. We rely on international trade and tourism and the officers at the border are accountable for processing the goods and people who pass through the POEs each day.

In 2009, 327 POEs—including land, air and sea—processed about 360 million passengers and 120 million cars, trucks, rail cars and cargo containers. This amounts to about one million passengers and pedestrians, including over 240,000 air passengers, and over 270,000 conveyances a day.[2] Overall, about 1 percent of travelers are denied entry. In 2009, approximately 88 million passengers were processed at the airports, 17 million passengers were processed at the seaports and over 257 million passengers were processed at POEs along 5,500 miles of the northern land border with Canada and 1,970 miles of southern land border with Mexico. This means that approximately 75 percent of travelers use the land ports as entry points.

These statistics are typical of the workload of CBP, although there are fluctuations from year to year. Revenues accruing from the tourism industry that relies on passenger processing at the borders are about $99.1 billion[3] and the industry employs about seven million people. Each year millions of visitors, tourists and nonimmigrants come from all around the world.

The current dispensation of border security combines three streams: legal immigration, customs, and agriculture inspections of plants and animals. Historically, these three operations have regulated the flow of commerce and people—to promote the growth of the American free-market economy and maintain the freedoms of a democratic society. The free-market system allows for bargains and competitive exchange of goods. Travelers and tourists come because of the alloy of American culture—diverse and dynamic. They travel to the United States because of the promise and opportunities in education and business. Each year more than four hundred million visits are made to the United States by travelers from countries all over the world. Over the past five years, an average of six million nonimmigrant visas were issued by the U.S. Department of State annually.[4]

VULNERABILITIES

Border security in its two basic forms—screenings and inspections of people and goods—is a balancing act of ensuring the free flow of commerce and travel and keeping counterfeit goods, contraband and false personas out. At the POE, officers must conduct three critical duties: screen passengers and commercial traffic, determine eligibility for lawful entry, and collect the proper duties and fees in short order to expedite the movement of people and goods across the border.

The American free and open market is not without risks; at the same time that CBP and its sister agencies facilitate commerce and travel, there is the corollary of deterring threats and containing our vulnerabilities. With the responsibility of enforcing trade laws, immigration policy and agricultural regulations, the approximately twenty thousand officers at the POEs, including designated land borders, airports and seaports, have to ensure that requirements are met for all the variety of traffic flowing through the borders. At the POE, CBP officers are the first line of defense against outside threats to the safety of our public health and agricultural infrastructure. In 2009, CBP made approximately 39,000 arrests of criminals at POEs, refused entry to 224,840 inadmissible travelers, apprehended approximately 781,000 illegal travelers at and between POEs, and seized approximately 26,000 fraudulent documents. In addition, seizures of undeclared or illicit currency totaled about $110,000,000, illegal drug seizures amounted to about 2,400,000 kilograms and there were 1,700,000 seizure incidents involving agricultural officers who intercepted prohibited plant, meat or animal byproducts and agricultural pests.[5] The bureau is also authorized to inspect and seize, if warranted, electronic media such as phones, video cameras, laptop computers, thumb drives and other types of portable electronic media in the federal inspection sections at the POEs.

CBP officers also review and inspect thousands of manifests from parcels arriving from all around the world at international mail facilities each day. At the POE each day, officers have to evaluate the relative risks of allowing the entry of cargo and people—they must be able to spot illegal or harmful materials and keep out potentially dangerous people. These responsibilities include intercepting the flow of illegal weapons, drugs and currency. The officers are at some risk of violence as well. At certain POEs with low volume of traffic, officers must be on the lookout for port runners—those who openly evade a customs inspection at a POE by ramming their vehicles through the border post.

Inspections at the airports and seaports are aided by the availability of advance information that allows officers to conduct checks against existing security databases. The seaports process the vast majority of the cargo that arrives in the country. Advance manifest information (see below) is important for screening, inspecting and examining cargo shipments before they arrive at our borders; but the same process of advance checking does not occur at the land borders where millions of passengers pass through. The land borders have programs (see below) that expedite travel through prior screening. And yet the uncomfortable truth is that because of the sheer volume of passengers and conveyances at the land borders, it is impossible to screen and inspect every passenger or vehicle that comes through the border post. To inspect every passenger or conveyance would slow commerce to a crawl; this would have a ripple effect as goods and travelers would not be able to arrive on time. The costs of a slow commercial process would be catastrophic for our economy. At the same time, the officers must be unremitting in ensuring the safety of all travel and trade.

Officers utilize technologies that can detect improvised explosive devices (IEDs), portable harmful weapons and chemical, biological and radiological agents, illegal drugs, ammunitions, undeclared currency, and human trafficking. Since the creation of DHS, extant programs have been improved and new programs have been created to enhance the security infrastructure at the border. Some of these programs are described below in alphabetical order:[6]

- Admissibility Review Office (ARO) provides agency-wide uniform oversight for evaluating admissibility and inadmissibility. The ARO reviews waiver requests for nonimmigrants to travel legally and all government nonimmigrant waiver requests under the Immigration and Nationality Act (INA).
- Advance Passenger Information System (APIS) is the prenotification information system for commercial and private aircraft. The system covers both departures and arrivals and relies on biographical and travel information for primarily air and sea passengers and (in limited cases) for land passengers traveling on commercial buses and on trains.
- Air and Marine of CBP combines aerial and maritime surveillance in detecting and identifying threats and illegal activities at the border. This is an integrated program that uses advanced communication equipment and sensors for interdictions.
- Automated Commercial Environment (ACE) is a system for processing cargo. It consolidates information on international trade and transportation and expedites and enhances security through an integrated submission system.
- Automated Targeting System (ATS) is used to review the bill of lading and manifest data. The ATS is used to collect, analyze and disseminate information so as to deter threats from entering the United States. ATS is also used by CBP to identify other violations of U.S. laws.

- Border Intelligence Centers (BICs) are dedicated to analysis and dissemination and sharing of intelligence on weapons, smugglers, and human trafficking.
- Border Patrol Checkpoint Operations is a program that conducts traffic checks at certain points between POEs along the border, located within about one hundred miles of the border. This is part of the roving activities of Border Patrol to reduce smuggling. These operations also involve the use of the Vehicle and Cargo Inspection System (VACIS), which is a nonintrusive inspection mechanism.
- Canine enforcement teams use highly trained and specialized detector dogs to identify concealed weapons and explosives. The dogs also perform rescue missions.
- Caribbean Border Interagency Group (CBIG) addresses illegal immigration of Cuban migrants to Puerto Rico.
- The Carrier Liaison Program (CLP) is managed by the Fraudulent Document Analysis Unit (FDAU), which is responsible for reducing the number of inadmissible passengers traveling to the United States in partnership and cooperation with other countries. This is another program to detect and deter the use of fraudulent travel documents.
- Consolidated Trusted Traveler Program (CTTP) covers all programs that expedite travel for enrollees who have been deemed low risk through verification of identification, biometric validation and screening. These programs include NEXUS (on the northern land border), SENTRI (on southwest land border), Free and Secure Trade program or FAST (commercial carriers) and Global Entry. The Global Entry program offers frequent air travelers expedited processing at selected preclearance and U.S. airports. The CTTP is meant to free up officers at the border to concentrate on other travelers who may pose higher risks. The program enhances security by allowing CBP officers to concentrate their efforts on potentially higher-risk travelers and goods.
- Container Security Initiative (CSI) provides a system for identifying and examining containers that pose a security risk; this includes partnerships with foreign governments that allow officers to work within counterpart countries to screen containers. CBP obtains a bill of lading and manifest information on vessel containers twenty-four hours before containers are loaded and shipped to the United States. The United States reciprocates this arrangement with partner countries, so that they have the opportunity to send their customs officers to POEs of the United States. CSI uses advance targeting information, prescreening and advanced detection technologies.
- Cooperative enforcement efforts—Operation Jumpstart originally started on June 15, 2006, and ended on July 15, 2008, and involved the use of

National Guard troops to support border patrol. The program was reauthorized in August 2010.

- Customs-Trade Partnership Against Terrorism (C-TPAT) is a program that monitors the security process in the supply chain of cargo shipments. As part of the program, partner countries are required to monitor security practices and verify that security guidelines have been followed before shipment. The process involves supply chain security specialists (SCSSs) from partner countries who collaborate on validating security processes in the supply chain.
- Electronic System for Travel Authorization (ESTA) allows DHS to determine eligibility to travel to the United States under the auspices of the Visa Waiver Program (VWP). Under ESTA, DHS is able to determine whether there are any security risks associated with travelers seeking to enter the United States. The program is meant to add another level of security through advance assessment of risk. Enrollees are screened against lookout databases.
- Expedited removal program put to an end the practice of "catch and release" where some aliens were released after apprehension with the agreement to appear at a hearing. The program involves mandatory detention of cases who can be removed without immigration hearing.
- Forward operating bases (FOBs) is a program to enable Border Patrol officers to deploy to areas between POEs that are relatively inaccessible. The program allows CBP officers to increase operational control of the border.
- The Fraudulent Document Analysis Unit of CBP (FDAU) analyzes fraudulent travel documents seized by the bureau. The unit is responsible for ensuring that these fraudulent documents are not in circulation. The FDAU works collaboratively with other DHS agencies such as the Transportation Security Administration (TSA) and the Citizenship and Immigration Services (USCIS).
- Immigration Advisory Program (IAP) is a cooperative initiative with foreign governments and commercial airlines to identify travelers who are deemed high risk and prevent them from boarding. The program uses advanced analysis and targeting.
- Integrated Border Enforcement Teams (IBETs) are mobile response resources combining air, land and marine. There are five core agencies that coordinate law enforcement operations including CBP Office of Border Patrol (OBP), Immigration and Customs Enforcement (ICE), U.S. Coast Guard (USCG), the Royal Canadian Mounted Police (RCMP) and Canada Border Services Agency.
- International Liaison Unit (ILU) facilitates active and progressive collaboration with foreign counterparts working toward greater border security.

The ILU has been instrumental in the response to border violence on the southwest border and the Operation Against Smugglers Initiative on Safety and Security (OASISS) that was a U.S.-Mexican agreement for prosecuting criminal cases.

- Model Ports of Entry Program was created to enhance the efficiency in processing passengers and to reduce wait times for legitimate travel at some of the busiest airports without compromising security measures. The increase in security checks has contributed to longer wait times for processing at the border generally, but more acutely at the airports. At the airports, wait times are measured by calculating the time it takes to process the last passenger on the flight after the plane arrives and is blocked at the terminal. Wait times generally vary by time of year (seasonality), day of the week and time of day. Efficiencies are achieved through queue management and informational videos to greet travelers and to provide guidance. Selected international airports are: New York (JFK), Miami, Los Angeles, Newark, Chicago (O'Hare), Honolulu, San Francisco, Atlanta, Dallas/Ft. Worth, Orlando, Detroit, Boston, Las Vegas, Sanford (Florida), Seattle, Philadelphia, San Juan and Ft. Lauderdale.
- National Targeting Center–Cargo (NTCC) is a counterpart to the National Targeting Center–Passenger (NTCP) that focuses on collecting targeting data and information on cargo-related activities for all modes of conveyance. The center works collaboratively with the Food and Drug Administration, (FDA), the Department of Agriculture, and U.S. Coast Guard (USCG).
- The NTCP is dedicated to providing research to support antiterrorism efforts. The program collects information on admissibility of nonimmigrants and identifies security and public health risks. The NTCP works collaboratively with the Federal Bureau of Investigation (FBI), TSA, and Terrorist Identities Datamart Environment (TIDE).
- Non-Intrusive Inspection (NII) relies on technologies such as radiation portal monitors (RPMs) and personal radiation detectors (PRDs) to detect radioactive materials, and gamma-ray and X-ray imaging systems to scan the contents of those containers which have been flagged as security risks for contraband such as illegal drugs, weapons, explosives, ammunition and human smuggling. Equipment using NII technology is deployed after the reviews have been conducted using the ATS.
- Operation Streamline involves several offices of DHS and Department of Justice (DOJ) to prosecute and remove illegal aliens and threats.
- Remote video surveillance systems (RVSS) are operated by the OBP and complement the operations of Air and Marine and the Unmanned Aircraft

System (UAS) program. RVSSs are deployed on both land borders and provide advanced detection technologies to spot illegal activities between POEs. The RVSSs include static and mobile video systems.

- Secure Border Initiative (SBI) is the framework to foster improved communications and integration of systems (SBI*net*), implement and maintain standard practices, and develop infrastructure to secure the borders. This includes the construction of virtual and actual fences (mainly on the southwest border).
- Secure Freight Initiative (SFI) provides another level of security to the supply chain before shipments reach the U.S. border. It incorporates the International Container Security (ICS) program and Security Filing. The SFI allows for improved screening of cargo using NII and other integrated equipment. The SFI deploys technology that is able to detect weapons of mass effect (WME) in maritime cargo.
- Threat-based surge operations are run by the OBP to contain threats and risks between POEs.
- The UAS is a program that supplements the Air and Marine operations. The UAS surveils the southwest border to detect smuggling activities (especially under the cover of darkness) and to gather intelligence on illegal operations in remote areas between POEs.
- U.S. Visitor and Immigrant Status Indicator Technology (US-VISIT) uses advanced equipment at primary and secondary inspection stations to detect fraud by providing unalterable and unique information on traveler identity.
- Western Hemisphere Travel Initiative (WHTI) strengthens the infrastructure of detection and reduces security risks at the border by requiring all travelers to present a passport or other approved documents that signify identity and citizenship when entering the United States. The requirement provides another level of security because it ensures reliability in the identification technologies and methods used by officers at the border to verify the documents of travelers.

An integral part of these programs is the effort to maintain cybersecurity in the aviation and maritime sectors. The computer-reliant infrastructure of border security reduces and mitigates disruptions in trade and travel. Additionally, the autonomous operations of the CBP are aided by the World Customs Organization (WCO), which has established the Standards to Secure and Facilitate Global Trade to help safeguard legitimate global trade from terrorism and crime. The WCO standards unify international efforts and procedures to maintain safety. Many of these programs were recommended by the National Commission on Terrorist Attacks upon the United States created in November 2002 by President George W. Bush.

Officers at the border also rely on their experience from processing several thousands of travelers and the ability, based on this expansive knowledge of traveler demeanor, to detect deception based on facial or behavioral cues, or to identify certain telltale signs of a nervous traveler who may be trying to conceal something. Kinesic analysis is an important part of current research[7] to detect concealed intent. This falls within the orbit of work being done by researchers to detect emotions from facial signs or microexpressions. These techniques include automated identification of nonverbal gestures to determine a traveler's intent (also known as automated intent determination) and speech act profiling, which is a method of analyzing and visualizing conversations. Speech act profiling is useful for detecting deception because deceivers often exhibit telltale communication patterns. However, the accuracy of deception detection can be chancy. The odds of detecting deception are sometimes no more than 0.5 according to researchers, indicating that it has the same odds as flipping a coin and landing on heads. The indicators of deception are oftentimes subtle, dynamic and "micro." Officers who have to determine whether a traveler is telling the truth must rely on tracking cues or configurations of the face and body that can be linked to certain emotional states.

Figure 1.2. The Port of Los Angeles/Long Beach is the largest and busiest port in the United States, handling about 45 percent of all containers processed by Customs and Border Protection. Photo by Charles Csavossy.

Figure 1.3. Protecting America's agricultural resources. These Miami-based CBP agriculture specialists inspect incoming flowers as part of the pre-Valentine's Day rush. Photo courtesy of CBP.

Figure 1.4. Canine enforcement. At a nearby warehouse a detection dog searches for explosives. Photo by James R. Tourtellotte.

The officers couple their experience with interviewing and interrogation methods that significantly improve deception detection. Officers become aware of deceptive communications by asking travelers to verify the accuracy of the information they are offering, and inspecting the equipment travelers are carrying. At the primary and secondary inspections areas, officers use real-time feedback to enhance deception detection. Through these techniques and methods, officers at the border have been able to thwart the schemes of many would-be bad guys. But the task is difficult and needless to say, by sheer random chance alone, some travelers who come to do harm would slip in (what statisticians call false negative), and by the same token, some travelers are turned back not because of their intent to do harm, but because they may have unwittingly exhibited signs of deception (what statisticians call false positive).

Even as the goal of these programs is to contain vulnerabilities at the border, to make commerce safer and travel more secure, two events in the recent past have underscored the limits of the diligence with which officers are supposed to perform their duties. The first incident was not a terrorist plot but had significant public health implications. For unknown reasons, the alerts that were put out did not lead to the interception that was supposed to occur. This was the incident involving a CBP officer who ignored the computer alert to detain a traveler who had reportedly contracted a rare, dangerous and drug-resistant form of tuberculosis in June 2007. The officer allowed entry to the traveler despite warnings transmitted system-wide. The officer who finally processed the traveler at the U.S.-Canada border in Champlain received the alert but thought the warning was "discretionary."

The second incident underscores the incapability of border security to thwart threats—it depicts the boundaries of border security. This is the case of the attempted attack that occurred on Christmas Day 2009. The only reason the attack was not successful was because the bomb equipment failed. Umar Farouk AbdulMutallab's father had become distressed about his son, and had gone as far as contacting Nigerian security agencies as well as the American Embassy in Nigeria because the father was concerned that his son was becoming radicalized and was in the process of planning an attack or something of the sort. The embassy reportedly forwarded the father's concerns to other agencies, but these forewarnings never prevented Farouk from boarding a plane headed to the United States. While AbdulMutallab did not reach a U.S. POE, all the warnings that were meant to prevent him from traveling in the first place were not effective.

These incidents uncover what officers can and cannot do at the border crossing: officers at the POE cannot exercise any control over threats that have already entered the United States or already exist within the homeland; officers cannot screen passengers for *intent* or "inspect" the *animus* of passengers. This signals the *end of authority* of border security. Beyond the border, primary responsibilities for securing the homeland against threats shift to other agencies such as the Federal Bureau of Investigation (FBI), U.S. Citizenship and Immigration Services (USCIS) and Immigration and Customs Enforcement (ICE). As for impulsion, the generalized hope is that our values, norms and beliefs will deter any malicious intentions. We rely on socialization and resocialization in the form of assimilation to fundamentally combat countercultures and terrorism within the boundaries of our society. But, in an open and free society, compliance and conformity cannot be foisted.

ASSIMILATION

It is the greatest migration story of humankind in the past three hundred years; over two hundred million people from diverse ethnicities have left their places of birth, familiar faces and kin to settle in a new land. More people have migrated to the United States than any other country over the past years. In the past two hundred or more years, we have been engaged in this grand production of the American reality. And, over the years, immigration laws have been revised or rewritten to calibrate the flow of new people coming here, and although immigration has ebbed during some periods, it has mainly flowed.

Immigration begets the ethos of assimilation—how we conduct into one alloy and how we channel the value of equality of all men and women, the norms of freedom as expressed in the Bill of Rights, and the belief in the pursuit of life, liberty and happiness. We are all engaged, in one way or the other, in the production of the objective reality of the American experience: different peoples, old minorities, new immigrants, our human terrain. The production reveals that our interpretive experiences are contingent on the *social distance* among us: what we think of one another, how we interact with one another and therefore how we decide to treat one another.

Even as the purpose of assimilation is to become socialized and resocialized as Americans, politicians have had to declare "war" in response to deviations from core values. When the war on crime was declared, it signaled the resolve to wage battle against deviant countercultures; it was the same edict that was made when President Richard Nixon declared drugs "America's public enemy number one" in 1971;[8] in fact this "war on drugs" had been raging on and off since the late 1800s, first on the opium trade and then during Prohibition. The war on terror has been the latest waged to maintain core values—terrorism is the latest challenge to the production of the American reality. When President George W. Bush declared the "war on terror," he was signaling the American resolve to fight the good fight against "the unlawful use of force and violence against persons or property to intimidate or coerce a government, the civilian population, or any segment thereof, in furtherance of political or social objectives."[9] All three wars are not merely metaphorical, but virtual and actual in varying degrees. The term "war" is meant to muster the same national resolve and conviction used to wage a military war. Compared to the wars on crime and drugs, the war on terror is relatively more recent. What we know is that terrorists may have a different motivation from drug dealers and criminals.[10]

So how powerful is assimilation within the homeland? It does not deter drug lords and criminals, and it did not deter Timothy McVeigh and other would-be American terrorists. McVeigh was perhaps the most prominent local terrorist in a line of over three dozen noteworthy terrorist attacks in the United States since the end of the Civil War: from the Haymarket Square bombing in Chicago in May 1886 and the bombing of the Sixteenth Street Baptist Church in Birmingham in September 1963 to the U.S. Capitol bombing in November 1983.[11] (Between 1980 and 2001, the FBI catalogued 294 terrorist incidents in the United States.) Some Americans have even attained principal roles in international terror networks. These Americans have become "the single biggest change in terrorism over the past several years . . . not just as foot soldiers but as key members of Islamist groups and as operatives inside terrorist organizations, including al-Qaida. These recruits . . . are now helping enemies target the United States."[12] These are the so-called jihadists "who have risen to positions of prominence in the world of radical Islam. They have emerged as masterminds, propagandists, enablers and media strategists who, because of their understanding of America, pose a new challenge for law enforcement."[13]

Two Americans who are thought to be among al-Qaida's leadership are Adam Gadahn and Adnan Shukrijumah, now considered one of al-Qaida's top lieutenants. Two other Americans were, until recently, in leadership positions: Samir Khan from North Carolina, who was editor of a new English-language magazine for al-Qaida's arm in Yemen, and Anwar al-Awlaki, who was thought to be involved in global recruitment efforts for the terrorist organization, were killed on September 30, 2011. Since 2002, when the war on terror was declared, over twenty terrorist attempts within the United States have been foiled by law enforcement[14] and in 2010, four terrorist attempts were uncovered:

Najibullah Zazi—February 2010. Najibullah, a U.S. legal permanent resident of Afghan descent, pleaded guilty and admitted he was trained by al-Qaida to attack New York City's underground transit system. Zazi pleaded guilty to conspiring to use weapons of mass destruction; conspiring to commit murder in a foreign country; and providing material support for foreign terrorist organizations. His accomplice was Zarein Ahmedzay.

Colleen Renee LaRose—March 2010. Allegedly nicknamed Jihad Jane, Colleen is an American citizen accused of being a terrorist and faces criminal charges of recruiting others to her jihadist cause and providing material support to terrorists. She faces life in prison.

Faisal Shahzad—June 2010. Faisal, a Pakistani American, placed a bomb in Times Square in May 2010 and confessed to ten counts based on the bombing attempt with material support from al-Qaida. In October 2010, Shahzad was sentenced to life imprisonment without the possibility of parole.

Farooque Ahmed—October 2010. Farooque is a Pakistani American charged with plotting a terrorist attack targeting the capital's subway system. He is accused of providing material support to al-Qaida. On April 11, 2011, he was sentenced to twenty-three years in jail.

As a society, we are faced with the challenge of not relying on or feeding into stereotypes about specific groups even as we are focused on reducing threats in our contemporary world. The ideas of plurality, equality and liberty that weave us, through assimilation, into a great nation are in constant tension with the threads of prejudice, stereotype and profiling. At the border crossing, it is probable that legitimate targeting efforts will conflate with profiling and indeed there are documented instances of what appears to be racial profiling at the POEs[15] and aggressive security checks that "are sweeping up some foreign college students and researchers who are in the country legally."[16] At the border, Muslim Americans have also reported being asked "about their religion, where they pray and how often."[17] While the use of data for targeting is legitimate in addressing terror threats, it cannot be replaced by law enforcement actions that rely primarily on race, ethnicity, religion or national origin as an indicator of threat. This is antithetical to our assimilation ideal.

PREJUDICE AND PROFILING

Our prejudices are recurrent and affect how we stage ourselves in everyday interactions—we may, as individuals, decide on specific occasions to perform our identities differently based on the audience.[18] We stage or present ourselves in ways to overcome the context or frame of race/ethnicity or other attributes that become our master defining trait. The shorthand descriptors we use can explain almost everything about the other person (even before we have engaged them) and allows us, in the anonymity of the public arena, to input their status. It is a vexing problem in the grand American narrative. It does not help that we are socially distant from one another—that is, the different racial and ethnic groups largely live separately from one another in separate communities and areas—and so residential segregation keeps us distant from one another.[19]

It is an output of our interaction space as Americans: the social episodes of stereotype and discrimination based on race and ethnicity (and religion). Race or ethnicity is used as a shorthand to understand our social environment and to simply make sense of our lives. This makes it difficult to experience the American space without engaging in racial thinking. We impart the idea of race with value in our daily interpretations of events. This is what creates "otherness," and allows us to stereotype and be prejudicial.[20] With new waves of new peoples, the conductivity of the American alloy grows more challenging and interactions rely more on shorthand definitions; we are likely to use canned descriptors of one another especially in public spaces. Is it easier for Americans to stereotype one another? Is stereotype or profiling (born of a certain prejudging) a part of the culture? How different are we in this characteristic from other countries? It is not right, using this shorthand to characterize people we don't know; it is convenient to do so in the anonymity of public spaces.

Researchers who study this phenomenon of prejudice and stereotype in America have identified what they call "color blindness" as the new progressive thinking that seemingly has replaced the stark practices that existed before the Civil Rights Act of 1964.[21] But as a lived experience, recurring encounters of prejudice as told by the "victims" of them are painful and stressful and affect interpretations of their American lives—these experiences have a cumulative effect and have not disappeared from our social spaces. When we experience prejudice and stereotype, it becomes part of the collective story of how the persistence of racial consciousness undermines the American alloy.[22] Prejudice and discrimination are "seldom just a personal matter . . . a victim frequently shares the incident with family and friends, often to lighten the burden, and this sharing creates a domino effect of anguish and anger rippling across an extended group. An individual's discrimination becomes a family matter."[23] The collective memory of the group experiencing prejudice and discrimination is translated into collective storytelling of negative recollections of the encounters with the groups that perpetuate prejudice. Within the American space, racial consciousness becomes tightly woven with personal and group memories of prejudice, which ultimately affects the production of our American lives—racial consciousness, born of prejudice, stereotype and discrimination makes us understand America differently and increases social distance between groups.

The current war on terror has opened a new dimension in our attitudes; security agencies must be seen not to be prejudging and/or profiling. The challenge is not to base our deterrence, screening and targeting activities on stereotypes and profiling of specific racial and ethnic groups. We must, as a nation, guard against using whatever vulnerabilities we face (as we have opened our doors to immigrants and travelers) as justification for prejudging and stereotyping any group. But, this is exactly what has been happening since September 11, 2001, as Muslims, Arabs, Sikhs and South Asians have become targets of prejudice and discrimination. According to Thomas Perez, the U.S. assistant attorney general for civil rights, "anti-Muslim harassment cases are now the largest category of religious discrimination in education cases and there has been a 163 percent increase in workplace complaints from Muslims to the Equal Employment Opportunity Commission."[24] What is becoming clear is the shift in national mood towards Muslim Americans that permits stereotyping and profiling. In this, other groups suffer as well; for instance, American Sikhs and Americans of South Asian ancestry have reported encounters of prejudice and stereotype even though they are not Muslims.

NOTES

1. U.S. Census Bureau, Foreign Trade Division. 2009. Exhibit 5: Exports, imports, and trade balance of goods. http://www.census.gov/foreign-trade/Press-Release/current _press_release/exh5s.pdf. Accessed October 2010. See also U.S. Customs and Border Protection. 2006. *Securing America's borders at ports of entry: Office of Field Operations strategic plan fy 2007–2011*. Washington, DC: U.S. Customs and Border Protection.

2. Customs and Border Protection. 2010. On a typical day in fiscal year 2009, CBP . . . http://www.cbp.gov/xp/cgov/about/accomplish/previous_year/fy2009_stats/fy09_typical _day.xml. Accessed February 2011.

3. Ibid.

4. U.S. Travel Association. 2010. Talking points and facts. http://www.ustravel.org/ marketing/national-travel-and-tourism-week/talking-points-and-facts. Accessed October 2010; U.S. Department of State. 2011. Table I: Immigrant and nonimmigrant visas issued at Foreign Service posts fiscal years 2006–2010. http://www.travel.state.gov/pdf/ FY10AnnualReport-TableI.pdf.

5. Customs and Border Protection. 2010. On a typical day in fiscal year 2009, CBP . . . http://www.cbp.gov/xp/cgov/about/accomplish/previous_year/fy2009_stats/fy09_typical _day.xml. Accessed February 2011.

6. Customs and Border Protection. 2008. Performance and accountability report. Washington, DC: U.S. Customs and Border Protection.

7. Paul Ekman. 2003. *Emotions revealed: Recognizing faces and feelings to improve communication and emotional life*. 2nd edition. New York: Holt Paperbacks. See also Shan Lu, Gabriel Tsechpenakis, Dimitris N. Metaxas, Matthew L. Jensen, and John Kruse. 2005 (January 3–6). Blob analysis of the head and hands: A method for deception detection. *Proceedings of the 38th Hawaii International Conference on System Sciences*. See also the work of Jay Nunamaker at the University of Arizona.

8. Gary Lafree. 2009. Criminology's third war. *Criminology and Public Policy*, *8*(3): 431–44.

9. Federal Bureau of Investigation. 2004. *Terrorism 2000/2001*. Washington, DC: Government Printing Office.

10. Gary Lafree. 2009. Criminology's third war. *Criminology and Public Policy*, 8(3):431–44.

11. Joseph T. McCann. 2006. *Terrorism on American soil: A concise history of plots and perpetrators from the famous to the forgotten.* Boulder, CO: Sentient Publications.

12. Dina Temple-Raston. 2010 (October 14). Two Americans become al-Qaida media strategists. National Public Radio. See also Frank J. Cillufo, Jeffrey B. Cozzens, and Magnus Ranstorp. 2010. Foreign fighters: Trends, trajectories and conflict zones. Washington, DC: George Washington University, Homeland Security Policy Institute.

13. Ibid.

14. Leigh Montgomery and Elizabeth Ryan. 2009 (September 26). Terrorists plots uncovered in the US since 9/11: At least 21 plots to launch attacks on American soil have been thwarted. *Christian Science Monitor.*

15. Anita Ramasastry. 2002. Airplane security: Terrorism prevention or racial profiling? CNN.com. http://edition.cnn.com/2002/LAW/10/02/ramasastry.security. Accessed November 2010.

16. David Sommerstein. 2010 (October 15). Border patrol asserts authority up north. National Public Radio.

17. Dina Temple-Raston. 2011 (March 10). Muslim Americans question scrutiny at border. National Public Radio.

18. Erving Goffman. 1959. *The presentation of self in everyday life.* New York: Doubleday.

19. John R. Logan. 2007. Who are the other African Americans? Contemporary African and Caribbean immigrants in the United States. In Yoku Shaw-Taylor and Steven Tuch (eds.), *The other African Americans*, pp. 49–68. Lanham, MD: Rowman & Littlefield. See also Douglas S. Massey and Nancy A. Denton. 1993. *American apartheid: Segregation and the making of the underclass.* Cambridge, MA: Harvard University Press.

20. Ana Liberato and Yoku Shaw-Taylor. 2009 (January 28). Resisting systemic racism from two immigrants. Racismreview.com.

21. Eduardo Bonilla-Silva. 2006. *Racism without racists: Color-blind racism and the persistence of racial inequality in the United States.* Lanham, MD: Rowman & Littlefield.

22. Joe Feagin and Melvin P. Sikes. 1994. *Living with racism: The black middle-class experience.* Boston: Beacon Press.

23. Ibid., p. 16.

24. Michelle Boorstein and Felicia Sonmez. 2011 (March 30). Familiar sparring in hearing on civil rights of Muslims. *Washington Post*, p. A3.

Chapter 2

Securing the Border since 1789

Customs, Immigration and Agriculture Inspections

A ll three inspection operations at the border—people, cargo, and plant and animal—are consolidated under Customs and Border Protection within the Department of Homeland Security: Animal and Plant Health inspections were combined with a largely intact Customs Service and the Immigration and Naturalization Service, now known as the U.S. Citizens and Immigration Service. These combined services are a significant component of the inspection operations of the department. On January 24, 2003, CBP, along with other directorates and agencies began functioning as part of the integrated operations ushering in another phase of a long history of regulations and enforcement.

On July 31, 1789, George Washington signed into existence the first and now the oldest federal agency of the government of the United States. The act establishing the Customs Service was passed by the First Congress of the United States as it met in New York City to consider the affairs of the very young nation; the Customs Service was created before the Department of War (August 7, 1789), the Department of the Treasury (September 2, 1789), the Supreme Court, and district and circuit courts (September 24, 1789). John Adams, the second president of the United States, presided over the Senate in Federal Hall as the details of the act were crafted.

The mandate of the U.S. Customs Service was contained in Article I, Section 8 of the Constitution:[1] "The Congress shall have Power To lay and collect Taxes, Duties, Imposts and Excises, to pay the Debts and provide for the common Defense and general Welfare of the United States; but all Duties, Imposts and Excises shall be uniform throughout the United States." The July 31, 1789, act was preceded by two important acts: the Tariff Act of July 4, 1789, which imposed duties on imports and the Duties on Tonnage

Statute of July 20, 1789, to regulate and collect duties on the tonnage of ships and vessels.

Article I conferred upon the Congress the initial and necessary powers to conduct the affairs of the state. The Customs Service's mandate to assess, collect and protect the revenue accruing to the United States based on duties, taxes and fees has essentially remained the same since this article was written more than two hundred years ago. Nonetheless, the role of the service has expanded in its enforcement of several hundred regulations related to trade and travel.[2]

The July 31 act created fifty-nine collection districts in eleven states: New Hampshire, Massachusetts, Connecticut, New York, New Jersey, Pennsylvania, Delaware, Maryland, Virginia, South Carolina and Georgia. North Carolina and Rhode Island became part of the Union in November 1789 and May 1790 respectively. There were three principal officers in each district: the collector, the naval officer, and the surveyor. Each of these officers had a share of the revenue from fines, penalties and forfeitures: "if an informant supplied information which led to a fine, etc., half of the moiety was given to the informant. To help ensure that Customs officers did not abuse the system, they had to post bonds. If found guilty of wrong-doing, Customs officers were subject to fines of up to $2,000 for each offense."[3]

The foundational years of the Customs Service were necessarily devoted to regulations and to defining the structure of this new and important agency. While regulatory activities and enforcement responsibilities overlapped in the evolving service, the regulatory regime was needed first to make the service functional.

The early Customs Service played an important role in enforcing immigration laws. Long before immigration and naturalization services were formally organized at the ports, the specialized immigration officers who processed travelers were employees of the Customs Service or were under its authority. It was thirty years after the Customs Service was created that Congress passed an act requiring the collection of immigration data. This was the very first substantive law on immigration by the U.S. Congress; the Steerage Act of March 2, 1819, had the following provisions:

a. Established the continuing reporting of immigration to the United States by requiring that passenger lists or manifests of all arriving vessels be delivered to the local collector of customs, copies transmitted to the secretary of state, and the information reported to Congress.
b. Set specific sustenance rules for passengers of ships leaving U.S. ports for Europe.
c. Restricted the number of passengers on all vessels either coming to or leaving the United States.[4]

Forty-five years later, Congress created the position of commissioner of immigration within the Department of State to oversee immigration and the work of the U.S. Emigrant Office in New York City, but Congress repealed this act four years later and the secretary of state was given the responsibility for immigration in the Act of July 4, 1864. Almost eleven years later, the Act of March 3, 1875, gave collectors at the ports the authority to inspect immigrants. After seven years, Congress passed a *general* law of immigration.[5] This was the Act of August 3, 1882, which reverted oversight of immigration matters to the Department of the Treasury. Under this law, the secretary of the treasury became responsible for enforcing the immigration laws restricting entry into the United States; the law also levied a tax of fifty cents on each immigrant. Finally, on March 3, 1891, the predecessor to the Immigration and Naturalization Service (INS) was created; the Bureau of Immigration and a superintendent of immigration were established under the Department of the Treasury.

With the establishment of the Bureau of Immigration, the immigration operations of Customs transferred to the new bureau. The 1891 law establishing the Bureau of Immigration gave the agency complete, broad and definite authority to administer all immigration laws and to deport those who enter the United States unlawfully. This bureau took on the duties of processing, admitting and declining entry to immigrants.

Twenty-one years after the Immigration Bureau was established, the authority to protect and promote agricultural exchange and our food supply was given to the Animal and Plant Health Inspection Service (APHIS) to inspect all agricultural and food products entering the country. The service was originally incubated at the U.S. Department of Agriculture (USDA) to oversee livestock research. The 1912 Plant Quarantine Act gave APHIS responsibility for enforcing the Lacey Act which had been passed in 1900 to protect plant and wildlife from illegal trade, the Virus-Serum-Toxin Act of 1921 ensuring the safe supply of animal vaccines, the Honeybee Act of 1922 restricting the importation of live adult bees in reaction to worldwide infestation, the Federal Seed Act of 1939 which established standards for trade in commercial seeds and the Endangered Species Act of 1973 to protect imperiled species from extinction.[6] When DHS was created, the responsibilities of the Department of Agriculture to inspect animal and plant imports were transferred to the new department.

THE REGULATORY REGIME OF CUSTOMS

As the fifty-nine collection districts were being organized under a uniform system, the larger debate about how to streamline the operations of all the officers in the eleven states loomed. The flow of revenue managed by customs officers was expectedly a temptation for fraud and the flow of commerce through the borders undoubtedly created opportunities for smuggling. The customs houses in these districts were operational in the colonies years before the United States was formed. The immigrant colonizers had started settlements and created customs services under the auspices of the British Empire. In Virginia, customs services had been in operation since 1671; in Maryland, Lord Baltimore's authority to collect customs and duties was established in 1644.[7]

Between the Declaration of Independence and the establishment of the foundations of an effective Customs Service, there wasn't a unified system; the establishment of the Treasury Department ensured a level of uniformity in the collection and securing of revenues. Under Section 2 of the Act to Establish the Treasury Department, its regulatory duties were defined:

> That it shall be the duty of the Secretary of the Treasury to digest and prepare plans for the improvement and management of the revenue, and for the support of public credit; to prepare and report estimates of the public revenue, and the public expenditures; to superintend the collection of revenue; to decide on the forms of keeping and stating accounts and making returns, and to grant under the limitations herein established, or to be hereafter provided, all warrants for monies to be issued from the Treasury, in pursuance of appropriations by law; to execute such services relative to the sale of the lands belonging to the United States, as may be by law required of him; to make report, and give information to either branch of the legislature, in person or in writing (as he may be required), respecting all matters referred to him by the Senate or House of Representatives, or which shall appertain to his office; and generally to perform all such services relative to the finances, as he shall be directed to perform.[8]

The secretary of the treasury was the head of the Customs Service with the responsibility to devise a uniform system for collection and accounting. Alexander Hamilton, the first secretary of the treasury, had the singular responsibility of establishing the foundations for an effective service. Before the formal establishment of the service, customs operations were not systematically regulated and enforced. Alexander Hamilton's initial activity, through a series of "circular letters" from the Department of the Treasury, provided the basis for education and communication among the districts. At the time, the Treasury Department with its customs officers was the largest department of the nascent government and was the major contributor of income to the country. From 1789 to 1800, the Customs Service contributed 88 percent of the young country's income.[9] The Customs Service continues to yield considerable revenues to the federal government. According to the historical account, the service returns over sixteen dollars to the government for every dollar that the agency receives in appropriations from Congress.[10]

During those early years, the secretary asked for and received advice from customs officers on the operations of this unified system. After all, these officers were experienced in the field and had firsthand knowledge of operations. (This is another practice that continues to this day—senior management at headquarters regularly asks for field operational advice about procedures in order to issue "musters" or advisories about changes in policy.)[11] Moreover, these customs officers had been at their posts under the various sovereign states before the U.S. government was formed. The transfer of local authority of the various ports of the sovereign states to the federal government of the United States required formal organization and gradual realignment of field operations because of the considerable authority wielded by local jurisdictions. The story is told of a local gentleman in Rhode Island who, in addition to being the customs officer, was also the municipality's "principal village trader, postmaster, and printer."[12]

Before the creation of the federal Customs Service, many of the customs officers in the local jurisdictions possessed considerable political power due to the status of their occupation and the income that accrued to them. "These officers had handsome salaries and fees, continued without exception to reside in their native communities, and were not barred from politics or business by law or mores. All in all, the Customs Service constituted the best official reservoir for political cadre in this decade of its inception."[13] The first secretary of the treasury necessarily had to rely on the expertise of these local officers until a unified agency was organized across the initial eleven states.

During this period of process establishment, the agency's initial enforcement activities were marine oriented, but the Customs Administration Act of March 2, 1799, expanded the purview of the Customs Service to include land borders. The organizing principles were based on (1) process for enforcement of the customs and navigation laws, (2) protection of officers, (3) mechanisms for rewarding informants who provided information about abuses and (4) responsibilities and rules for auditing and checking records.[14] Following the foundational years, the operations of the service were shaped by sentinel events. The Embargo Acts of 1807 and 1808 and the enforcement of the ban on importation of slaves required more customs officers to search and seize all vessels violating the laws. The protective tariffs of 1816, 1824, 1828 and 1832 (portending distally, perhaps, the Civil War) reduced the volume of operations at the ports and increased the incidence of smuggling. Then, during the Civil War, operations became increasingly difficult in a divided country, and loyalty among the ranks of the service had to be affirmed through an oath of allegiance to the Union (as a blockade to the Confederate states took effect).

The Civil War was indeed a test for the Customs Service:[15] "War pressures were nowhere more in evidence than at the border ports, some of which lay in a virtual no-man's-land between Union and Confederacy. Alexandria and Baltimore in the East and Louisville and Cincinnati in the West. . . . All the regulations in the world, and even broad new powers were not sufficient to stop contraband traffic. So compelling was the Confederacy's need for northern manufactures, and so ambivalent the border states' populations that the U.S. Customs Service had all it could do just to keep the lid on the flow of contraband from North to South." There were also reforms to contain corruption (the Pendleton Civil Service Reform Act of January 16, 1883) due to persistent political patronage within the service at the various major ports, but particularly at New York as reported by the Jay Commission in 1877: "officers are appointed through political influence, and are expected to make their offices contribute in turn to support the party."[16]

Over the past hundred years, the officers in the Customs Service have been called upon to increase vigilance in searches and seizures along the border during two world wars, and they continue to do so at the ports in the "wars" against crime, drugs and terror. New regulations for inspecting and screening travelers and cargo have made enforcement actions more targeted, but no less difficult.

Figure 2.1. Old Customs House, Yorktown, built circa 1721. Photo courtesy of the Virginia Department of Historic Resources, State Historic Preservation Office.

THE REGULATORY REGIME OF IMMIGRATION

It was in New York Harbor that the new federal Bureau of Immigration began its operations in January 1892. Of the initial staff of 180 immigration officers, slightly more than half of them were employed at Ellis Island.[17] Many of the staff of the new bureau were former customs officers, who had considerable experience already with inspecting and processing at the ports. On the authority of the 1891 act, immigration regulations were codified into operational guidelines at the border.

Even as the emergent prosperous country opened its gates to immigrants, over time, there were controls and restrictions on who was welcome. The language of the 1891 law was clear in its proscriptions: the class of inadmissible persons included "persons likely to become public charges, persons suffering from certain contagious disease, felons, persons convicted of other crimes or misdemeanors, polygamists, aliens assisted by others by payment of passage."[18] The "intelligent and effective restrictions"[19] reversed an open-door policy that politicians thought had caused an increase in the ranks of the poor; at the time, the stark photos of journalist Jacob Riis depicted slums in New York and squalid living of the indigent, many of whom were recent immigrants.

In 1891, the new Bureau of Immigration had twenty-four border stations on the eastern coast and along the northern and southwestern border at Baltimore, Boston, Barnstable, Brunswick, Galveston, Gloucester, Jacksonville, Key West, Mobile, New Orleans, New York, New Bedford, Norfolk, Newport News, Philadelphia, Providence, Portland (Maine), Portland (Oregon), Port Townsend, Pensacola, San Francisco, San Diego, Savannah, and Wilmington. The Bureau of Immigration relied on the Marine Hospital Service to conduct medical inspections. As mandated by law, the bureau began producing statistics on the distribution of immigrants arriving in the country. The bureau formally began its operations on July 12, 1891, and produced its first report on November 30, 1892, showing the distribution of admissible and inadmissible immigrants based on quality of character including categories such as "idiots," "insane," "paupers," "diseased persons," "convicts," "assisted immigrants," "prostitutes" and "contract laborers."[20] Other excludable classes were added in 1907: "imbeciles, feeble-minded persons, persons with physical or mental defects which may affect their ability to earn a living, persons afflicted with tuberculosis, children unaccompanied by their parents, persons who admitted the commission of a crime involving moral turpitude, and women coming to the United States for immoral purposes."[21] In 1917, "illiterates" were added to the excludable classes.

As the bureau evolved into a mature institution, several changes took place: the head of the bureau became a commissioner general, instead of a superintendent, and the Division of Naturalization was created to regulate the naturalization process. By 1906, the number of staff increased to twelve hundred. An act of Congress transferred the agency from the Department of the Treasury to the newly created Department of Commerce and Labor and the functions of the bureau included oversight of naturalization. The agency was now known as the Bureau of Immigration and Naturalization with a complete division responsible for processing the acquisition of citizenship.[22] However, operations were still dispersed throughout the border states that had immigration stations. At the federal level, the workload was policy oriented and consisted of written communications, correspondences with officers at the various border crossings to enforce uniformity. It was during these formative years that the bureau formalized the classification of traveler status by requiring aliens to declare intention of permanent or temporary stay in the United States. The official categories designating travelers as immigrants or nonimmigrants were created during this time. The bureau, also, for the first time, developed the formal requisites of an assimilation process for immigrants in the form of a literacy test.[23] By 1913, the bureau had changed again as the Department of Commerce and Labor was split in two. The bureau was transferred to the Department of Labor and divided into two sections: the Bureau of Immigration and the Bureau of Naturalization. In 1924, the U.S. Border Patrol was created within the Bureau of Immigration.

Expectedly, there was greater scrutiny of immigrant processes during the two world wars. By 1933, the two sections of the bureau had been combined again to achieve greater uniformity in the approval and dismissal of petitions. The Immigration and Naturalization Service (INS), the immediate predecessor to CIS, was created by an executive order in June 1933 only a few years before World War II. The mission of the service when it was created by the executive order has become its operative mandate until now: "to inspect and identify every man, woman, and child, whether citizen or alien, entering the United States at a legal port of entry, and to prevent any alien from entering this country at any point other than a legal port of entry."[24] As the war effort ramped up in the years following the creation of the INS, the agency was transferred to the Department of Justice as a security precaution and new enforcement protocols were put in place.

The immigration service and its naturalization operations now oversee the formal pathway for assimilation in America by (1) asking travelers to declare their immigrant intentions at the border and (2) using literacy tests as a most basic entry requisite to indicate readiness for assimilation into the American society.[25]

THE ANIMAL AND PLANT
HEALTH INSPECTION SERVICE

The history of APHIS can be traced to May 15, 1862, when the USDA was created by Abraham Lincoln. The department was charged with the following duties: "to acquire and to diffuse among the people of the United States useful information on subjects connected with agriculture in the most general and comprehensive sense of that word, and to procure, propagate, and distribute among the people new and valuable seeds and plants."[26] By this act, the administration and management of agriculture activities and operations moved from the Patent Office, which had been responsible for the distribution of plants and seeds that were not indigenous to the United States.[27] According to the historical account, the precursor of APHIS in the Department of Agriculture was the Veterinary Division, which became the department's initial arm for regulating animal research when it was renamed the Bureau of Animal Industry.[28] Leading up to the formal creation of APHIS was the creation of the Horticultural Board (later to become the Plant Quarantine and Control Administration and then the Bureau of Plant Quarantine) with enforcement powers. It was under the auspices of the Plant Quarantine and Control Administration that agricultural inspections focusing on plant, fruit and vegetable restrictions began in earnest at major U.S. ports and along the southwestern border between 1913 and 1928. The regulatory mandate of APHIS derives from the Plant Quarantine Act passed by Congress on August 20, 1912.

Before plant and animal quarantine operations were consolidated under one umbrella in the USDA's Agricultural Research Service (ARS) in 1953, the Bureau of Plant Quarantine was restructured to include a research arm focusing on entomology (Bureau of Entomology and Plant Quarantine) and management of research activities (Agricultural Research Administration). The ARS was the harbinger of the current structure that separates regulatory activities from research or control operations. After nineteen years, another restructured design was implemented that consolidated regulatory and enforcement activities under the Animal and Plant Health Inspection Services—this agency combined the plant regulatory responsibilities of the divisions of Plant Pest Control and Plant Quarantine into Plant Protection and Quarantine (PPQ) within the USDA. The animal regulatory responsibilities of the Animal Health and Veterinary Biologics were combined into the Veterinary Services. Inspections at the POEs were under the functional operations of APHIS and remained within its scope till APHIS became part of the newly created DHS. This regulatory framework also includes the Agricultural Quarantine Inspection (AQI) program that oversees inspection policy, training and user fees.

Agricultural inspectors received U.S. Foreign Service status (as members of diplomatic missions) to enable them to better enforce agricultural laws while promoting trade with partner countries.

Inspectors at the border are authorized to safeguard our agriculture through the identification of potential disease threats at the ports, but at the same time, they are mandated to allow legitimate trade in animals and plants. Two recent laws have strengthened the hand of APHIS to investigate and enforce the laws restricting and prohibiting pests, weeds, animal products and biologic agents that could pose a danger to our public health and harm our plant and animal health. The Plant Protection Act of June 20, 2000, and the Agricultural Bioterrorism Protection Act of June 12, 2002, consolidated several laws into comprehensive regulations that have increased the authority of APHIS.

ENFORCEMENT ACTIVITIES

Customs

In the transition from a unified regulatory system to enforcement and then consolidation under the DHS, the three border inspection operations have one primary goal: ensuring the security and safety of the traffic that flows through our ports. Before these three functional areas of border inspections were consolidated, the officers in each bureau or agency faced challenges unique to their enforcement operations.

One of the first major responsibilities assigned to the Customs Service was the enforcement of the Embargo Acts of 1808, but the most challenging during the first hundred years of the service was the coordination of the Chinese Exclusion Act of May 6, 1882. It fell to the Customs Service to enforce what was essentially an immigration issue when the legislation was first enacted. The Customs Service created a "Chinese Bureau" at the Port of San Francisco to attend to this obligation assigned by Congress because Chinese settlement was greatest in that area. The act itself depicted the bane of prejudice and stereotype in our society; before the act was passed, anti-Chinese sentiment was rife and there were riots and looting of Chinese establishments in San Francisco.[29]

There were reports and documentation of smuggling of Chinese girls and women sold into prostitution[30] and it was the task of the Customs Service to stem the flow of this inhumane trade. The task was a difficult one mainly because customs officers, especially on the West Coast, were not adequately trained; the Port of San Francisco had to retain the use of Chinese interpreters to explain to detainees their impending fate of deportation. There was not enough staff to monitor all the reported attempts of smuggling of Chinese girls and women that were reportedly occurring at the ports and between ports. In 1910, the new Bureau of Immigration took over the task of enforcing this racial exclusionary law enacted by the U.S. Congress.

Before the ratification of the Eighteenth Amendment to the U.S. Constitution, the Customs Service took primary responsibility for stemming the flow of smuggled alcoholic beverages. The National Prohibition Act was destined to be the only amendment to the Constitution to be repealed, but before its repeal in 1933, the prohibition on the manufacture, sale, transport, import or export of alcoholic beverages spurred coordinated smuggling attempts on the northern land border (the New York-to-Vermont border and the Great Lakes region), at the southern seaports in Florida and at the land border region around El Paso. The creation of the Bureau of Prohibition separating it from Customs within the Department of the Treasury was meant to support enforcement of the prohibition law. The Coast Guard and Border Patrol were also involved in these antismuggling efforts—as they have been ever since in combating current drug, contraband and human smuggling. In 1930, the Bureau of Prohibition estimated that more than five hundred million gallons of alcohol had been smuggled into the United States, depicting the scope of the smuggling operations to bring alcohol into the country.[31] The Customs Service retired its alcohol inspection protocols after the repeal of Prohibition, but it is still waging the war on drugs.

The Customs Service was given authority to seize drugs not meeting standards of pharmacopeia when Congress passed the Import Drugs Act of 1848. The authority allowed Customs to confiscate contaminated, diluted, adulterated, or decomposed drugs being imported into the country. The 1909 Opium Exclusion Act was the first federal law to curtail importation of opium and the Customs Service was duty bound to keep any form of this drug out of the country. Cocaine came to prominence as a recreational drug during the early 1900s when it was the preferred substitute for the addictive morphine prescribed by physicians. The Harrison Narcotic Act of 1914 limiting the possession and sale of opium and cocaine and the Marijuana Tax Act of 1937 providing penalties for the possession of marijuana gave the Customs Service authority to inspect travelers and cargo for all three drugs.[32] In 1970, Congress passed the Comprehensive Drug Abuse Prevention and Control Act (containing the Controlled Substances Act) and consolidated all drug laws. The authority of the Customs Service was strengthened by these new legislative activities by Congress as it received more appropriations to search and seize the implements of smuggling.

Immigration

The immigration enforcement story begins with the challenge posed by the transfer of responsibility from the Customs Service to the Bureau of

Immigration for enforcing the Chinese Exclusion Act. The bureau was also responsible for enforcing the passport-permit system established during World War I and monitoring the immigration status of contract laborers from Mexico who came to the United States to work on the farms, railroads and other construction projects in the country during both world wars. The required literacy test for these contract laborers was suspended because of an acute shortage of labor.

However, the most challenging enforcement activity of the agency was when the Alien Registration Act was passed during World War II. This act required all aliens in the United States to register at local post offices throughout the country—in all, approximately five million aliens were registered; over six hundred thousand Italians, three hundred thousand Germans and ninety thousand Japanese were registered under this act. The agency was transferred to the Department of Justice and it received broad powers and responsibilities for internment, parole and deportation of enemy aliens. Naturalization and expatriation laws were changed to increase national security.[33] The internment of U.S. citizens and legal residents of Italian, German or Japanese descent during that war was justified by the provisions of the national emergency acts. Many more thousands of Japanese Americans were interned and the episode portrayed the existing national mood; several thousand Japanese Americans renounced their citizenship because of this treatment as the INS exercised its broad powers to detain American citizens.

When the Internal Security Act of 1950 was passed, the INS was tasked with enforcement of a law that was meant to track "the presence of aliens in the United States whose activities are or may be detrimental to the safety and security of this country."[34] The prevailing mood of suspicion of Communist infiltration made membership in Communist organizations the basis for entry refusal, deportation or denial of naturalization. According to the historical record, this act gave INS broad powers to conduct investigations, to deport naturalized people and to revoke citizenship or "denaturalize" citizens. Several thousand investigations were conducted by the INS and are documented in its annual reports of 1951 and 1952. The aim was to safeguard the homestead from un-American activities; these restrictions were based on membership in stigmatized associations rather than race or ethnicity. After World War II, the INS faced the task of enforcing a law that rested on heightened sense of nationalism. But, the contemporary enforcement mandate to track the whereabouts of nonimmigrants is difficult because most of those who are admitted do not generally notify the agency about their change of address or their movements within the country as they are required to do. There are inadequate controls for operational efficiency to ensure that enforcement of status is not based on race, ethnicity or religion.

Agriculture

Enforcing agriculture regulations at the busy ports requires epidemiologic vigilance to detect and quickly react to pests that are harmful to our food supply. The officers at the ports are on constant lookout for invasive plants and animals, but these efforts are limited because only a small percentage of plant and animal products are inspected even as threats from invasive or exotic plants have increased with the uptick in the volume of food imports.[35] The enforcement operations of APHIS require effective biodefense or biosecurity controls that can identify a threat, determine the nature of the threat and intercept it before it spreads across the continental United States—to be effective, the capability to inspect has to increase. The Plant and Animal Protection and Quarantine operations also rely on early identification and transmission of information about potential outbreaks. There has to be coordination among all agencies responsible for safeguarding our food supply to increase capabilities and prevent threats.

In October 2010, for instance, CBP agricultural specialists at a seaport in Houston identified three "hitchhiking" insects that were found in a shipment of tile from Europe. These insects and other agricultural pests can have potentially disastrous impact on our food supply if allowed to spread within the homeland. The USDA's specialists identified these pests as *Ceralaptus gracilicornis*, *Chorthippus albomarginatus*, and *Kervillea conspurcata*, or grasshopper, green stinkbug, and brown plant hopper. Although these pests are commonly known, the specific species discovered in the cargo shipment are not native to America and are known to be harmful to crops.

Agricultural specialists have discovered other agricultural pests such as *Emmelia trabealis* or a moth known for its appetite for feeding on farm produce. In March 2009, agricultural specialists at Newark Liberty International Airport intercepted the pest *Hallodapus sp (Miridae)* which was discovered on a cargo shipment from the Middle East and was identified as a "quarantine pest that had the potential to cause economic damage to the trillion dollar U.S. agriculture industry."[36] Agriculture specialists have also discovered a pathogen identified as *Pleurophomorousis salicina* in shipments at the northern border on routine inspections of cut flowers; these pathogens had previously been discovered in central Europe. At the Port of Buffalo another plant pest was discovered when a prohibited fruit, langsat, was intercepted. Upon inspection of the fruit, an adult insect was found that was identified as *Isunidothrips serangga kudo (Thripidae)*. At the Port of Wilmington, agriculture specialists also intercepted a prohibited invasive species known as *mile-a-minute weed* which was discovered during routine inspections of a shipment of pineapples from the Caribbean.[37] The weed is particularly harmful because it grows quickly and has the capability to overtake native species. The active inspections of plant and animal shipments are part of the important work of ensuring agrosecurity at the border and within the homeland.[38]

SECURING THE BORDER SINCE 2003

Before the establishment of DHS, homeland security activities were spread across more than forty federal agencies and an estimated two thousand separate congressional appropriations accounts. Historical reports note that there were two congressional efforts to create a unified homeland security agency in February and March 2001; the first was a recommendation in the Hart-Rudman Commission on National Security Report and the second was a bill proposed by Representative Mac Thornberry.[39]

By November 25, 2002, when Congress passed the Homeland Security Act, two previous executive orders, in October 2001 and March 2002, and one presidential directive had provided a framework for establishing this new department. This is the newest department since the Department of Education was created in 1980 by President Jimmy Carter. The uniform duty of CBP as contained in the larger framework of DHS is based on a legacy of enforcement that has been in place for over two hundred years.

The responsibility of DHS to secure the homeland lies at the intersection of border screenings and immigration flows. However, the effectiveness of inspections at the border is bounded by our screening technologies, even as security in the homeland is strengthened by the PATRIOT Act. The challenge is that our tracking programs beyond the border must match the motivations of the deviant behaviors and activities that undermine the production of the American reality. The new global threats cannot slow legitimate trade and travel, and our deterrence activities should not overrun the scope of our vulnerabilities. The fight against countercultures and terror should not undermine how we become one as Americans and the creep of prejudice and stereotype should not be the overriding justification for screenings at the ports and within the homeland.

NOTES

1. U.S. Constitution, Article 1, Section 8. http://www.usconstitution.net/xconst_A1Sec8.html. Accessed November 2010.

2. U.S. Department of the Treasury. 1988. *A history of enforcement in the United States Customs Service 1789–1875*. Washington, DC: Author, p. 1.

3. Ibid., p. 9.

4. Carl E. Prince and Mollie Keller. 1989. *The U.S. Customs Service: A bicentennial history*. Washington, DC: Department of the Treasury, p. 171.

5. Sharon D. Masanz. 1980. *History of the Immigration and Naturalization Service: A report*. Washington, DC: Congressional Research Service.

6. Ruth Ellen Wasem, Jennifer Lake, Lisa Seghetti, James Monke, and Stephen Vina. 2004. *Border security: Inspections practices, policies and issues*. Washington, DC: Congressional Research Service, Library of Congress, pp. 8–9.

7. National Society of the Colonial Dames of America. 1972. *Three centuries of custom houses*. Washington, DC: Author.

8. U.S. Department of the Treasury. Act of Congress establishing the Treasury Department. http://www.ustreas.gov/education/fact-sheets/history/act-congress.shtml#a. Accessed November 2010.

9. Carl E. Prince and Mollie Keller. 1989. *The U.S. Customs Service: A bicentennial history*. Washington, DC: Department of the Treasury, p. 36.

10. U.S. Customs Service—More than 200 years of history. http://www.cbp.gov/xp/cgov/about/history/legacy/history2.xml. Accessed October 2010.

11. Another example of a muster was given after the Haitian earthquake in 2010: "After a quick muster with last minute instructions, CBP officers at Orlando-Sanford fanned out to their inspection booths while a second team approached the plane. CBP officers facilitated the processing of Haitian orphans and their caregivers in the wee hours of the morning." See http://www.cbp.gov/xp/cgov/newsroom/highlights/haiti_relief/haiti_orphan.xml. Accessed October 2010.

12. Carl E. Prince and Mollie Keller. 1989. *The U.S. Customs Service: A bicentennial history*. Washington, DC: Department of the Treasury, p. 38.

13. Ibid.

14. U.S. Department of the Treasury. 1988. *A history of enforcement in the United States Customs Service 1789–1875*. Washington, DC: Author, p. 12.

15. Carl E. Prince and Mollie Keller. 1989. *The U.S. Customs Service: A bicentennial history*. Washington, DC: Department of the Treasury, p. 127.

16. Ibid., p. 148.

17. Marian L. Smith. 1998. Overview of INS history to 1998. Originally published in *A historical guide to the U.S. government*, edited by George T. Kurian. New York: Oxford University Press.

18. *Immigration legal history: Legislation from 1790–1900*. Washington, DC: U.S. Citizenship and Immigration Services.

19. Aristide R. Zolberg. 2006. *A nation by design: Immigration policy in the fashioning of America*. New York and Cambridge, MA: Russell Sage and Harvard University Press, pp. 199–242.

20. I am indebted to Zack Wilske, historian at the U.S. Citizenship and Immigration Services (USCIS) History Office, for these data.

21. *Immigration legal history: Legislation from 1901–1940*. Washington, DC: U.S. Citizenship and Immigration Services.

22. Sharon D. Masanz. 1980. *History of the Immigration and Naturalization Service: A report*. Washington, DC: Congressional Research Service.

23. Ibid., pp. 13–23.

24. Ibid., p. 42.

25. Aristide R. Zolberg. 2006. *A nation by design: Immigration policy in the fashioning of America*. New York and Cambridge, MA: Russell Sage and Harvard University Press, pp. 199–242.

26. Abraham Lincoln and agriculture: An act to establish a department of agriculture. http://riley.nal.usda.gov. Accessed November 2010.

27. U.S. Customs and Border Protection. U.S. Department of Agriculture, Animal and Plant Health Inspection Service—Protecting America's agricultural resources. http://www.cbp.gov/xp/cgov/about/history/legacy/aqi_history.xml. Accessed December 2010.

28. U.S Department of Agriculture, Animal and Plant Health Inspection Service. About APHIS. http://www.aphis.usda.gov/about_aphis/history.shtml. Accessed November 2010.

29. Carl E. Prince and Mollie Keller. 1989. *The U.S. Customs Service: A bicentennial history*. Washington, DC: Department of the Treasury, pp. 171–93.

30. Carol Green Wilson. 1950. *Chinatown quest: The life adventures of Donaldina Cameron*. Palo Alto, CA: Stanford University Press.

31. Dennis Cashman. 1981. *Prohibition: The lie of the land*. New York: Free Press.

32. Carl E. Prince and Mollie Keller. 1989. *The U.S. Customs Service: A bicentennial history*. Washington, DC: Department of the Treasury, p. 227.

33. Sharon D. Masanz. 1980. *History of the Immigration and Naturalization Service: A report*. Washington, DC: Congressional Research Service, pp. 47–52.

34. Ibid., p. 55.

35. I. Miley Gonzalez. 2010. *Border security: The relationship between CBP and APHIS*. Washington, DC: American Association for the Advancement of Science, Center for Science, Technology and Security.

36. CBP makes important pest discovery. 2010 (Winter). *Frontline*, *3*(1): 34.

37. Agriculture specialists discover '1st in nation' pests. 2009 (Summer). *Frontline*, *2*(2): 45.

38. Ibid.

39. Elizabeth C. Borja. 2008. *Brief documentary history of the Department of Homeland Security 2001–2008*. Washington, DC: Department of Homeland Security History Office.

Chapter 3

A Nation of Immigrants

The Required Background Story of Immigration

In the past three hundred years, more than two hundred million men, women and children have come to America. Two other countries were settled by waves of immigrants in our times—Canada and Australia. Geographically, Canada is larger than the United States and Australia is only slightly smaller than the United States, but there are more people in the United States than in Canada and Australia combined. Through the years, immigration laws have moderated the flow of immigrants, and there have been periods when immigration policy has encouraged or discouraged people from different parts of the world. Our ethnic diversity is the backdrop of two realities: the old reality of voluntary and involuntary migration and restrictions on entry based on quality of character and the new reality of increasing racial and ethnic variation and vulnerabilities in the homeland. There is a compulsory reading of the American immigrant history and the contemporary narrative based on patterns of settlement. This reading has the following themes: the changing immigrant profile since 1965 and the issues that occupy or dominate the contemporary public mood including undocumented immigrants, immigration policy and threats at the border.

THE INDIGENES AND SETTLERS BEFORE 1965

We have to take that mandatory tour of our American immigrant history, noting important events and immigration laws of the past—we know some of the historical facts already and in this section, I discuss the early immigration of the English, Africans, Irish, Germans, Chinese, Italians, Jews, Japanese and Mexicans. Immigration to North America is described in this book in two major waves. The initial wave of immigration was mainly from Europe, after the colony had been settled in 1607 at Jamestown, Dominion of Virginia, and then in 1629, when the Puritans arrived in Massachusetts from England. The immigration from Europe began in earnest during the 1700s and continued through the 1800s, and then ebbed after 1924. The second substantive and significant wave is the current "new" voluntary immigration from Asia, Africa, the Caribbean and South America, which began after 1965, when immigration laws were changed to allow entry to more people from areas other than Europe.

It is through conquest and competition that America became a nation. That, and differential power gave the European immigrant colonizers dominance over the Native Americans. The Native Americans consisted of the societies and communities in the southeast, principally the Cherokee, who were among the first to come into contact with the English colonists;[1] the communities in the Great Plains and in the northwest; the Navaho and Pueblo in Arizona and New Mexico; the desert communities of southern Arizona and New Mexico; and the communities in Alaska including the Eskimo.[2]

The colonial subordination of these indigenous groups took the form of forced internal migration, relocations, and attempts at enslavement as European colonists expanded their immigrant communities.[3] At the time, there were no "American Indians" per se but rather a great number of diverse ethnic groups, viewing themselves as being as different from one another as they were from the European "invaders."[4] Contact between the native people and the colonizers occurred around 1492 and during the early decades of the 1500s. The tremendous waves of immigration to North America gave birth to the moniker "nation of immigrants"[5] as the United States of America came into being and the natives were displaced from their lands.

We know that the English settlers were not the first Europeans to come to America; the Spanish and the Portuguese had reached the Americas in the late 1400s. Some historical accounts suggest that the Vikings may have reached the Americas earlier in the eleventh century.[6] But we know more about the man born in Genoa, Cristoforo Colombo, a.k.a. Christopher Columbus, whose explorations opened up the Americas to the rest of Europe and the world for that matter; at Union Station in Washington, DC, he casts an imposing figure in the memorial fountain dedicated to him.

It is the English, however, who were the first colonial settlers in North America.[7] Their migration to and settlement in North America in large waves did not abate till perhaps World War I.[8] At the time of the American Revolution, the English colonizing migrants numbered about two million. Other early European immigrants to North America—such as the Germans and the Irish—did not have to engage in the process of colonizing; this brutal work had already been done for them by the English. Among these early waves were settlers from the British Isles including the Scottish and Welsh. The English continued to contribute a sizable number of immigrants to North America through the early 1900s; between 1820 and 1950 approximately three million immigrants from Britain came. However, there has been considerable decline in the trend of immigration from Britain. Their proportion has declined when compared to other white ethnic groups who have migrated to the United States since the late 1700s.[9]

The Africans came after the early English migrants and settlers. In 1619, twenty Africans landed at Jamestown on a Dutch ship and by the time the Puritans arrived in Massachusetts in 1629, the status of these Africans had become fully regulated. In Colonial Williamsburg in Virginia (the first English colony in North America), these were "slave laws" or "slave codes." The Colonial Williamsburg Foundation has collated these laws passed in Virginia between 1639 (only twenty years after the Africans landed in Jamestown) and 1705.[10] It is estimated that approximately 15 million Africans were brought to the Western Hemisphere from 1625 to the 1860s. These Africans came from the west and southwest regions of Africa, stretching from present-day Senegal to Angola. Of course, untold millions more died on the high seas. Most of these Africans were eventually located in the West Indies and South America, but approximately 7 percent of them came to North America. By 1790, there were approximately 760,000 Africans spread across several states including Virginia, Maryland, North Carolina, South Carolina, New York, New Jersey, Georgia, Delaware and Pennsylvania.[11, 12, 13, 14] In March 1807, Congress passed an act banning the importation of slaves. At the end of the slave trade, the voluntary migration of Africans to America was almost nonexistent, except from the Cape Verde Islands off the coast of Senegal. Migration of Africans to the United States continued in the form of movement from the Caribbean, but these migration flows were significant not in numbers but in the type of immigrants allowed: the Caribbean immigrants during the early to mid-1900s were comparatively literate, skilled professionals or white-collar workers.[15] The very few Africans who came to the United States during the late 1800s were mostly students.

The first Irish came to North America almost thirty years after the Africans landed at Jamestown; the 550 Irish men and women who came in 1650 to New England on Captain John Vernon's ship from southern Ireland were mostly servants and workers.[16] Later immigration was largely from Ulster or Northern Ireland. The Irish immigrants settled mainly in New England, New York, Pennsylvania and Maryland. Approximately three hundred thousand left for North America in the 1700s and by the mid- to late 1800s, about 1.6 million Irish had landed on the shores of the United States. The Irish who came to the United States from Northern Ireland were of mixed Scottish ancestry, but their primary identification was Irish. While immigration increased in the late 1800s, it declined in the early 1900s. Immigration from Ireland included not only Irish Catholics; there are accounts of Celtic migrants crossing the Atlantic. The early immigrants were both Protestant and Catholic.

Compared to the English and the Irish, the Germans did not migrate in large numbers until the 1680s and by the early 1700s, they had created a settlement (Germantown) in Pennsylvania. It is noted that there were a few German settlers among the first English migrant colonizers in Jamestown.[17] By the mid-1800s, approximately one million Germans had migrated to the United States. The mid-1800s to the early 1900s was the peak period of German immigration after which time migration dropped significantly.

Among Asian immigrants, the Chinese are the largest single group and they have been here longer than any other Asian immigrant group. In terms of time of migration and numbers, the Chinese are the next significant group in the chronology of the "old" immigration. They arrived in the decades before the Civil War, but immigration surged in the decades after the war. By the late 1800s, there were over two hundred thousand Chinese living on the West Coast. Chinese migration in fact instigated the *first act of Congress to regulate immigration*: The Act of March 3, 1875, established the policy of direct federal regulation of immigration by prohibiting for the first time entry to so-called undesirable immigrants. This act had the following provisions:

a. Excluded criminals and prostitutes from admission.
b. Prohibited the bringing of any Oriental persons without their free and voluntary consent; declared contracting to supply labor a felony.
c. Entrusted the inspection of immigrants to collectors of the ports.[18]

The Act of March 3, 1875, was purportedly passed to prohibit the importation of Chinese women as prostitutes. Seven years later, Congress went further in passing the first act prohibiting immigration based on race/ethnicity. The Chinese Exclusion Act of May 6, 1882, had the following provisions:

a. Suspended immigration of Chinese laborers to the United States for ten years.
b. Permitted Chinese laborers already in the United States to remain in the country after a temporary absence.
c. Provided for deportation of Chinese illegally in the United States.
d. Barred Chinese from naturalization.
e. Permitted the entry of Chinese students, teachers, merchants, or those proceeding to the U.S. . . . from curiosity.[19]

This exclusion act was effective in reducing the number of Chinese immigrants, which had surged in the early to mid-1800s. Of course, the Chinese population in the United States declined precipitously through the early 1900s. This racial exclusion act was extended in 1904: "Act of April 27, 1904 reaffirmed and made permanent the Chinese exclusion laws. In addition, the Act clarified the territories from which Chinese were to be excluded."[20] (Prior to the 1904 act, the Immigration Acts of 1903 had expanded the authority of the immigration commissioner and codified existing immigration law.) It was not until 1943, when China became a U.S. ally in World War II, that the exclusion act was repealed: "Act of December 17, 1943 amended the Alien Registration Act of 1940, adding to the classes eligible for naturalization Chinese persons or persons of Chinese descent. A quota of 105 per year was established."[21]

Chronologically, Italians are the next wave of immigrants to the United States. It was an Italian explorer and an Italian navigator who made the colonization of North America possible. But the Italians were not the immigrant colonizers who made North America their home in large numbers. Very few Italians immigrated and settled in North America during the early years of settlement.[22] It is recorded however that several accomplished Italians contributed to the young country, among them Filippo Mazzei, who was among the settlers in Virginia and who was a friend to Thomas Jefferson. Jefferson is said to have invited other Italian experts and craft workers to Virginia and brought an Italian architect to design his Monticello home. Other Italian musicians were invited to form the first U.S. Marine Corps band.[23]

However, the Immigration Act of 1924 was instrumental in slowing the immigration of Italians due to its quota system: the Immigration Act of May 26, 1924, was the next substantive legislation that set limits on immigration and established the "national origins quota system." In conjunction with the Immigration Act of 1917 and the Quota Law of May 19, 1921 (the first quantitative immigration law limiting the number of aliens admitted into the country), the 1924 act dictated American immigration policy until the Immigration and Nationality Act of 1952 was passed. The 1924 act contained the following:

a. Two quota provisions:
   1. In effect until June 30, 1927—set the annual quota of any "quota" nationality at 2 percent of the number of foreign-born persons of such nationality resident in the continental United States in 1890 (total quota: 164,667).
   2. From July 1, 1927 (later postponed to July 1, 1929) to December 31, 1952—used the national origins quota system: the annual quota for any country or nationality was related to the number of inhabitants in the

continental United States in 1920. Preference quota status was established for: unmarried children under twenty-one; parents; spouses of U.S. citizens age twenty-one and over; and for quota immigrants age twenty-one and over who are skilled in agriculture, together with their wives and dependent children under age sixteen.

b. Nonquota status was accorded to wives and unmarried children under age eighteen of U.S. citizens; natives of Western Hemisphere countries, with their families; nonimmigrants; and others. (Subsequent amendments eliminated certain elements of this law's inherent discrimination against women but comprehensive elimination was not achieved until 1952 [see the Immigration and Nationality Act of 1952].)

c. Established the "consular control system" of immigration by mandating that no alien may be permitted entrance to the United States without an unexpired immigration visa issued by an American consular officer abroad. Thus, the State Department and the Immigration and Naturalization Service shared control of immigration.

d. Introduced the provision that no alien ineligible to become a citizen shall be admitted to the United States as an immigrant. This was aimed primarily at Japanese aliens.

e. Imposed fines on transportation companies who landed aliens in violation of U.S. immigration laws.

f. Defined the term "immigrant" and designated all other alien entries into the United States as "nonimmigrant" (temporary visitor). Established classes of admission for nonimmigrant entries.[24]

The 1924 act, together with the Immigration Act of February 5, 1917, "codified all previously enacted exclusion provisions" by barring entry to illiterate aliens and aliens with mental health problems, further restricting immigration of Asian persons and creating another class of inadmissible aliens from the Asia-Pacific triangle, expanding the classes of deportable aliens and introducing the requirement of deportation without statute of limitation.[25]

Two acts in 1929 expanded the reach of the 1924 act: the first was the Registry Act of March 2 that "amended existing immigration law authorizing the establishment of a record of lawful admission for certain aliens not ineligible for citizenship when no record of admission for permanent residence could be found and the alien could prove entrance to the U.S. before July 1, 1924 (subsequently amended to June 3, 1921 by the Act of August 7, 1939) and then later incorporated into the Alien Registration Act of 1940."[26] The other was the Act of March 4 which had the following provisions:

a. Added two deportable classes, consisting of aliens convicted of carrying any weapon or bomb and sentenced to any term of six months or more, and

aliens convicted of violation of the Prohibition law for which a sentence of one year or more is received.
b. Made reentry of a previously deported alien a felony punishable by fine or imprisonment or both.
c. Made entry by an alien at other than a designated place or by fraud to be a misdemeanor punishable by fine or imprisonment or both.
d. Deferred the deportation of an alien sentenced to imprisonment until the termination of the imprisonment.[27]

Historians note that there was nativist ferment by Anglo-Protestant groups[28] that led to the 1924 act and subsequent legislation. The act set a small quota for Italians, while giving the countries of Britain, Germany, Ireland and Scandinavian countries high quotas. Italian remigration was high.

Jewish Americans are the next group of immigrants in the chronology of the waves of movement to North America and the United States. According to historical accounts, twenty-three Jews arrived in the United States in 1654 as they fled Brazil due to the Catholic Inquisition;[29] these Sephardic Jews (descendants from modern Spain and Portugal) settled in New Amsterdam and were later joined by the Marrano Jews (who had been publicly forced to convert to Christianity) in the early 1700s; the Ashkenazi Jews from England, Germany and Poland immigrated to North America around the same time. The numbers of the migrant Jews were small and they generally settled in port cities along the eastern coast from New York to Atlanta. During the early to mid-1800s, increasing numbers of Jews came to the United States from Europe due, in part, to the push factors of anti-Semitism. In the later part of the 1800s, eastern European Jews migrated in large numbers mainly from Russia due to the pogroms. Immigration increased generally during this period through the early 1900s until the Immigration Act of 1924 was implemented. By the time World War II began, the flow of Jews from Europe had slowed considerably because admissibility requirements for refugees fleeing Hitler's death camps were onerous. Postwar immigration picked up somewhat, but nowhere near the numbers before the 1924 act.

Japanese migration to the United States follows the Jews in terms of their numbers. Immigration from Japan to the United States is the second oldest from Asia, after the Chinese. The Japanese began migrating to the United States in large numbers during the mid-1800s through the early 1900s and their first destination was Hawaii; approximately 230,000 migrated to this colony during this period. (Hawaii came under the territorial control of the United States in 1898.) The 1882 Chinese Exclusion Act created opportunity for more Japanese to be admitted. Many of the immigrants came under labor contract as farm workers to work in the Hawaiian plantations. There was immigration to the mainland as well, with approximately three hundred

thousand Japanese entering the continental United States in the late 1800s
and the early 1900s.[30]

Much has been written about the Gentlemen's Agreement in 1908 that curtailed immigration of the Japanese in the early to mid-1900s. Historians note
that there were nativist tensions on the West Coast (especially San Francisco)
because the immigrants were seen as a threat to established white entrepreneurs. Because of this, "President Theodore Roosevelt arranged for a prohibition of Japanese migrants. In negotiations in 1907 and 1908, Roosevelt
persuaded the Japanese government to agree to the infamous Gentlemen's
Agreement whereby no passports would be given by Japan to any Japanese
workers except those already in the U.S. and their close relatives."[31] After this
agreement, the Immigration Act of 1924 went even further in restricting immigration from Japan.[32] Japanese Americans were placed in detention camps
en masse during World War II after the military victories of the Japanese and
the attack on Pearl Harbor.

We close out the early history with the migration of Hispanics/Latinos or
more precisely Mexicans, who, by their numbers, are the largest Latino group
in the United States. After Mexico won its independence from Spain in 1821,
the province of Texas was part of the newly established country. Following the revolt by citizens of the province against the central government of
Mexico (beginning in October 1835 and ending in April 1836), the independent Republic of Texas was annexed by the United States in 1845, becoming
the twenty-eighth state. The annexation of Texas precipitated conflict with
Mexico; in 1848, the Mexican government ceded the southwest area (including Texas, New Mexico and parts of California) to the United States for $15
million after a bloody war. Most of the Mexicans living in the area chose to
remain there rather than move to Mexico in the south. The Latinos were given
assurances of protection of their rights and cultural heritage under the Treaty
of Guadalupe Hidalgo.[33]

The population in the southwest grew due to settlers from other parts of the
United States. At the same time, immigration from Mexico picked up after
the U.S.-Mexican war; there are estimates of millions of immigrants crossing
the border between 1910 and 1930. Due to contiguity of southwest United
States and Mexico, some of the Mexicans who came to work in the United
States had short-term permits but lived in Mexico; others were commuters
or seasonal farm workers. There was undocumented immigration as well.
Immigration slowed after the 1930s due to deportations and the literacy test
required for citizenship.[34]

Over the years, other groups migrated to the United States as well, including Puerto Ricans, Cubans, Jamaicans and other black Caribbean Islanders,
Filipinos, Koreans, Vietnamese and Asian-Indians. Immigration from eastern
and southern Europe has also contributed to the diversity of our human terrain.

IMMIGRATION SINCE 1965

More than any other, the Immigration and Nationality Act of October 3, 1965, has altered the immigrant landscape in the United States in the past forty-five years.

Eleven years before the 1965 act was signed into law, Congress had passed the Immigration and Nationality Act of June 27, 1952, which "brought into one comprehensive statute the multiple laws which, before its enactment, governed immigration and naturalization in the United States,"[35] and preserved and consolidated the laws of 1917, 1924, and 1929. Before 1965, the 1882 Exclusion Act stood out as the only law that specifically restricted one ethnic/racial group from entering the United States and immigration flows were largely from Europe. During the Depression, the numbers of immigrants from all around the world declined significantly and the immigrant quotas act of 1924 was calculated to reduce flows to the United States. The act of 1929 updated the 1924 act with additional provisions. While retaining the system of national origins quota, the 1952 act added a system of preferences as well. These preferences were mostly based on occupation and supported reunification of families.[36]

The 1965 act, also known as the Hart-Celler Act, ended all the previous regulations that were seen as racially unfair and unduly restrictive including the laws from 1917, 1924, 1929 and 1952. The changes in immigration policy in 1965 altered the immigration terrain of the country and encouraged naturalization. The act had the following important provisions:

a. Abolished the national origins quota system, eliminating national origin, race, or ancestry as a basis for immigration to the United States.
b. Established allocation of immigrant visas on a first-come, first-served basis, subject to a seven-category preference system for relatives of U.S. citizens and permanent resident aliens (for the reunification of families) and for persons with special occupational skills, abilities, or training (needed in the United States).
c. Established two categories of immigrants not subject to numerical restrictions:
   1. Immediate relatives (spouses, children, parents) of U.S. citizens, and
   2. Special immigrants: certain ministers of religion; certain former employees of the U.S. government abroad; certain persons who lost citizenship (e.g., by marriage or by service in foreign armed forces); and certain foreign medical graduates.
d. Maintained the principle of numerical restriction, expanding limits to world coverage by limiting Eastern Hemisphere immigration to 170,000 and placing a ceiling on Western Hemisphere immigration (120,000) for

the first time. However, neither the preference categories nor the twenty-thousand-per-country limit were applied to the Western Hemisphere.

e. Introduced a prerequisite for the issuance of a visa of an affirmative finding by the secretary of labor that an alien seeking to enter as a worker will not replace a worker in the United States nor adversely affect the wages and working conditions of similarly employed individuals in the United States.[37]

The significance of the 1965 act is that it created the basic structure of today's immigration regulations; this law and subsequent ones (1986 and 1990) established family unification as the cornerstone of U.S. immigration policy. Under this law, immediate relatives of immigrants (spouses, minor children, and parents of U.S. citizens over the age of twenty-one years) were not counted as quota immigrants and were not counted as part of either the hemispheric or country ceiling. The new immigration reforms also removed country limits for Caribbean Island nations as they are part of the Western Hemisphere. Caribbean Island nations could also take advantage of the 120,000 immigrant quota allowed to all countries in the hemisphere. (The 1976 amendment imposed a limit of twenty thousand immigrants for nations in the hemisphere.) The 1965 act had the effect of increasing immigration from the Caribbean Islands. It is noteworthy that the passage of the Hart-Celler Act coincided with the growing tide of civil rights legislation during the same period. Subsequent acts, in 1986 and 1990, provided important changes that have increased immigration from regions other than Europe.

The next major act that reshaped immigration policy is the Immigration Reform and Control Act (IRCA) of November 6, 1986. This act was consequential because of the following provisions:

a. Authorized legalization (i.e., temporary and then permanent resident status) for aliens who had resided in the United States in an unlawful status since January 1, 1982 (entering illegally or as temporary visitors with authorized stay expiring before that date or with the government's knowledge of their unlawful status before that date).
b. Created sanctions prohibiting employers from knowingly hiring, recruiting, or referring for a fee aliens not authorized to work in the United States.
c. Increased enforcement at U.S. borders.
d. Created a new classification of seasonal agricultural worker and provisions for the legalization of such workers.
e. Extended the registry date (i.e., the date from which an alien has resided illegally and continuously in the United States and thus qualifies for adjustment to permanent resident status) from June 30, 1948, to January 1, 1972.

Figure 3.1. CBP officer checks fingerprints of individuals entering the United States. Photo by Gerald L. Nino.

f. Authorized adjustment to permanent resident status for Cubans and Haitians who entered the United States without inspection and had continuously resided in the country since January 1, 1982.
g. Increased the numerical limitation for immigrants admitted under the preference system for dependent areas from six hundred to five thousand beginning in fiscal year 1988.
h. Created a new special immigrant category for certain retired employees of international organizations and their families and a new nonimmigrant status for parents and children of such immigrants.
i. Created the nonimmigrant Visa Waiver Pilot Program allowing certain aliens to visit the United States without applying for a nonimmigrant visa.
j. Allocated five thousand nonpreference visas in each of fiscal years 1987 and 1988 for aliens born in countries from which immigration was adversely affected by the 1965 act.[38]

The IRCA of 1986 provided amnesty to undocumented immigrants in the United States whose numbers were estimated to be slightly more than three million at the time; of these eligible immigrants, approximately 60 percent or 1.7 million applied and received legal status.[39] On November 10, 1986, Congress passed amendments to the IRCA. The next consequential legislation was the Immigration Act of November 29, 1990, which was major in that it revamped immigration policy. The provisions of this major act were:

a. Increased total immigration under an overall flexible cap of 675,000 immigrants beginning in fiscal year 1995, preceded by a 700,000 level during fiscal years 1992 through 1994. The 675,000 level consists of: 480,000 family sponsored; 140,000 employment based; and 55,000 diversity immigrants.
b. Revised all grounds for exclusion and deportation, significantly rewriting the political and ideological grounds. For example, repealed the bar against the admission of Communists as nonimmigrants and limited the exclusion of aliens on foreign policy grounds.
c. Authorized the attorney general to grant temporary protected status to undocumented alien nationals of designated countries subject to armed conflict or natural disasters.
d. Revised and established new nonimmigrant admission categories:
    1. Redefined the H-1(b) temporary worker category and limited the number of aliens who may be issued visas or otherwise provided nonimmigrant status under this category to 65,000 annually.
    2. Limited the number of H-2(b) temporary worker category aliens who may be issued visas or otherwise provided nonimmigrant status to 66,000 annually.
    3. Created new temporary worker admission categories (O, P, Q, and R), some with annual caps on the number of aliens who may be issued visas or otherwise provided nonimmigrant status.
e. Revised and extended the Visa Waiver Pilot Program through fiscal year 1994.
f. Revised naturalization authority and requirements:
    1. Transferred the exclusive jurisdiction to naturalize aliens from the federal and state courts to the attorney general.
    2. Amended the substantive requirements for naturalization: state residency requirements revised and reduced to three months; added another ground for waiving the English-language requirement; lifted the permanent bar to naturalization for aliens who applied to be relieved from U.S. military service on grounds of alienage who previously served in the country of the alien's nationality.
g. Revised enforcement activities:
    1. Broadened the definition of aggravated felony and imposed new legal restrictions on aliens convicted of such crimes.
    2. Revised employer sanctions provisions of the Immigration Reform and Control Act of 1986.

3. Authorized funds to increase Border Patrol personnel by one thousand.
4. Revised criminal and deportation provisions.
h. Recodified the thirty-two grounds for exclusion into nine categories, including revising and repealing some of the grounds (especially health grounds).[40]

The 1990 act introduced the lottery visa system and increased employment visas for underrepresented countries in the immigration flow to America. These visas were developed to increase ethnic diversity and contained minimal eligibility requirements. A significant proportion of immigrants who are granted visas under the diversity program are managerial and technical professionals who leave their countries of origin where their services are most needed to come to the United States. Additional provisions of the 1990 act limited the number of immigrants thereby setting some restrictions on the flow of immigrants. While overhauling immigration policy to allow for more diversity, the numerical limits provided in this legislation contrasts with the unlimited immigration from Europe that the United States allowed before 1910.[41]

Data from the Office of Immigration Statistics (tables 3.1 and 3.2) show patterns of immigration before and after 1965. These shifts must be put in perspective. The collection and monitoring of information on legal permanent status began in 1820. Prior to 1965, more than half of all immigration had been from Europe, followed by immigration from Canada, Newfoundland and Mexico; immigration from Asia accounted for less than 7 percent and voluntary immigration from Africa and South America accounted for less than 2 percent of overall immigration during this period. After 1965, the distribution of immigrants has shifted; immigration from Europe accounts for less than 20 percent and Asia and Africa contribute over 29 percent and 6 percent respectively.

UNDOCUMENTED IMMIGRATION, IMMIGRATION REFORM AND THE NEW AMERICANS

As the U.S. economy was emerging from the worst recession in its history in 2010, there were reports that the annual flow of undocumented (also known as illegal or unauthorized) immigrants had declined by almost 65 percent from 2000 to 2009.[42] The anemic economy had undoubtedly made jobs scarce, but all the talk and activities regarding secure borders and increased enforcement had also made it more difficult for migrants to cross illegally between POEs.

The undocumented are those who come here legally and then overstay their visas and therefore become illegal aliens, or those who cross the border

Table 3.1. Percentage of Immigrants Obtaining Legal Permanent Status by Region, 1920–2009

	Europe	Asia	America*	Central America	South America	Africa	Oceania	Not Specified
1920–1929	58.8	2.9	36.5	0.4	1.0	0.1	0.2	0
1930–1939	62.0	2.7	32.2	1.0	1.4	0.3	0.5	—
1940–1949	52.7	3.9	36.6	2.2	2.2	0.7	1.6	0
1950–1959	53.7	5.2	35.2	1.5	3.0	0.5	0.4	0
1960–1969	31.8	10.1	47.0	2.8	7.0	0.7	0.7	0
1970–1979	17.8	30.3	41.0	2.6	5.9	1.5	0.9	0
1980–1989	9.6	34.2	38.6	4.9	5.7	2.0	0.6	4.4
1990–1999	12.3	26.1	46.9	5.6	5.2	3.2	0.5	0
2000–2009	11.5	29.5	37.8	5.0	7.3	6.5	0.6	1.8

Source: Office of Immigration Statistics, Department of Homeland Security. 2010. *Yearbook of Immigration Statistics 2009.*
*America = Canada and Newfoundland, Mexico, Caribbean

Table 3.2. Persons Obtaining Legal Permanent Status by Region, 1820–2009

	Europe	Asia	America*	Central America	South America	Africa	Oceania	Not Specified
1820–1829	99,272	34	9,655	57	405	15	3	19,523
1830–1839	422,771	55	31,905	94	957	50	7	83,593
1840–1849	1,369,259	121	50,516	297	1,062	61	14	7,366
1850–1859	2,619,680	36,080	84,145	512	3,569	84	166	74,399
1860–1869	1,877,726	54,408	130,292	70	1,536	407	187	18,241
1870–1879	2,251,878	134,128	345,010	173	1,109	371	9,996	754
1880–1889	4,638,677	71,151	524,826	279	1,954	763	12,361	790
1890–1899	3,576,411	61,285	37,350	649	1,389	432	4,704	14,112
1900–1909	7,572,569	299,836	277,809	7,341	15,253	6,326	12,355	33,493
1910–1919	4,985,411	269,736	1,070,539	15,692	39,938	8,867	12,339	488
1920–1929	2,560,340	126,740	1,591,278	16,511	43,025	6,362	9,860	930
1930–1939	444,399	19,231	230,319	6,840	9,990	2,120	3,306	—
1940–1949	472,524	34,532	328,435	20,135	19,662	6,720	14,262	135
1950–1959	1,404,973	135,844	921,610	40,201	78,418	13,016	11,353	12,472
1960–1969	1,133,443	358,605	1,674,172	98,560	250,754	23,780	23,630	119
1970–1979	825,590	1,406,544	1,904,355	120,374	273,608	71,408	39,980	326
1980–1989	668,866	2,391,356	2,695,329	339,376	399,862	141,990	41,432	305,406
1990–1999	1,348,612	2,859,899	5,137,743	610,189	570,624	346,416	56,800	25,928
2000–2009	1,348,904	3,470,835	4,442,226	591,130	856,593	759,742	65,793	211,930

Source: Office of Immigration Statistics, Department of Homeland Security. 2010. *Yearbook of Immigration Statistics 2009.*
*America = Canada and Newfoundland, Mexico, Caribbean

illegally between POEs. In the main, the undocumented immigrants who cross the border illegally do so at the southern border.

There is a long history of farm laborers crossing the southern border to come to the United States to work; among the authorized workers who came here under the 1942 Emergency Farm Labor Agreement between the United States and Mexico were undocumented immigrants who came here essentially to find work. The Immigration Act of 1929 (see the earlier discussion) made illegal entry into the United States a crime and based on authority of this act, many of the undocumented Mexican workers were deported.

Immigration researchers have argued that there was an increase in the number of undocumented after the 1965 act, probably because the demand for entry jobs by immigrants from the sending countries far exceeded the legal limits allowed. As important, the 1986 act did not have the necessary provisions to establish a nationwide system of verifications for legal status after the amnesty program.[43]

Current estimates peg the total number of undocumented immigrants at approximately 11.9 million as reported by the Pew Hispanic Center in their 2009 report. The center estimated that the growth of undocumented immigrants occurred between 1990 and 2008. This estimate is approximately the same figure that was released by DHS in February 2010.[44] Approximately 70 percent or eight million of the undocumented are in the labor force. The major flow of undocumented immigrants comes from Central and South America and the Caribbean across the southern border of the United States. Eight states, California, Texas, Florida, New York, New Jersey, Arizona, Georgia and Illinois, are home to most of these undocumented immigrants. (California had the largest proportion in 2008.) The undocumented are among the poorest in America—their median household income in 2007 was $36,000, approximately one-third less than the median household income for residents. Most of the undocumented do not have health insurance.[45]

The majority of undocumented immigrant adults live with their spouses or children. In 2008, the majority of the children of undocumented immigrants, approximately 73 percent, were citizens by birth and the number of second-generation immigrants in mixed-status families (undocumented immigrant parents and citizen children) has grown considerably since 2003. Using census data, the Pew Hispanic Center estimates that undocumented immigrants are 4 percent of the nation's population and approximately 5 percent of its workforce. The second-generation children of undocumented immigrants make up about 7 percent of the students enrolled in the nation's elementary and secondary schools.[46]

Under President Barack Obama's administration, deportations of undocumented immigrants have increased, according to data from Immigration and

Customs Enforcement (ICE) as shown in figure 3.2.[47] The agency reports that considerable proportions of these deportations are criminals, and this is in keeping with the new mandate of DHS to use immigration enforcement as a crime-fighting tool.[48] Under this program, employers who hire undocumented immigrants are also targeted; 180 such employers have been criminally charged and fines of up to $50 million have been imposed.

President Obama has been "drawing flak from those who contend the administration is weak on border security and from those who are disappointed he has not done more to fulfill his campaign promise to help the country's estimated 11 million illegal residents. Trying to thread a needle, the president contends enforcement—including the deployment of fresh troops to the Mexico border—is a necessary but insufficient solution."[49] Specifically, the Secure Communities program and Section 287(g) of the Illegal Immigration Reform and Immigrant Responsibility Act are the tools used by DHS to snare the undocumented. Section 287(g) authorizes the secretary of DHS to enter into agreements with state and local law enforcement agencies to carry out immigration enforcement activities. As such, ICE has set priorities to capture, detain and deport, in descending order of importance, illegal immigrants convicted of a misdemeanor, those caught near the border and those who have failed to obey deportation orders. Working with local law enforcement

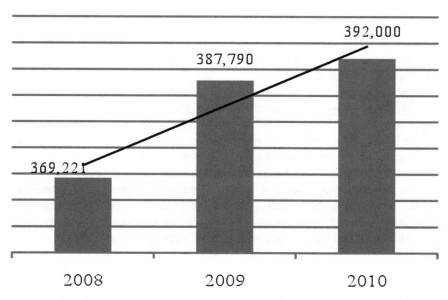

Figure 3.2. Deportations of undocumented immigrants, 2008 to 2010. *Source*: Immigration and Customs Enforcement.

agents, the Secure Communities program provides an integrated approach to identify and deport criminal aliens. Indeed, state and local jurisdictions cannot opt out of this program.

The efforts to target criminal undocumented immigrants sweep up non-criminal undocumented immigrants as well. While it is important to make the distinction between immigrants who overstay their visas and those who have committed crimes, the current process of targeting has given concern about the potential for racial profiling.[50] The topic of undocumented immigrants has become a hot-button political issue and a robust policy solution has not yet been found. Immigration advocates argue that these programs target otherwise law-abiding undocumented immigrants and wreak havoc in mixed-status families because of deportations. Also, businesses pay hefty fines for employing undocumented immigrants. At the same time, supporters of more stringent enforcement policies maintain that undocumented immigrants have broken immigration laws and cannot be allowed to remain in the country. Arizona's controversial SB 1070 immigration law captures the current tenor of the debate in the absence of a comprehensive federal law. The law criminalizes illegal immigration by categorizing it as trespassing. By this definition, local law enforcement agents are authorized to question anybody they suspect of being an illegal immigrant. Approximately 50 percent of all arrested illegal immigrants attempted a crossing at the Arizona border and lawmakers in the state are under pressure from its citizens to solve the border problem because the federal government has failed to provide comprehensive policy reform.

Current immigration policy reform has been discussed since May 2005 when Senators John McCain and (the late) Ted Kennedy proposed the Secure America and Orderly Immigration Act. In July 2005, Senators John Cornyn and Jon Kyl proposed the Comprehensive Enforcement and Immigration Reform Act. In May 2006, another attempt was made by Senator Arlen Specter titled the Comprehensive Immigration Reform Act of 2006, which was passed by the Senate but did not have any traction in the House. In two attempts, the Comprehensive Immigration Reform Act of 2007 failed to pass the Senate even though it had the support of President George W. Bush.[51] The track of failure has continued with the DREAM (Development, Relief and Education for Alien Minors) Act, proposed in September 2010 by Senator Dick Durbin, that would have provided a path to citizenship for undocumented youth who came to the United States as children (under the age of sixteen). In another bid, Senators Robert Menendez and Patrick Leahy proposed the Comprehensive Immigration Reform Act of 2010 as a fair and practical solution to the current system of targeted enforcement of immigration laws and arbitrary state solutions to the problem of illegal border crossings.

It is not clear when comprehensive immigration reform will take place. The history of immigration laws has tracked the political will and the public mood; what we know is that there are at least four core provisions that any contemporary bill would have to contain: (1) border enforcement, (2) interior enforcement, (3) nonimmigrant programs and (4) legalization of undocumented immigrants.[52] On September 22, 2010, United Press International carried a story on President Obama speaking about immigration reform in an interview with the TV network Telemundo; President Obama is quoted as saying: "You know, it is a very difficult thing to do administratively, because we want comprehensive reform." The news item added that the president doubted Congress would pass immigration reform just as midterm elections were looming in November 2010. Politicians must take the pulse of their electorate, but on the current issue of immigration reform, there is no consensus on solutions even as the second-generation children of immigrants from mixed-status families come of age as the new Americans.

Since 1996 when the Census Bureau began collecting data on this generation, the numbers of these "new" Americans have grown. The "new" Americans are the children of post-1965 immigrants who come primarily from Latin America, Asia and Africa. The Immigration Policy Center observes that this group accounted for about 10 percent of all registered voters in 2008; there are 11.6 million Latinos comprising 8 percent of registered voters and four million Asians accounting for 3 percent of registered voters; "This group of voters and potential voters includes not only immigrants who have become U.S. citizens (naturalized Americans), but also the U.S.-born children of immigrants who were raised during the current era of large-scale immigration from Latin America and Asia which began in 1965 (the post-1965 children of immigrants)."[53]

Inexplicably, the center's data do not include estimates for African and Caribbean immigrants, who are also an important bloc of new Americans. Between 1990 and 2000, the Caribbean immigrant population grew by 67 percent and the population of African immigrants grew by 167 percent. Together, these two groups contributed about 17 percent of the increase in the non-Hispanic black population. Caribbean and African immigrants outnumber and are growing faster than groups such as Cubans and Koreans.[54] What is most important about the new Americans is their connection to recent immigrant experience in America. It is this contemporary connection to the experiences of their parents and grandparents which makes the new Americans more sensitive to immigration policy and immigration reform. In its political analysis, the Immigration Policy Center concludes: "As public opinion polls reveal, anti-immigrant political rhetoric is likely to motivate many New Americans to cast ballots, but is unlikely to win many votes for candidates perceived as anti-immigrant."[55] The results of the analysis conducted by the Immigration Policy Center are not merely descriptive but potentially predictive:

> The number of New American Registered Voters *Exceeded* 2008 Presidential Victory Margins in 12 States:
>
> 1. This was the case in Arizona, California, Florida, Georgia, Indiana, Missouri, Montana, Nevada, New Jersey, North Carolina, Texas, and Virginia. In similarly close Presidential, Congressional, state house, or local elections today, the votes of New Americans could be decisive.
> 2. In North Carolina, New Americans accounted for 177,291 of the state's registered voters, while the margin of victory in the Presidential race was only 14,177 votes.
> 3. In Virginia, New Americans comprised 367,745 of all registered voters, while the margin of victory in the Presidential race was 234,527 votes.
>
> The Number of Latino and Asian Registered Voters *Exceeded* 2008 Presidential Victory Margins in 15 States:
>
> 1. This was the case in Arizona, California, Colorado, Florida, Georgia, Hawaii, Indiana, Missouri, Montana, Nevada, New Jersey, New Mexico, North Carolina, Texas, and Virginia. In similarly close Presidential, Congressional, state house, or local elections today, the votes of Latinos and Asians could be decisive.
> 2. In Arizona, Latinos and Asians accounted for 449,774 of the state's registered voters, while the margin of victory in the Presidential race was 195,404 votes.
> 3. In Missouri, Latinos and Asians comprised 42,629 of all registered voters, while the margin of victory in the Presidential race was only 3,903 votes.[56]

THREATS AT THE BORDER

One of the outcomes of the PATRIOT Act was the Secure Border Initiative (SBI). The law called for an effective program to secure the border with new fencing and to unify systems that are needed to control the spaces between POEs. The law also called for integrating the work of patrol, customs, agriculture and immigration officers. The systems approach created the SBI*net* that enhances communication among all the component parts of border security. This was a major initiative and the government spent a lot of money— over three billion dollars, according to one estimate—on new fencing and other virtual security measures to keep out smugglers, traffickers and illegal immigrants especially on the southwest border.[57]

Figure 3.3. Illegal immigrants often find themselves abandoned and disoriented in the desert, unable to find a way out. Dozens of these rescue beacons offer a lifeline to safety and medical care, with the stark reminder: "You are in danger of dying if you do not summon help." Photo courtesy of *Frontline*, Fall 2010.

The goal to achieve effective control and maintain comprehensive surveillance of the borders is important because the vast spaces between the POEs are vulnerabilities that terrorists may exploit. Included in this initiative is the mobile surveillance system (MSS), which combines ground surveillance radar, infrared cameras, and laser range finders/designators. The SBI also deployed unattended ground sensors (UGSs) that support surveillance and detections along the border. These systems have had limited effectiveness because of problems in program implementation. According to the Government Accountability Office (GAO), "these weaknesses can be attributed in part to limitations in the defined verification and acceptance of the deliverable process, a program office decision to exclude certain deliverables from the process, and insufficient time to review technical documentation. All told, DHS has not effectively managed and overseen its SBI*net* prime contractor, thus resulting in costly rework and contributing to SBI*net*'s well-chronicled history of not delivering promised capabilities and benefits on time and within budget."[58] When the secretary of the DHS, Janet Napolitano, declared that the SBI program was being stopped, she was finally admitting the need for improvement in the program: "Not only do we have an obligation to secure our borders, we have a responsibility to do so in the most cost-effective way possible, the system of sensors and cameras along the southwest border known as SBInet has been plagued with cost overruns and missed deadlines."[59] A congressman concluded that the program had been "a grave and expensive disappointment."[60] But whether the SBI program was ill conceived or not, the need to secure our border, especially after September 11, 2001, is palpable.

(In light of the ineffectiveness of SBI, the National Guard was deployed again to the southwest border in August 2010 by President Obama, continuing a practice that was initiated by his predecessor, President Bush. In all, 1,200 National Guard troops will support the work of Border Patrol by being "extra eyes and ears."[61] Critics have said the deployment is not adequate because of the size of the border, although the troops are credited with apprehending illegal immigrants on their trek across the southwest border.)

The reach of the PATRIOT Act is prescriptively broad and it covers not just border security, but infrastructure for processing at the borders, such as the ESTA program that allows DHS to determine eligibility to travel to the United States under the auspices of the VWP, the Global Entry program and the WHTI program (see chapter 1).

These measures as called for by the PATRIOT Act have had unintended consequences as well. The "watch lists" that are used to screen travelers include names of people who have no links to terrorism networks at all, ensnarling and inconveniencing travelers whose names are similar to alleged terrorists. Reports by civil liberties groups have documented incidents of harassment and discrimination at the borders because of these lists and screening methods. Asian and Muslim travelers have reported that they are threatened with detention for not answering questions about their religious practices and political beliefs, leading to charges by these groups of troubling patterns of profiling and discrimination based on race, ethnicity, national origin and religion.[62] But the system is a dynamic one and analysts are responsible for updating and reviewing these lists daily to ensure their validity. Also, travelers can file complaints about treatment at the border and DHS has to review these cases for redress. Currently there are approximately a half-million unduplicated names on the "no fly" lists, the vast proportion of which are names of foreigners.

There have been other unintended results as well. For all the expense of the SBI, more illegal immigrants are taking riskier chances, and with more personnel to patrol, Border Patrol officers are covering more ground and making more discoveries. On October 6, 2010, National Public Radio reported on *Morning Edition* that "more than 250 bodies have been discovered in the Arizona desert in the past year. That's a record. They are the remains of migrants who died trying to cross into the U.S. illegally."[63]

NOTES

1. Kirkpatrick Sale. 1990. *The conquest of paradise*. New York: Knopf.

2. Joe Feagin and Clairece Booher Feagin. 1999. *Racial and ethnic relations*, 6th ed. Upper Saddle River, NJ: Prentice Hall, p. 200.

3. Russel Thornton. 1987. *American Indian holocaust and survival: A population history since 1492*. Norman: University of Oklahoma Press.

4. Martin N. Marger. 2000. *Race and ethnic relations: American and global perspectives*, 5th ed. Stamford, CT: Wadsworth.

5. John F. Kennedy. 1958 (2008 reprint). *A nation of immigrants*. New York: Harper.

6. European colonization of the Americas. http://en.wikipedia.org/wiki/European_colonization_of_the_Americas. Accessed October 2010.

7. Joe Feagin and Clairece Booher Feagin. 1999. *Racial and ethnic relations*, 6th ed. Upper Saddle River, NJ: Prentice Hall, p. 77.

8. Wilbur S. Shepperson. 1957. *British emigration to North America*. Oxford: Basil Blackwell.

9. Stanley Lieberson and Mary C. Waters. 1988. *From many strands*. New York: Russell Sage, pp. 40–41.

10. Slavery and the law in Virginia. http://www.history.org/history/teaching/slavelaw.cfm. Accessed October 2010.

11. John Hope Franklin and Alfred A. Moss Jr. 2004. *From slavery to freedom: A history of African Americans*, 8th ed. New York: Knopf. See also Philip D. Curtin. 1969. *The Atlantic slave trade*. Madison: University of Wisconsin Press, pp. 87–93; U.S. Bureau of the Census. 1960. *Historical statistics of the United States*. Washington, DC: Author, p. 770.

12. Philip Morgan. 1998. *Slave counterpoint: Black culture in the eighteenth-century Chesapeake and lowcountry*. Chapel Hill: University of North Carolina Press.

13. Edwin G. Burrows and Mike Wallace. 1999. *Gotham: A history of New York to 1898*. New York: Oxford University Press.

14. Graham R. Hodges. 1999. *Root and branch: African Americans in New York and East Jersey 1613–1863*. Chapel Hill: University of North Carolina Press.

15. Winston James. 2002. Explaining Afro-Caribbean social mobility in the United States: Beyond the Sowell thesis. *Comparative Studies in Society and History*, *44*(2): 218–62.

16. Joe Feagin and Clairece Booher Feagin. 1999. *Racial and ethnic relations*, 6th ed. Upper Saddle River, NJ: Prentice Hall, p. 106. See also James Leyburn. 1962. *The Scotch-Irish*. Chapel Hill: University of North Carolina Press.

17. Compare the historical account in John F. Kennedy. 1958. *A nation of immigrants*. New York: Harper.

18. *Immigration legal history: Legislation from 1790–1900*. Washington, DC: U.S. Citizenship and Immigration Services.

19. Ibid.

20. *Immigration legal history: Legislation from 1901–1940*. Washington, DC: U.S. Citizenship and Immigration Services.

21. *Immigration legal history: Legislation from 1941–1960*. Washington, DC: U.S. Citizenship and Immigration Services.

22. Philip di Franco. 1988. *The Italian American experience*. New York: Tom Doherty Associates.

23. Giovanni Schiavo. 1934. *The Italians in America before the Civil War*. New York: Vigo Press.

24. *Immigration legal history: Legislation from 1901–1940*. Washington, DC: U.S. Citizenship and Immigration Services.

25. Ibid.

26. Ibid.

27. Ibid.

28. John Higham. 1975. *Strangers in the land*. New York: Atheneum.

29. Arthur Hertzburg. 1989. *The Jews in America*. New York: Simon & Schuster.

30. Hilary Conroy. 1953. *The Japanese frontier in Hawaii 1868–1898*. Berkeley: University of California Press.

31. Joe Feagin and Clairece Booher Feagin. 1999. *Racial and ethnic relations*, 6th ed. Upper Saddle River, NJ: Prentice Hall, p. 383.

32. *Immigration legal history: Legislation from 1901–1940*. Washington, DC: U.S. Citizenship and Immigration Services.

33. Carl N. Degler. 1959. *Out of our past*. New York: Harper, p. 109.

34. See Joe Feagin and Clairece Booher Feagin. 1999. *Racial and ethnic relations*, 6th ed. Upper Saddle River, NJ: Prentice Hall, p. 66.

35. *Immigration legal history: Legislation from 1961–1980*. Washington, DC: U.S. Citizenship and Immigration Services.

36. John R. Weeks. 1986. *Population: An introduction to concepts and issues*. Belmont, CA: Wadsworth.

37. *Immigration legal history: Legislation from 1961–1980*. Washington, DC: U.S. Citizenship and Immigration Services.

38. *Immigration legal history: Legislation from 1981–1996*. Washington, DC: U.S. Citizenship and Immigration Services.

39. Jacqueline Maria Hagan and Susan Gonzalez Baker. 1993 (Fall). Implementing the U.S. Legalization Program. *International Migration Review, 27*: 514.

40. *Immigration legal history: Legislation from 1981–1996*. Washington, DC: U.S. Citizenship and Immigration Services.

41. Joe Feagin and Clairece Booher Feagin. 1999. *Racial and ethnic relations*, 6th ed. Upper Saddle River, NJ: Prentice Hall, p. 460.

42. Jeffrey S. Passel and D'Vera Cohn. 2009. *A portrait of unauthorized immigrants in the United States*. Washington, DC: Pew Hispanic Center.

43. Fixing a broken immigration system. 2009 (December). *Centerpoint, Woodrow Wilson International Center for Scholars Newsletter*, pp. 1–2. See also Mae M. Ngai. 2005. *Impossible subjects: Illegal aliens and the making of America*. Princeton, NJ: Princeton University Press.

44. Spenser S. Hsu. 2010 (February 10). U.S. illegal immigrant population declines for second year. *Washington Post*, p. A1.

45. Jeffrey S. Passel and D'Vera Cohn. 2009. *A portrait of unauthorized immigrants in the United States*. Washington, DC: Pew Hispanic Center.

46. Ibid.

47. Shankar Vedantam. 2010 (October 7). U.S. deportations reach record high. *Washington Post*, p. A10.

48. Peter Slavin. 2010 (July 26). Deportation of illegal immigrants increases under Obama administration. *Washington Post*, p. A9.

49. Shankar Vedantam. 2010 (October 7). U.S. deportations reach record high. *Washington Post*, p. A10.

50. Shankar Vedantam. 2010 (November 2). Destined for deportation. Salvadoran woman targeted by program designed to catch undocumented criminals. *Washington Post*, p. B1.

51. Comprehensive Immigration Reform Act of 2007. http://en.wikipedia.org/wiki/Comprehensive_Immigration_Reform_Act_of_2007. Accessed October 2010.

52. Aristide R. Zolberg. 2006. *A nation by design: Immigration policy in the fashioning of America*. New York and Cambridge, MA: Russell Sage Foundation and Harvard University Press. See also Carol M. Swain (ed.). 2007. *Debating immigration*. Cambridge: Cambridge University Press.

53. Immigration Policy Center. 2010. *The new American electorate: The growing political power of immigrants and their children*. Washington, DC: Author.

54. John R. Logan. 2007. Who are the other African Americans? Contemporary African and Caribbean immigrants in the United States. In Yoku Shaw-Taylor and Steven Tuch (eds.), *The other African Americans*, pp. 49–68. Lanham, MD: Rowman & Littlefield.

55. Immigration Policy Center 2010. *Executive summary. The new American electorate: The growing political power of immigrants and their children*. Washington, DC: Author.

56. Ibid.

57. Stephen S. Hsu. 2010 (March 16). Work to cease on virtual fence along U.S.-Mexico border. *Washington Post*, p. A4.

58. Government Accountability Office. 2010. *Secure Border Initiative: DHS needs to strengthen management and oversight of its prime contractor*. Washington, DC: Government Printing Office.

59. Stephen S. Hsu. 2010 (March 16). Work to cease on virtual fence along U.S.-Mexico border. *Washington Post*, p. A4.

60. Ibid.

61. Amanda Lee Myers. 2010 (October 8). Feds touting National Guard mission in Arizona. Associated Press.

62. Spencer S. Hsu. 2009 (April 20). U.S. border screening under fire. *Washington Post*, p. A13.

63. Ted Robbins. 2010. Illegal immigrant deaths set record in Arizona. National Public Radio, October 6.

Chapter 4

Assimilation in America

A ssimilation is the process by which immigrants remake themselves
as Americans through the acculturation of our values, norms and beliefs; new immigrants are socialized to believe in the value of equality of all men and women, the norms of freedom and the pursuit of liberty in
America. Immigrants eventually intermarry with citizens or the natives and
they take on new identities as Americans.

But there are barriers to this process in the form of prejudice, stereotypes
and discrimination, and the assimilation process is always tempered by the
adoption of transnational identities which is an attribute of each successive
wave of immigrants since this great land was settled by immigrant colonizers.
Transnationalism is also the extension of family and social networks beyond
the United States. There are limits to the effect of assimilation as well, and
the maintenance of transnational identities may be strained by the sweeping
surveillance provisions contained in the PATRIOT Act. The challenge of assimilation in America is to create and recreate an inclusive American identity
based on different regional and transnational expressions of culture without
perpetuating prejudice, stereotype and social distance.

THE STAGES

When the erstwhile Bureau of Immigration and Naturalization Service began testing immigrants for literacy in English (the 1917 act), it was the first
formal process determining the requisites for assimilation in America. Even
though our ethnic ancestries create "hybrid" identities (Irish American, Pol-
ish American, Jamaican American, Nigerian American, etc.), we become a

somewhat distinctive national culture through assimilation. Our ethnic terrain produces an "ecumenical" (or inclusive) American culture[1] that derives its strength from its diverse constituent parts.

In our society, there are social forces that encourage integration or conformity to the generalized culture and value system; newcomers shed their "outsider" status and take on the beliefs and customs of Americans. In chapter 3, the cultural evolution of America was traced to show the significance of English Americans in the new nation; the English were immigrant colonizers and they influenced the adoption of language, customs and social institutions. These early immigrants also became dominant through their economic and political power. During the early immigration, the Africans, Irish, Germans, Chinese, Italians, Jews, Mexicans, Japanese and other groups had to conform to the culture of the immigrant colonizers. It is true the other immigrants have added to the ecumenical American character, but it is the English who have formed the cultural and institutional basis of this country.

Assimilation ideas and concepts tell us about the nature of immigrant incorporation into and adaption to American society; it is a process during which immigrants embrace our cultural philosophy. But assimilation and ethnic identification in America is a two-way, recursive and dynamic process. As social scientists began writing about assimilation generally and about assimilation in America in particular, their original focus was on the early immigrant flows from Europe and how these groups would become integrated into the Anglo-based American culture. But current research on immigrants from South America, Asia and the Caribbean is changing the way we think about how immigrants become incorporated or integrated. The assimilation process is a gradual one—it involves the "interpenetration and fusion" of people and groups during which immigrants "acquire the memories, sentiments, and attitudes of other persons or groups, and by sharing their experience and history are incorporated with them in a common cultural life."[2] During this process of fusion, groups take pains to reduce the incidence of conflict and manage competition so that there is a certain level of assurance that the newcomers will not undermine the extant social structure.

The original ideas about the process of immigrant incorporation described a process that eventually ends in the assimilation phase. Before assimilation, there is the initial phase involving contact between immigrants and native groups. The phase of competition follows the initial phase as immigrants attempt to gain economic advantage in their new land of settlement. During the accommodation phase, barriers between the newcomers and the natives decline and in the final assimilation phase, the newcomers take on the attributes of the natives.[3] The phases of incorporation, according to this explanation, lead progressively to the final phase of assimilation. The pull of the United States of America is a global one—all immigrants have a globalized view of

America even before they set foot here. As immigrants move toward assimilation, the process is moderated by other factors such as race and ethnicity. Researchers have noted that when the ethnic and racial attributes of immigrants are not similar to those of the host culture, the incorporation process leading to assimilation may take longer and the competition and accommodation phases may be prolonged.[4]

During the early immigration from the seventeenth to nineteenth centuries, the pressures to conform to the still-evolving Anglo American culture were higher than they are now—in one publication, groups were ranked based on their similarity or cultural adaptability to that of the Anglo immigrant colonizers.[5] The ethnicity of certain groups was used as a predictor of the level of their eventual assimilation into the culture and therefore an indicator of how quickly they would move up in social status. Based on the cultural and physical attributes of the immigrant group, researchers could predict the social and economic advantages they would receive in America. These were the early years of understanding ethnic and racial hierarchies in America and how certain groups created enclaves because they couldn't readily get into the mainstream society. Our history books relate the struggles of so-called white ethnics such as Irish Americans and Italian Americans, and nonwhites from Asia, South America, the Caribbean and Africa.

The early writings about the process of assimilation in America necessarily focused on the pull of the American culture. Anglo conformity was a requirement for moving up in the emergent American space. However, "unlearning" one's culture or identity is a severe proposition. Immigrants do not "unlearn" their culture or their identity as they become assimilated; rather they go through stages of integration and then take on attributes that do not unmake their identities, but remake them. The stages of assimilation (the final phase of immigrant incorporation) have been described as follows:[6]

1. Acculturation: cultural or behavioral assimilation or the adoption of customs and language
2. Structural assimilation: entry into cliques, clubs and institutions
3. Marital assimilation: intermarriage
4. Identification assimilation: development of new identities
5. Attitude reception assimilation: decrease and eventual absence of prejudice
6. Behavior reception assimilation: decrease and eventual absence of discrimination
7. Civic assimilation: decrease and eventual absence of conflict

These stages show how the process of assimilation takes shape in America according to Milton Gordon. But these stages could take place in any given

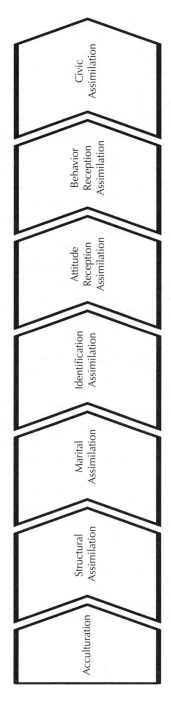

Figure 4.1. The stages of assimilation.

society. Progressively, intermarriage shows that the social distance between immigrant groups and the host American society has diminished to the point where immigrants are accepted into the community as kin, as family. Before intermarriage occurs, immigrant groups must be accepted into the closed social clubs usually reserved for "members only." The immigrant must demonstrate the characteristics of belonging and must project his or her willingness to become American. According to this trajectory, you cannot, as an immigrant, expect to be considered a bona fide community member if you do not accept the general guidelines of membership in terms of rules of behavior. Belonging in any community also entails individual responsibilities in terms of acceptance of the generalized value system of ownership.

While most marriages occur within an ethnic or racial group, the incidence and prevalence of intermarriages show that racial or ethnic boundaries are being crossed and that the social distance between groups is reducing. This is ultimately a good thing and an important indicator of assimilation. In 2010, a research report by the Pew Center showed how this indicator of assimilation was bearing out in the United States:

- Rates of intermarriages among newlyweds in the United States more than doubled between 1980 (6.7 percent) and 2008 (14.6 percent). A record 14.6 percent of all new marriages in the United States in 2008 were between spouses of a different race or ethnicity from one another. This includes marriages between a Hispanic and non-Hispanic as well as marriages between spouses of different races—be they white, black, Asian, American Indian or those who identify as being of multiple races or "some other" race.
- Among all newlyweds in 2008, 9 percent of whites, 16 percent of blacks, 26 percent of Hispanics and 31 percent of Asians married someone whose race or ethnicity was different from their own.
- Among all new marriages in 2008, 22 percent in the West were interracial or interethnic, compared with 13 percent in both the South and Northeast and 11 percent in the Midwest.
- Most Americans say they approve of racial or ethnic intermarriage—not just in the abstract, but in their own families. More than six in ten say it "would be fine" with them if a family member told them they were going to marry someone from any of three major race/ethnic groups other than their own.
- Thirty-five percent of adults say they have a family member who is married to someone of a different race. Blacks say this at higher rates than do whites; younger adults at higher rates than older adults; and westerners at higher rates than people living in other regions of the country.[7]

Intermarriages signify that groups are moving closer to one another metaphorically and geographically.[8] This is not to say that social distance between and among groups has been completely bridged (in some kind of "postracial"

Figure 4.2. Assimilation in America. Photo courtesy of CBP.

environment). There is still evidence of residential segregation; that is, clusters of specific ethnic groups living in sections of a given city and areas where there is little to no diversity in terms of the racial makeup of residents.[9]

The stages of assimilation after intermarriage show how new identities will emerge and how prejudice, stereotypes, discrimination and conflict decline based on incorporation. And it is the promise of America that the values of equality, freedom and liberty trump prejudice, stereotypes and discrimination.

PREJUDICE, STEREOTYPES, DISCRIMINATION AND PRESENTATION OF THE SELF—PROFILERS ARE US

The experience of assimilation also exposes us to prejudice—mostly in the form of negative attitudes about other groups used as shorthand descriptors. Sometimes, these prejudices would lead to discrimination or actions that have harmful effects on others. Stereotypes flow from prejudice, in that the negative attitude about a group is used as a generalization to define a person of the group. Profiling is a form of prejudice that can lead to discrimination. All of this happens within the context of culture, which is the powerful basis of any ethnic group—it signifies language and ways of thinking, behaving and

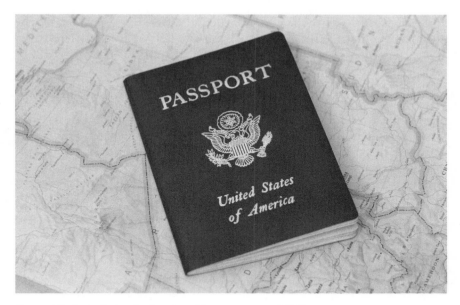

Figure 4.3. Assimilation in America. Photo courtesy of CBP.

acting as prescribed by a common natural history. People from a particular country may share a national culture—but within that country there may be different ethnic groups based on their histories; generally, ethnic groups have a cultural basis and racial groups are defined by phenotypes or physical characteristics.

There are many historical and current examples of prejudice, stereotypes and discrimination against relatively new immigrants. Despite the significance of these experiences, I will not repeat the hurtful and harmful affairs or episodes of prejudice, stereotypes and discrimination that have been an inauspicious part of our culture since our nation was founded—suffice it to say that most of the racial and ethnic groups have experienced this unpalatable aspect of our culture. This was what the Civil Rights Act of 1964 formally attempted to correct.

One assimilation lesson we learn as we come to terms with prejudice, stereotypes and discrimination is that we all become "racialized"[10] as we become American. In the process of becoming American, there is some kind of "hazing" that comes with the primal awareness of racial differentiation. In the extreme, it emboldens fringe Americans to kill. The reckoning is that "race consciousness" is a requisite for becoming American. When sociologists have studied prejudice, stereotypes and discrimination, they have highlighted how our individual defining characteristics become significant; the cumulative effects of the lived experience of differential treatment and the perception of hostility in public areas (such as restaurants, hotels, department stores) show that we cannot, as individuals, take for granted how we will be received in public areas where we are anonymous.

In our daily interactions with others, we are all interested in presenting ourselves in the best possible light—based on whatever conception we have of ourselves. We seek the same from others, that they would treat us within the same framework of how we define ourselves; we attempt to define the encounter based on our appearance and other indicators of our social status. We are interested in calling forth certain desired responses. Any public social encounter is a situation where the dialogue and interaction are negotiated between presentation of the self and the disruptive perception that traps us in the other person's prejudice and stereotype; "life may not be much of a gamble, but interaction is."[11]

These interactions require negotiations based on our identity and the un-remitting possibility of negative attitudes and unflattering stereotype that the other person may harbor about us. All the other person relies on is the way we look, the way we appear; so it doesn't matter what our station in life is. This reliance on stereotype means that we are essentially caught within the other person's prejudice based on the American racial taxonomy. The ethnic or racial features that lead to prejudice and stereotyping permit discrimination because the assumed imperfections about the other person allow us to impute, without hesitation, that unequal or harmful treatment is warranted based on the other's presumed undesirable attributes.

The unfortunate outcome of profiling and discrimination is the reinforcement of stratification in the American society. It is the promise of America that we call out these patterns of racial or ethnic antagonism whether they are based on the occurrence of discrimination or even the *perception* of its occurrence. The reality is that because of the racialized setting, some of us must constantly be vigilant and on the lookout for disruptions that our identities may generate from others. The ascriptions we desire cannot be taken for granted. A corollary of discrimination is *reverse* discrimination. Discrimination becomes reverse when it is practiced by the individuals or groups who have traditionally been victims of these unequal or harmful actions. An important distinction, however, is that reverse discrimination is not supported by any institutional or systemic framework of the kind that buttressed racial discrimination in a variety of forms before the Civil Rights Act of 1964.

In the stages of assimilation, the decline of prejudice and discrimination is an infinitely good thing for our society. However, as we come to terms with the cultural definitions of our identities as Americans, the production and presentation of the self is never a settled social phenomenon. The barriers to assimilation mean that some groups do not fully identify as being part of the American alloy. There is "segmented" assimilation[12] based on prejudice, stereotype and discrimination that make it difficult for some immigrants to follow the path to civic assimilation as described by Milton Gordon in his stages of assimilation.

TRANSNATIONALISM AND RECREATING AN AMERICAN IDENTITY

Second-generation immigrants are really no longer immigrants; we call them children of immigrants, but they are more American than their parents. At the same time, there is a continuing process of transnationalism. Researchers have written about the development of transnational "consciousness"[13] among the second generation through contact with their parents' birthplaces and maintenance of family and social relations in these countries. This process of transnational migration is an involved one, because individuals must maintain "multi-stranded social relations that link together societies of origin and settlement."[14] This involves sustaining multiple identities and loyalties. The study of transnational migration is focused on the reorganization of the lives of immigrants and the emergent social, economic and political outcomes in the countries of origin and settlement. This is different from state or governmental activities relating to citizenship rights; it is also different from global nonstate or nongovernmental organizations and corporations that involve transnational or international economic relations or social movements.

Transnationalism is not new. Transnational migration is a process that first-generation immigrants have undertaken in one form or another; these activities have included maintaining social links and sending remittances to families back home. Early immigrants kept in close touch with families through letters and created identities based on the culture of their places of birth. In 1916, a writer noted that "America is coming to be, not a nationality, but a trans-nationality, a weaving back and forth, with the other lands, of many threads."[15] As a contemporary process, transnationalism is happening within the context of the "global village." It is a process facilitated and sustained by technology and relative prosperity, such as the Internet, cell phones, and inexpensive airline tickets. In our era, it is possible to distinguish two kinds of transmigrants or transnationals: the core type who are frequent travelers to their ancestral countries and places of birth versus transmigrants whose travel to their places of birth is sporadic or infrequent and whose engagement in transnational activities is limited.[16]

However, the practice of transnationalism bears risks. The historical ties, loyalties and practices that define the identity of the American transmigrant can lead to greater scrutiny under our new awareness about threats and

vulnerabilities in the homeland. Frequent travel to certain places raises suspicion and new provisions under the PATRIOT Act may allow seemingly
innocuous activities by ordinary citizens to be monitored by the government.
And yet, transmigration is another dimension of our "nation of immigrants."
First-generation immigrants are merely ordinary citizens who necessarily
live their lives across borders and across cultures. Some first-generation immigrants maintain business connections and are entrepreneurs whose circle
of business activities involves frequent travel and transactions across borders.

For the children of immigrants, or the second generation, the ties that bind
them to the places of birth of their parents will not be as strong. People of
this generation have to manage their transnational ties just as they are defining themselves as American. If they are of a darker hue or are phenotypically
different, their American peers may not perceive them as fully American
because of their cultural ties or the way they look. The children of first-
generation immigrants may be more engaged in the symbolic culture of their
parents—perhaps wearing certain types of attire on special occasions to show
their cultural affiliation. But they may attach less significance to the cultural
ties that their parents maintain across borders.[17]

If we understand assimilation to be an interactive process during which
the affirmation of ethnicity becomes part of the American identity, then
transnationalism does not challenge assimilation but rather reaffirms cultural
affiliations. Assimilation is not necessarily a "homogenizing" process, but
rather the integration of the "natural histories"[18] of different ethnic groups.
In the absence of prejudice, stereotypes and discrimination, assimilation is
the significant rewarding experience of immigrants. And it remains the most
important dimension of intergroup relations in our homeland[19] because it is
the path through which immigrants are able to attain economic prosperity and
recreate themselves as Americans through resocialization.

THE LIMITS OF RESOCIALIZATION

It is not only first-generation immigrants and their children who assimilate
into our American culture. We are all socialized to become Americans in ex-
plicit ways (such as how to dress, how to behave) and implicit ways (mores
and moral values). There are powerful "agents" who help mold us into good
citizens. Our families are the primary agents of socialization, for it is within
our families that we first learn about our identities, intimate relationships and
group life. Our schools are powerful agents of socialization where conformity
to rules and regulations is taught and enforced. Our peers mold us through
the usual give and take that occurs among equals as we experience the consequence of nonconformity to rules. The mass media (print and electronic, but

especially the television) are the other significant socializing agents, project-
ing and depicting specific roles and sometimes reinforcing stereotypes. With
all these agents, the socialization process is an enduring one. Immigrants
learn to assimilate from Americans who have already been socialized to accept the beliefs, norms and values of our society. Immigrants learn new roles
and self-identities as they resocialize as Americans.

When Timothy McVeigh bombed the Alfred P. Murrah Federal Building
in Oklahoma in 1995, it was the most egregious and most serious act of an
American whose socialization into the American way of life had severely
deviated from what was expected. That bombing was the most destructive
terrorist act by an American on our soil—killing 198 people including nineteen children. Almost six years later, another terrorist act was committed
by foreigners who had been allowed into the United States. Terrorism by
Americans against fellow Americans was only perfected by McVeigh in its
scale; thirty years before, a terrorist act by Americans at the Sixteenth Street
Baptist Church in the morning of a September day killed four young girls in
Birmingham.

As we have grappled with how our open and largely welcoming society
can become so threatened after the events of September 11, 2001, we have
become more aware of the impact of deviance and countercultures in our
society and the limits of socialization or resocialization. When individuals or
groups deviate from the accepted norms of our society, their actions are in *op-
position* to the larger society—these are countercultures. Deviance becomes
a significant problem when individuals act in oppositional ways that elicit
negative sanctions.[20] There is an important distinction between countercultures and subcultures. Subcultures are differentiated norms and values that
exist within our society but are not opposed to society's norms and values.
The content of subcultures may be distinguishable from the culture of the
society at large but is not opposed to the culture of society. The content of
counterculture is distinguishable from the culture of the society at large and
also opposed to the culture of society. Crime—"actions that are deemed in-
jurious to the public welfare or morals or to the interests of the state and is
legally prohibited"[21, 22]—is the most pervasive type of deviant behavior, and
there are certain types of crime, *mala in se* (bad in themselves), that elicit
universal condemnation: murder, rape, robbery, burglary and assault.

Awareness of our vulnerabilities has made the national mood more sensitive to deviance and countercultures over time.[23] The Uniting and Strengthening America by Providing Appropriate Tools Required to Intercept and
Obstruct Terrorism Act of 2001 (the PATRIOT Act) was signed into law by
President George W. Bush on October 26, 2001, to attend to the threats that
undermine the production of our American reality. The act expanded authority for surveillance and tracking and "reduced restrictions on law enforcement

agencies' ability to search telephone, e-mail communications, medical, financial, and other records; eased restrictions on foreign intelligence gathering within the U.S.; expanded the Secretary of the Treasury's authority to regulate financial transactions, particularly those involving foreign individuals and entities; and broadened the discretion of law enforcement and immigration authorities in detaining and deporting immigrants suspected of terrorism-related acts. The Act also expanded the definition of terrorism to include domestic terrorism, thus enlarging the number of activities to which law enforcement powers could be applied."[24]

The unprecedented nature of the authorizations to monitor Americans and the removal of walls between criminal investigations and surveillance may be necessary safeguards for our homeland, but how do these new powers affect our socialization, assimilation or resocialization as Americans? For those of us with transnational identities, there is the question of whether competing cultural loyalties challenge assimilation into our American culture. This is a strain on the integration of a diversity of identities as we "hold the line" on what is American and what is not. Some researchers have argued that these new policies will negatively impact particularly Arab and Muslim Americans and non-Christian immigrants based on the provisions that allow (1) for the control of entry into the United States, (2) monitoring of foreigners, (3) voluntary interview program or community reporting, and (4) intelligence gathering that justifies secret detentions and the Foreign Intelligence Surveillance Act (FISA). The Migration Policy Institute (MPI) believes that "rather than concentrating its efforts on investigation, surveillance and law enforcement based on individualized suspicion, the government has essentially used national origin as a proxy for evidence of dangerousness. By the discriminatory action of targeting specific ethnic groups with its new measures, the government has violated a core principle of American justice."[25] For whatever identity we choose, there is feedback in the form of prejudice, stereotype, discrimination or rewards and advantages that our identities bestow upon us. Some of us must be on the lookout for how our identities may call out unwanted reactions and treatment.

In their report on the experiences of Americans with Middle Eastern heritage and American Muslims after September 11, 2001, the MPI notes that: "Many Muslims in the U.S. today feel that they are under a microscope. On the one hand they have been the objects of suspicion by the government and hate by ordinary citizens; on the other hand they feel they must defend and serve as ambassadors of Islam, . . . Arab and Muslim Americans feel under siege. They believe there is an aura of fear and suspicion."[26] It is palpable.

Sociologists have argued that officers of the law make decisions about where and what to look for and whether to make an arrest based on perceived or actual patterns of crime. Surveillance efforts involve spending a considerable amount of time on areas and particular groups that they believe, rightly or wrongly, have a higher incidence or prevalence of the phenomenon of interest. The problem of such a focus on particular types of people and places is the potential for profiling, an offshoot of prejudice and stereotype.[27] These practices, the researchers say, bias the data on prevalence and incidence of events because of the focus on particular areas and groups. It is of course unlawful to use race, gender, or class as a basis for any law enforcement action, and there will be no law enforcement agency that will admit to doing anything that is unlawful. But it is exactly the perception of some groups that they are under scrutiny and are being profiled. Take, for instance, the issue of racial profiling in motorist stops. In 2000, the GAO released the results of a comprehensive study of traffic stops and concluded that African American motorists in particular, and minority motorists in general, were proportionately more likely than whites to be stopped on the roadways studied,[28] but this was not a nationwide phenomenon.

The challenge for enforcement agencies is to consistently rely on careful analysis of data to forecast and contain potential threats, and not to use shorthand descriptors to predict deviance or crime. Within the public space of social encounters, we moderate the use of these shorthand descriptors if only because the law requires that we do so. It may be the case that prejudice and its ancillary dimensions are the subtext of the grand assimilation narrative in America. This explains why profiling at the border and within the homeland has again dominated the public mood. It is not a new phenomenon; various groups over the years have been victims of prejudice and profiling in our evolution as a country. The public mood *shifts* and rightly or wrongly, there is a collective gaze that refocuses our attention.

At the borders, there is no substitute for actionable intelligence and data. In the anonymity of the public space in the federal inspection station (FIS), and when there are no firm data on the risk level a traveler poses, officers at the border may rely on shorthand descriptors and identifiers to assess the people they are processing; officers have, on average, less than five minutes to do this assessment. In public, we mutually prejudge and stereotype one another because we are all anonymous even as we attempt to call forth favorable impressions about ourselves from the other person in the interactive space; it is a kind of gambit.

ECUMENICAL AMERICA[29]

There is an American cosmos made up of regional expressions and integrated transnational peoples—these regional orbits have been described as the Atlantic, Tex-Mex, California and the Northwest, depicting multicultural influences

Figure 4.4. Prejudice and profiling: Portraits of America. Photo by Greg Gorman.

in particular spheres of our American spaces. We are still largely a Christian society and our culture is anchored by the legacy of the English settlers whose language we use. But we become one alloy through assimilation, and we contribute to this alloy by negotiating the racial/ethnic signifiers or markers that make us vulnerable to stereotype. The American identity we adopt as immigrants is ecumenical and it is universally recognized around the globe.

However, in the orbit of the American cosmos is the rotation and ubiquity of prejudice and stereotype. Consider the incident in October 2010 when the African American journalist Juan Williams made statements about "people in Muslim garb" on TV. I wondered: Is it easier for Americans to stereotype one another? How different are we in this characteristic from other cultures? Has September 11, 2001, given us more reason to do so? When stereotyping occurs—and it does on a daily basis—it signals that we are still very much socially distant from one another. Muslim Americans and Arab Americans have become targets of this public mood for prejudging. This is the subtext of assimilation in America.

At the border, Muslim Americans have reported what they deem as greater scrutiny and what they believe to be prejudice: the story is told of Samer Shehata, professor of Middle Eastern studies at Georgetown University, who was referred to secondary inspection at the border upon his return from vacation in Mexico with his wife and their four-year-old son. Shehata had never experienced this treatment before. After forty minutes Shehata began to worry about missing their connecting flight. He told one of the officers as much and a few minutes afterward he was summoned to speak to the supervisor of homeland security at Fort Lauderdale (Florida) airport. Shehata said what followed wasn't a question-and-answer session as much as it was an interrogation. "He asked me about my parents, what I studied in college, where I went to college, my sisters' names," Shehata said. "Then I suggested he look up my resume on the Georgetown University website because all the information he wanted was there." Then the interview took a bizarre turn. According to Shehata, after he told the border officer that he taught Middle Eastern politics, the officer asked, "Who's going to win?"[30] According to Shehata, the officer stated that "location of birth" was the reason for the secondary inspection. Shehata is an American citizen born in Egypt. "For the first time in my life, I felt my status in this country was tenuous, even though I have lived here for decades—ever since I was five or six years old," Shehata said.[31]

On March 10, 2011, U.S. Congressman Peter King, chairman of the House Committee on Homeland Security, held hearings on the "Extent of Radicalization in the American Muslim Community and that Community's Response." This was the fifteenth time Congress had held discussions about homegrown terrorism and radicalization of Muslims in America (or American Muslims). The hearing brought to the American foreground, once again, suspicions about Muslims in America and consequent Islamophobia experienced by American Muslims.[32, 33] This followed the shootings at Fort Hood in Texas by Nidal Malik Hassan that killed thirteen people and wounded another twenty-nine. Hassan is a Muslim and was a U.S. Army psychiatrist. Congressman King's hearings also followed the heated public arguments and debate about plans by Imam Feisal Abdul Rauf to build an Islamic center in Lower Manhattan, two blocks from the World Trade Center site. This proposal convulsed the media and the political class in the early fall of 2010. This public mood about Islam in America was captured conscientiously by

Akbar Ahmed, a professor at American University, in his opinion piece in the *New York Times*:

> Muslim leaders must acknowledge that many Americans are fearful of religiously motivated terrorism. Muslims should embrace the chance to explain their beliefs fully and clearly. But members of Congress also need to act responsibly. They should avoid broad accusations. . . . The actions of both groups will shape America's relationship with Islam, and the relationship of American Muslims with their country. . . . The diversity of the Muslim community is frequently obscured by ignorance and mistrust. We were often asked by non-Muslims whether Muslims could be "good" Americans. Too many Americans acknowledged that they knew virtually nothing about Islam and said they had never met a Muslim. At the same time, Muslims must realize that to be truly accepted as "good" Americans, they need to more explicitly embrace American identity, culture and history—from political debates like Representative King's hearing to the ideals of this country's founders. America, in turn, must realize its best aspirations by better understanding Islam. No appreciation of the founders is complete without an acknowledgment of their truly pluralist vision.[34]

Below is the social distance scale, first conceptualized by two sociologists, Robert Park and Ernest Burgess, and empirically calibrated by Emory Borgadus.[35, 36] The cumulative scale describes progressive degrees of social contact or social distance and is a valuable instrument in the toolbox of sociologists. Insert any group into the scale and measure your level of prejudice and bigotry as an American (or not) toward this group; this will be your temporal level of social distance from this group. Pick more than one group—indeed, pick all the identifiable racial/ethnic groups in America. And be true to yourself! For each question, give a yes or no response.

Would you be willing to admit or accept (insert group)

- To close kinship by marriage?
- To my club as personal friend?
- To live on the same street as my neighbor?
- To be a co-worker in the same occupation?
- To citizenship in my country?
- As only visitors in my country? Or
- Would you be willing to exclude (insert group) from my country?

NOTES

1. Orlando Patterson. 1994 (Summer). Ecumenical America: Global culture and the American cosmos. *World Policy Journal, 11*: 103–17.

2. Robert Park and Ernest Burgess. 1921. *Introduction to the science of sociology.* Chicago: University of Chicago Press.

3. Robert Park. 1950. *Race and culture.* Glencoe, IL: Free Press.

4. Lloyd W. Warner and Leo Srole. 1945. *The social systems of American ethnic groups.* New Haven, CT: Yale University Press.

5. Ibid.

6. Milton M. Gordon. 1964. *Assimilation in American life: The role of race, religion and national origins.* New York: Oxford University Press. See also Gordon Allport. 1979. *The nature of prejudice.* Reading, MA: Addison-Wesley.

7. Paul Taylor, Jeffrey S. Passel, Wendy Wang, Jocelyn Kiley, Gabriel Valasco, and Daniel Dockterman. 2010. *Marrying out: One-in-seven U.S. marriages is interracial or interethnic.* Washington, DC: Pew Center.

8. Regine O. Jackson and Yoku Shaw-Taylor. 2010 (June 12). Intermarriage among blacks in America. RacismReview.com.

9. John R. Logan. 2007. Who are the other African Americans? Contemporary African and Caribbean immigrants in the United States. In Yoku Shaw-Taylor and Steven Tuch (eds.), *The other African Americans*, pp. 49–68. Lanham, MD: Rowman & Littlefield.

10. Eduardo Bonnila-Silva. 1996 (June). Rethinking racism: Toward a structural interpretation. *American Sociological Review, 62*: 465–80. See also Yoku Shaw-Taylor. 2007. The intersection of assimilation, race, presentation of self. In Yoku Shaw-Taylor and Steven Tuch (eds.), *The other African Americans*, p. 19. Lanham, MD: Rowman & Littlefield.

11. Erving Goffman. 1959. *The presentation of self in everyday life.* New York: Doubleday, p. 243; see also Erving Goffman. 1961. *Encounters: Two studies in the sociology of interaction.* Indianapolis: Bobbs-Merrill; Erving Goffman. 1963a. *Stigma: Notes on the management of spoiled identity.* Englewood Cliffs, NJ: Prentice Hall; Erving Goffman. 1963b. *Behavior in public places: Notes on the social organization of gatherings.* New York: Free Press; Erving Goffman. 1971. *Relations in public: Microstudies of the public order.* New York: Basic Books; Erving Goffman. 1983 (February). The interaction order: American Sociological Association, 1982 presidential address. *American Sociological Review, 48*: 1–17.

12. Alejandro Portes and Min Zhou. 1993 (November). The new second generation: Segmented assimilation and its variants. *Annals of the American Academy of Political and Social Science, 530*: 74–96.

13. Milton Vickerman. 2002. Second-generation West Indian transnationalism. In Peggy Levitt and Mary Waters (eds.), *The changing face of home: The transnational lives of the second generation*, pp. 341–66. New York: Russell Sage Foundation.

14. Linda Basch, Nina Glick Schiller, and Cristina S. Blanc. 1994. *Nations unbound: Transnational projects, postcolonial predicaments and deterritorialized nation-states.* Langhorne, PA: Gordon and Breach, p. 7.

15. Randolph S. Bourne. 1916. Trans-national America. *Atlantic Monthly, 118*: 86–97, cited in Rubén G. Rumbaut. 2002. Severed or sustained attachments? Language identity and imagined communities in the postimmigrant generation. In Peggy Levitt and Mary Waters (eds.), *The changing face of home: The transnational lives of the second generation*, pp. 43–95. New York: Russell Sage Foundation.

16. Peggy Levitt and Mary C. Waters, eds. 2002. *The changing face of home: The transnational lives of the second generation.* New York: Russell Sage Foundation.

17. Milton Vickerman. 2002. Second-generation West Indian transnationalism. In Peggy Levitt and Mary Waters (eds.), *The changing face of home: The transnational*

lives of the second generation, pp. 341–66. New York: Russell Sage Foundation. See also Rubén G. Rumbaut. 2002. Severed or sustained attachments? Language identity and imagined communities in the post-immigrant generation. In Peggy Levitt and Mary Waters (eds.), *The changing face of home: The transnational lives of the second generation*, pp. 43–95. New York: Russell Sage Foundation.

18. Andrew M. Greeley. 1976. *Ethnicity in the United States: A preliminary reconnaissance*. New York: Wiley.

19. Richard Alba and Victor Nee. 2003. *Remaking the American mainstream: Assimilation and contemporary immigration*. Cambridge, MA: Harvard University Press.

20. Marshall B. Clinard and Robert F. Meier. 1995. *Sociology of deviant behavior*. Fort Worth: Harcourt Brace, p. 8.

21. Encyclopedia Britannica. 2008. Crime. Encyclopedia Britannica Online. http://www.britannica.com. Accessed November 2010.

22. Marshall B. Clinard and Robert F. Meier. 1995. *Sociology of deviant behavior*. Fort Worth: Harcourt Brace, p. 145.

23. Joseph T. McCann. 2006. *Terrorism on American soil: A concise history of plots and perpetrators from the famous to the forgotten*. Boulder, CO: Sentient Publications.

24. Wikipedia. The U.S. PATRIOT Act. http://en.wikipedia.org/wiki/USA_PATRIOT _Act. Accessed November 2010.

25. Chishti A. Muzaffar, Doris Meissner, Demetrios G. Papademetriou, Jay Peterzell, Michael J. Wishnie, and Stephen W. Yale-Loehr. 2003. *America's challenge: Domestic security, civil liberties, and national unity after September 11*. Washington, DC: Migration Policy Institute, p. 7.

26. Ibid., p. 87.

27. William J. Chambliss. 1988. *Exploring criminology*. New York: Macmillan, p. 38.

28. General Accounting Office. 2000. *Racial profiling: Limited data available on motorist stops*. Washington DC: Government Printing Office.

29. Orlando Patterson. 1994 (Summer). Ecumenical America: Global culture and the American cosmos. *World Policy Journal, 11*: 103–17.

30. Dina Temple-Raston. 2011 (March 10). Muslim Americans question scrutiny at border. National Public Radio.

31. Ibid.

32. David Nakamura. 2011 (March 9). United against radical Islam hearing. *Washington Post*, p. A6.

33. Michelle Boorstein. 2011 (March 12). U.S. Muslim groups split on the hearing's impact. *Washington Post*, p. B1.

34. Akbar Ahmed. 2011 (March 9). Fair to Muslims? *New York Times*, p. A27.

35. Robert Park and Ernest Burgess. 1921. *Introduction to the science of sociology*. Chicago: University of Chicago Press, p. 440.

36. Emory Borgardus. 1968 (January). Comparing racial distance in Ethiopia, South Africa, and the United States. *Sociology and Social Research, 5*: 149–56.

Chapter 5

Incident Logs from the Border

A t the border post, officers write incident reports to document any inspections that result in enforcement actions, such as seizures and arrests. Officers must process and screen to admit legitimate travelers and determine which travelers are imposters, impersonators, fraudsters and smugglers. The incident logs ensure the operational and legal integrity of passenger screenings. Supervisory review is meant to isolate any incidence of enforcement that does not rely on general admissibility rules.

The imperatives of free trade and travel require officers to admit most travelers, but officers must be able to identify and deter travelers with the intention to do harm to our homeland. Officers must also resist any temptations to rely on racial or ethnic attributes as primary indicators of admissibility. Enforcement actions and inadmissibility must be based on objective criteria and not shorthand descriptors of traveler virtues and motives. Given those requirements, officers at the border post "are trying to strike a delicate balance. Their job is to stop bad people or bad things from getting into this country. As they see it, they have about 45 seconds to one minute to decide whether someone might be a threat. The concern is that those quick assessments often seem driven by stereotypes."[1]

The virtual stories from the border post are a window into how inspections and enforcement actions take place. It is at the airport, land border or seaport that trade and travel are facilitated and counterfeit goods and false personas are intercepted; this world reveals the discrete events that determine traveler status and admissibility. It is also at the POE that officer integrity must be cultivated and monitored.

Along the long stretch of northern land border with Canada, there are more POEs and crossings than on the southwestern land border with Mexico.

But, in sheer volume of passengers and conveyances, the southwestern land border is the busier of the two even though it has fewer POEs. The northern land border is spread across ten states including Maine, Vermont, New York, Michigan, Minnesota, North Dakota, Montana, Idaho, Washington and Alaska. Along the southwestern land border with Mexico, the POEs are located in four states: California, Arizona, New Mexico and Texas.

Many of the POEs have more than one crossing, that is, one POE has administrative authority over more than one crossing location for enforcing export and import laws, immigration regulations and agriculture inspections. For instance, on the southwestern land border, the El Paso port has administrative authority for crossings at the Bridge of the Americas (BOTA), Yselta, Paso Del Notre-Santa Fe Street Bridge, and Stanton Street. The Laredo port also administers crossings at Bridge I-Convent Street, Bridge II-Lincoln Juarez, Bridge III-Colombia and Bridge IV-World Trade Bridge. On the northern border, the Buffalo port oversees the crossings at Niagara Falls/ Rainbow Bridge, Lewiston Bridge, Peace Bridge and Whirlpool Rapids. The Detroit port also covers the Ambassador Bridge and Windsor Bridge crossings. Along the northern land border, about half of all the POEs have only one crossing. A few of these POEs are unmanned because of their remote locations. Many of these POEs are also service ports; these are posts that provide a range of cargo processing operations including inspections, verifications and collections. Some of the large land POEs process both commercially operated vehicles (or COVs, such as trucks) and privately operated vehicles (or POVs, such as cars and buses) and their passengers. Hours of operations vary across the POEs, but most operate twenty-four hours daily.

In addition to international airports, there are "preclearance" airports which provide advance approval for entry into the United States; there are preclearance locations in the Caribbean, Canada and Ireland where inspections are conducted much in the same way that a traveler would expect if being inspected at a POE on U.S. soil. Travelers cleared at preclearance locations arrive at domestic terminals at the airport. Another category of airports is the "user-fee airport" which designates POEs that generally have a low volume of passengers but have been approved by CBP to process aircraft, their passengers and cargo arriving in the United States for a fee.

The workload of seaports involves processing cargo and a considerable volume of passengers and crew from cruise ships. There are discernable seasonal patterns in travel in all three environments—land border, airport, seaport—depending on region. In general, the volume of COVs is steady throughout the year except in October and December; there are a lot of POVs, buses and their passengers crossing the land border in July and August, but there is not much travel in January and February. Commercial aircraft and their passengers follow a seasonal pattern similar to POVs. However, the volume of private aircraft and passengers increases between March and July. There is considerable pedestrian traffic, especially on the southwestern border, in November and December. The volume of vessels and passengers arriving at the seaports peaks in the later part of the year and in early months of the year. Overall, there are more airports than seaports and land border ports, as shown in table 5.1. In terms of passengers, the land border ports in Texas, California and Arizona are the busiest; the airports in New York, Florida (Miami), and California (Los Angeles) have the highest volumes; and the seaports in Florida, California and New York have recorded the most traffic. The busiest land ports for cargo are Michigan (Detroit) and Texas (Laredo). At the airports, California (Los Angeles), Alaska (Anchorage), Florida (Miami), New York and Georgia (Atlanta) rank among the top ports that process cargo. At the seaports, California (Los Angeles) and Florida (Miami) are among the busiest.

Table 5.1. Ports of Entry

State/City	Airport	Seaport	Land Border
Alabama			
Birmingham	X		
Huntsville	X		
Mobile		X	
Alaska			
Alcan	X		X
Anchorage	X	X	
Dalton Cache		X	X
Fairbanks	X		
Juneau	X	X	
Ketchikan	X	X	X
Kodiak	X	X	
Nome	X	X	
Sitka	X	X	
Skagway	X	X	X
Valdez	X	X	
Wrangell	X	X	
Arizona			
Douglas			X
Lukeville			X
Naco			X
Nogales			X
Phoenix	X		
Phoenix-Mesa	X		
San Luis			X
Sasabe			X
Scottsdale	X		
Tucson	X		

(Continued)

Table 5.1. Continued

State/City	Airport	Seaport	Land Border
Arkansas			
Little Rock-North Little Rock	X		
Rogers	X		
California			
Andrade			X
Calexico West			X
Calexico East			X
Eureka	X		
Fresno	X		
Los Angeles-Long Beach	X	X	
Monterrey	X		
Ontario	X		
Otay Mesa (San Diego)			X
Palm Springs	X		
Port Hueneme		X	
Sacramento	X		
San Diego	X	X	
San Francisco-Oakland	X	X	
San Jose	X		
San Ysidro (San Diego)			X
Tecate			X
Victorville	X		
Colorado			
Denver (Centennial, Eagle County Regional, Rocky Mountain)	X		
Connecticut			
Bridgeport	X		
Hartford	X		
New Haven	X	X	
New London		X	
Delaware			
Wilmington		X	
District of Columbia			
Washington (National, Dulles)	X		
Florida			
Cape Canaveral		X	
Daytona Beach	X		
Fernandina Beach		X	
Fort Myers	X		
Jacksonville	X	X	
Key West	X	X	
Leesburg	X		
Melbourne	X		
Miami	X	X	
Orlando	X		

State/City	Airport	Seaport	Land Border
Panama City		X	
Pensacola		X	
Port Everglades/Fort Lauderdale	X	X	
Port Manatee		X	
Sanford	X		
Sarasota	X		
St. Augustine	X		
St. Petersburg	X		
Tampa	X	X	
West Palm Beach	X	X	
Georgia			
Atlanta	X		
Brunswick		X	
Savannah		X	
Hawaii			
Hilo	X	X	
Honolulu	X	X	
Kahului	X	X	
Kona	X		
Nawiliwili-Port Allen	X	X	
Idaho			
Boise	X		
Eastport			X
Porthill	X		X
Illinois			
Chicago	X		
Davenport-Moline/Rock Island	X		
Decatur	X		
Mascoutah/MidAmerica St. Louis	X		
Peoria	X		
Rockford	X		
Waukegan	X		
West Chicago	X		
Wheeling	X		
Indiana			
Evansville	X		
Fort Wayne	X		
Indianapolis	X		
Iowa			
Des Moines	X		
Kansas			
Wichita	X		
Kentucky			
Owensboro	X		

(Continued)

Table 5.1. Continued

State/City	Airport	Seaport	Land Border
Louisiana			
Baton Rouge	X	X	
Gramercy		X	
Lake Charles	X	X	
Morgan City		X	
New Orleans	X	X	
Shreveport-Bossier City	X		
Maine			
Bangor	X		
Bar Harbor		X	
Bath		X	
Belfast		X	
Bridgewater			X
Calais			X
Eastport	X	X	X
Fort Fairfield	X		X
Fort Kent			X
Houlton			X
Jackman	X		X
Jonesport			X
Limestone			X
Madawaska			X
Portland	X	X	
Rockland		X	
Van Buren			X
Vanceboro			X
Maryland			
Baltimore	X	X	
Massachusetts			
Boston	X	X	
Fall River		X	
Gloucester	X	X	
Lawrence	X		
New Bedford	X	X	
Plymouth		X	
Salem		X	
Springfield	X		
Worcester	X		
Michigan			
Battle Creek	X		
Detroit	X	X	X
Grand Rapids	X	X	
Lansing	X		
Port Huron	X	X	X
Saginaw/Bay City/Flint	X	X	
Sault St. Marie	X	X	X

State/City	Airport	Seaport	Land Border
Minnesota			
Baudette	X		X
Duluth	X	X	
Grand Portage			X
International Falls			X
Lancaster			X
Minneapolis-St. Paul	X		
Pinecreek			X
Roseau			X
Warroad	X		X
Mississippi			
Gulfport	X	X	
Pascagoula	X	X	
Vicksburg	X		
Missouri			
Kansas City	X		
Springfield	X		
St. Louis (Lambert)	X		
St. Louis (Spirit of St. Louis)	X		
Montana			
Butte	X		
Del Bonita	X		X
Great Falls	X		
Kalispell	X		
Morgan	X		X
Opheim	X		X
Piegan			X
Raymond			X
Roosville			X
Scobey			X
Sweetgrass	X		X
Turner			X
Whitetail			X
Whitlash			X
Wild Horse			X
Willow Creek			X
Nebraska			
Omaha	X		
Nevada			
Las Vegas	X		
Reno	X		
New Hampshire			
Manchester	X		
Portsmouth	X		

(Continued)

Table 5.1. Continued

State/City	Airport	Seaport	Land Border
New Jersey			
Morristown	X		
Newark-New York	X		
Perth Amboy		X	
New Mexico			
Albuquerque	X		
Columbus			X
Santa Teresa	X		X
New York			
Albany	X	X	
Alexandria Bay	X		X
Binghamton	X		
Buffalo-Niagara Falls	X	X	X
Champlain-Rouses Point	X		X
Massena	X		X
New York	X	X	
Ogdensburg	X	X	X
Rochester	X		
Syracuse	X		
Trout River			X
North Carolina			
Charlotte	X		
Morehead City-Beaufort	X	X	
Raleigh-Durham	X		
Wilmington	X	X	
Winston-Salem	X		
North Dakota			
Ambrose			X
Antler			X
Carbury			X
Dunseith	X		X
Fargo	X		
Fortuna			X
Grand Forks	X		
Hannah			X
Hansboro			X
Maida			X
Minot	X		
Neche			X
Noonan			X
Northgate			X
Pembina	X		X
Portal			X
Sarles			X
Sherwood			X
St. John			X

State/City	Airport	Seaport	Land Border
Walhalla			X
Westhope			X
Williston	X		
Ohio			
Ashtabula/Conneaut	X	X	
Cincinnati/Lawrenceburg	X	X	
Cleveland	X	X	
Columbus	X		
Dayton	X		
Toledo-Sandusky	X	X	
Wilmington	X		
Oklahoma			
Oklahoma City	X		
Tulsa	X		
Oregon			
Astoria		X	
Coos Bay		X	
Hillsboro	X		
Newport		X	
Portland	X	X	
Pennsylvania			
Erie	X		
Harrisburg	X		
Lehigh Valley	X		
Philadelphia	X	X	
Pittsburgh	X		
Wilkes-Barre/Scranton	X		
Puerto Rico			
Aguadilla	X		
Fajardo	X	X	
Isla Verde: Luis Munoz IA	X		
Mayaguez	X	X	
Ponce	X	X	
San Juan	X	X	
Rhode Island			
Newport	X		
Providence	X	X	
South Carolina			
Charleston	X	X	
Columbia	X		
Georgetown	X	X	
Greenville-Spartanburg	X		
Myrtle Beach	X		

(Continued)

Table 5.1. Continued

State/City	Airport	Seaport	Land Border
South Dakota			
Sioux Falls	X		
Tennessee			
Chattanooga	X		
Knoxville	X		
Memphis	X	X	
Nashville	X		
Tri-Cities	X		
Texas			
Addison	X		
Amarillo	X		
Austin	X		
Brownsville/Los Indios	X	X	X
Corpus Christi	X	X	
Dallas-Fort Worth	X		
Del Rio	X		X
Eagle Pass			X
El Paso	X		X
Fabens			X
Freeport		X	
Harlingen: Valley IA	X		
Hidalgo/Pharr/Anzalduas	X		X
Houston	X	X	
Laredo	X		X
Lubbock	X		
McKinney	X		
Midland	X		
Port Arthur-Beaumont	X	X	
Port Lavaca-Point Comfort		X	
Sabine		X	
Presidio	X		X
Progresso	X		X
Rio Grande City/Los Ebanos			X
Roma/Falcon Dam			X
San Antonio	X		
Sugar Land	X		
Utah			
Salt Lake City	X		
Vermont			
Beecher Falls			X
Burlington	X		
Derby Line			X
Highgate Springs/Alburg			X
Morses Line			X

State/City	Airport	Seaport	Land Border
Norton			X
Richford			X
St. Albans			X
Virginia			
Dublin: New River Valley IA	X		
Front Royal	X	X	
Newport News	X	X	
Norfolk	X	X	
Richmond-Petersburg	X	X	
Virgin Islands			
Charlotte Amalie/St. Thomas	X	X	
Cruz Bay/St. John		X	
St. Croix	X	X	
Washington			
Aberdeen	X		
Blaine			X
Boundary			X
Danville			X
Ferry			X
Frontier			X
Laurier			X
Longview			X
Lynden			X
Metaline Falls			X
Nighthawk			X
Oroville	X		X
Point Roberts			X
Port Angeles		X	
Seattle	X	X	
Spokane	X		
Sumas			X
Tacoma	X	X	
West Virginia			
Charleston	X	X	
Wisconsin			
Green Bay	X		
Milwaukee	X	X	
Racine	X	X	
Wyoming			
Natrona	X		

Source: Customs and Border Protection, www.cbp.gov.

ENFORCEMENT ACTIONS AT THE AIRPORT

At the border post and in the federal service areas, officers do not need probable cause to search the baggage, packages or the electronic media of the traveler entering the country. This is different from law enforcement within the country where officers rely on probable cause to conduct any searches. Indeed, officers at the border post possess the right to search anyone for no reason at all—they do not need to provide one.

Officers have to be well versed in agricultural inspections, immigration policies and customs regulations; this is the required cross-training program to make the agency more efficient. An immigration officer may process forty or more passengers of mixed ethnicities and races at a midsize airport such as Thurgood Marshall Baltimore Washington International when an international flight arrives. Some flights are preceded by alerts based on intelligence reports. If you have been processed through immigration after an international flight, you know the routine questions asked by immigration officers, such as why you were traveling and what you are carrying. Sometimes the officer may ask to see your itinerary in addition to your documents. Officers may ask to examine any electronic equipment you may be carrying such as video cameras, laptop computers, scanners or cell phones. If you have been referred for further questioning, this secondary inspection process means that you will be subjected to more searches and questions about your trip.

Some travelers who are referred to the secondary round may give all the wrong clues to the immigration officer, for instance, not making eye contact and giving responses that seem contrived or evasive such as uncertainty or incomplete information about destination address and ignorance about the occupation of the traveler's hosts. The traveler's papers may be fine—when scanned with the latest biometric technology to confirm traveler identity. When officers decide to send a traveler to secondary questioning for further processing, they are signaling that they are unsure whether the demeanor of the traveler conveys untruthfulness. Many first-time travelers may be naturally nervous about what to say as the immigration officer probes for details to determine admissibility.

Officers have to make important and critical decisions regarding the status of the traveler before them within the short time span. Consider the use of the carotid artery as an indication of nervousness or anxiety. Officers would quickly glance at this artery to gauge one's level of anxiety—of course this is not foolproof science. This artery runs down the side of your neck on both sides of your head. It is an important artery that supplies your neck and head with oxygenated blood. When you look at yourself in the mirror, you can identify the carotid artery by feeling for it at the side of your neck, right around the angle of your jaw. At the lower part of your neck, this artery is not superficial; it is deeper than the section on the upper part of your neck. The carotid artery can be used to measure your pulse and may indicate your cardiac function. So what does a pulsating carotid artery indicate? Could it be some kind of abnormality? When officers are looking for clues of truthfulness, they must rely on all the indicators at their disposal. In a scenario where a traveler exhibits anxiety with clearly visible indication of a pulsating carotid artery on the left side of his neck, an officer has to use this as a clue for something. But what, if anything, does this clue indicate?

Enforcement actions involve travelers who would make false claims about their travel plans or may be carrying documents that belie their intentions. Some travelers with immigrant intentions (to work and stay indefinitely) will present at the POE with a nonimmigrant visa; but they may inadvertently provide information that reveals their travel motives, such as responding affirmatively to the question about seeking employment. Some of these travelers are turned away at the airport, but there are others who are not barred from entry; the traveler who expresses credible fear about returning to his place of birth and carries incomplete travel papers may not be turned away even though his preliminary traveler status at the POE makes him inadmissible. Some of these inadmissible travelers used to be given notices to appear before an immigration judge at a later date. The problem is that many of them did not show up for the hearing. This practice has generally been discontinued.

Some travelers convey characteristics that raise flags at the POE such as frequent travel to the same country within in a year with short layovers and declaration of currency in the thousands of dollars. At secondary questioning, a supervisor with experience in intercepting drug traffickers may decide to let a traveler wait it out because of the officer's suspicions. After three hours, the traveler may ask to use the restroom with complaints about abdominal pains. If the traveler is female, a female officer will escort her to the restroom. During the short walk to the restroom, the officer will casually ask the traveler if she is carrying any substances in her body cavity. In the restroom, the officer may observe the distressed traveler removing what looks to be a pad from her vagina; the contents of the packages usually test positive for controlled substances such cocaine or heroin.[2]

Some of these carrier travelers or "mules" confess to ingesting drugs after several hours in secondary; the technique of letting them wait it out at secondary is effective—after several hours, they may complain of gastrointestinal pain and they will be eager to pass the substances concealed in condoms or wrapped in plastic in their belly, if they haven't already consented to an X-ray search. Over time, due to natural process of peristalsis, bowel movements will emit the contraband they are carrying. These travelers will generally refuse to use the restroom for long periods of time unless the discomfort they feel becomes unbearable. In some cases, the travelers would have to be escorted to a hospital for peristalsis to be induced due to the large number of pellets of drugs they have ingested. Other carriers conceal the contraband in their rectum. These mules normally take a constipating agent to prevent the passage of the contraband before they deplane. Each packet may contain anywhere from one to fifteen grams of the contraband drug. Of course drug sniffing canines cannot detect these substances carried by the mules, and so it falls on the officers to spot this type of traveler. In addition to the indicators mentioned above, some of the signs that raise suspicion include: (1) carrying no luggage or only one (small) piece of luggage, (2) arrival from a source city or country based on prior intelligence and data, (3) short stays and rapid return, (4) exhibition of a certain level of nervousness, (5) method of payment in purchasing ticket, and (6) exclusive reliance on public transportation when questioned about travel plans. Travelers whose names are matched on TIDE are also referred to secondary. There, the supervising officer conducts more searches and requests the intervention of officers from Immigration and Customs Enforcement (ICE) because such enforcement actions are national security intercepts. At secondary, agricultural inspections are equally important even though the significance of seizures is not immediately recognized. Animal and plant inspections occur only at secondary where examinations yield two types of seizures: interceptions which may have to be quarantined for further examination or evaluation, and violations which are misrepresentations of goods, infringements regarding import procedure, or obtuse attempts at smuggling.

Officers look for signifiers to identify false claims and to detect inadmissible travelers with fraudulent documents. But this kind of detection within a short span of human interaction is difficult. Motives cannot always be captured in that brief space of exchange between the officer at the border and the traveler who seeks permission to enter. What science gives the officer the tools to separate those making false claims and concealing contraband from those who are not? How does an officer know if the traveler seeking asylum is expressing credible fear and is protected under humanitarian grounds? Which travelers deserve to be paroled, and which ones must be expeditiously removed? The traveler who presents at the border with a story of political persecution with little or no luggage and incomplete documents that look fraudulent may be telling the truth after all; but the initial immigration stamp on the travel document may state the traveler's disposition as inadmissible.

The experiential stories of officers describe operational frustrations and job fatigue. The daily high-level early morning briefings held by the political appointees and career administrators are dominated by security and emergent threats. Managers must implement policies that support efficient field operations: to increase the incidence of positive personal searches and reduce the incidence of negative ones. Each day, our international and user-fee airports are engaged in all manner of episodes of interception which take place during brief human interaction.

ENFORCEMENT ACTIONS AT THE LAND BORDER

Bridge I at the Laredo POE is a heavily traveled crossing and typical of POEs that process a large volume of passengers; it is also known as the Gateway to the Americas International Bridge which straddles the Rio Grande. On most days, vehicular traffic is backed up for a mile or more. Without vehicle counters, the number of POVs and COVs and their passengers are estimates based on previous data streams and calculations of average vehicle occupancy. The technology provided by Vehicle Primary Client (VPC) counters will make these reports on conveyance and passenger volume more accurate, and license plate readers (LPRs) will reduce the error margins of the estimates of POV, COV and passenger volume reported by the bureau.

Inspections of all vehicles are impossible, but the use of nonintrusive methods for detecting contraband makes the work easier. The SENTRI Trusted Traveler Program helps the flow of traffic—so that not all travelers have to wait in the long lines that snake around the Mexican Federal Highway 85. All the lanes at this crossing are always staffed because of the high volume of traffic, but officers must rotate every so many hours to ensure integrity of enforcement operations. Every passenger that crosses the land border now is required to present some form of identification for travel. At the POE, name queries are conducted at primary inspections to confirm the identity of the traveler; vehicles are also queried. Further queries are conducted at secondary inspections using the database of the National Crime Information Center (NCIC) to access any alerts and warnings about travelers. Reviews of COVs are based on the Border Release Advanced Selectivity System (BRASS) to check the manifests and invoices of the cargo coming across the border.

News reports about drug busts at the port depict only the tip of the iceberg in terms of the volume of smuggling going on; smuggled contraband drugs are hidden in spare tires, engine compartments that have been retrofitted, the vehicle floor that has been hollowed out, false compartments in bumpers, and the oil pans of vehicles that are reconstructed to hold fewer quarts of oil. Undeclared currency in the hundreds of thousands of dollars is seized from outbound vehicles; weapons and hundreds of thousands of rounds of ammunition that are hidden in the undercarriage of trucks are seized.[3] These weapons, disguised weapons and accessories include machine guns, pistols, revolvers, assault rifles and shotguns, mortar, grenades, fireworks, missiles, bulletproof vests and silencers. The technology to detect smuggling ranges from the simple, such as a mirror to inspect the undercarriage of vehicles or ordinary rubber mallets used to examine vehicle panels, to the sophisticated such as telescopic instruments used to peek into barrels and tanks and X-ray machines that are part of nonintrusive inspections.

Travelers are not always who they say they are; a trucker who claims that he is transporting mangoes from across the border may indeed be carrying tons of marijuana and methamphetamine; the passenger in the pickup truck claiming to be a relative of the driver is not; they are carrying over forty thousand dollars in undeclared currency in small denominations under the truck bed liner. The sheer volume of vehicle traffic at the busy border crossing allows these smugglers to estimate that their chances of getting caught are low. For every seizure, apprehension or arrest that is made, there are several others that are missed.[4]

The six shuttle buses that run weekly across the border are actually human smuggling operations; the passengers on these buses will provide ready and reasonable answers to inquiries about their travel across the border northward; they have fake receipts of ordinary purchases they made in their make-believe world. When they come through the crossing and are led through primary inspections, they do not look like they have paid someone to smuggle them across the border with fraudulent documents. This is a bus service carrying travelers who are making false claims.[5] Other smugglers use less-complicated operational ruses; they pack the illegal migrants in the trunk of the POV or in the compact legroom on the front passenger side of the vehicle under the glove compartment. They are unlucky if they are selected randomly for an inspection; if the traffic volume is peaking and wait times are over one hour, the odds may be in their favor.

There are drivers who will obey the order to drive to the inspection area through the lanes between booths so that their identification papers can be verified. But on some occasions, drivers will disobey orders and ram their vehicles through the POE in order to avoid inspection; these are port runners. Some travelers who are being detained at secondary will attempt to elude inspection or arrest by fleeing—these are the absconders. The "Stop Stick" and other devices that are meant to deflate the tires of the vehicles that are port running have to be deployed quickly to stop the port runner or absconder in their tracks. These incidents may happen once every two months at the port, but they are nonetheless dangerous episodes that put the lives of officers at risk.

Officers become victims of physical assaults and gunfire in other episodes of border violence. Border patrol agents have identified traps such as metal wires between border posts meant to cut the throats of officers patrolling between POEs.[6] These incidents have to be taken seriously. Though there have been no officer fatalities at the POEs, patrol officers have been attacked

Figure 5.1. Landports. Photo by James R. Tourtellotte.

Figure 5.2. Cargo is removed from an incoming ship newly arrived at the Port of Los Angeles/Long Beach. Photo by Charles Csavossy.

Figure 5.3. Trucks bring products into the United States through the Otay Mesa border crossing, where CBP agriculture specialists inspect their cargo. Photo by James R. Tourtellotte.

Figure 5.4. Sophisticated X-ray equipment is used to detect contraband in packages and luggage. Photo by James R. Tourtellotte.

and killed.[7] In defending themselves against these acts of border violence, officers and agents are permitted to use lethal force.[8] At the land border, there are equally important tasks of producing standard reports describing port activities and operations; there are incident logs about seizures and arrests that have to be submitted via the Treasury Enforcement Communication System (TECS) for cross-checking approved entries.

ENFORCEMENT ACTIONS AT THE SEAPORT

Cargo operations at the seaport involve constant monitoring of early warning indicators of the supply chain security to prevent false shipments from entering the country. These include the review of cargo manifests before they arrive at the port. The inbound containers that arrive by the hundreds packed with tons of commercial goods that are off-loaded at a busy port such as Cape Canaveral would have to be examined with mobile truck X-ray machines.

The Customs-Trade Partnership Against Terrorism (C-TPAT) program mandates a stepwise process to verify that (1) the movement of the cargo shipments from the country of origin, transportation modes and transit points are mapped and tracked during the delivery chain; (2) threat and vulnerability assessments based on country of origin and transit points are accurate in order to reduce security breaches be they human smuggling, drugs, or other illegitimate forms of trade; and (3) the established protocols and strategies to address and attend to weaknesses or vulnerabilities in the delivery chain are transparent and documented. The analysis to determine security risks of inbound cargo generates targeted lists of containers deemed suspicious by the Automated Targeting System (ATS). The assessments are data that the National Targeting Center–Cargo (NTCC) uses to identify and screen high-risk cargo at foreign ports before these shipments leave for our shores. Inspections using the Vehicle and Cargo Inspection System (VACIS) allow for effective reviews of the contents of containers as they arrive at the port; the screenings performed by the VACIS technology are the end point of tracking and targeting for security of cargo. Electronic files of the manifest are entered in the Automated Broker Interface (ABI) to process commercial goods arriving at the port. This is a similar to the Automated Manifest System (AMS).

Unlike the land port and airport where travelers must come to federal service areas to be processed, the inspections of inbound vessels and crew sometimes occur on the vessel itself. (Note that officers have the authority to board any conveyance that presents at the port.) When vessels arrive, they must be boarded. The living quarters of the crew may be inspected for any traces of contraband and the cargo shipments are examined before they are off-loaded by cranes located at the freight terminals. It is during one of these routine examinations that containers that have been modified as living quarters for stowaways are discovered.[9] Sometimes stowaways are discovered hiding in life rafts in the vessel when officers board the ship.[10] To be constrained for several weeks in the steel compartment among several hundred containers in the hull of a vessel with a small hole for entry and exit may be unfathomable to many of us; but it is an indication of desperation that these stowaways risk death to leave their countries.[11, 12] The stowaways ask for asylum upon discovery and these incidents must be investigated to identify which transit points allowed the breach to occur. The cargo containers that are cleared must be recorded; all violations must be reported in the incident logs and the interceptions must be shared with sister agencies that focus on enforcement of immigration and customs regulations.

The cruise terminals are not as starkly constructed and designed as cargo terminals. The dedicated cruise terminals invite travelers to experience the sensations of easy living; the terminals depict tropical colors and set the scene of relaxation. Some of these cruise ships are massive vessels that can take three thousand or more passengers and require over a thousand feet of docking space and approximately seventy thousand square feet of embarkation and baggage-handling facilities. The terminals are built with glass towers, high atriums, terrazzo floors, gleaming stainless steel escalators and hydraulic gangways that carry passengers through an embarkation facility with tropical murals. The cafes in the terminal are all thematic, showing various vacation experiences. The parking garages for the cruise terminals are set apart from the general parking areas of the seaport.

OFFICER INTEGRITY

Program managers from CBP's Office of Internal Affairs are the custodians of integrity, "ensuring compliance with all . . . programs and policies relating to corruption, misconduct or mismanagement."[13] Officers who betray the public trust take bribes to look the other way and jeopardize the security of our homeland.

For smugglers, insider connections mean a more secure illegal operation— the likelihood of discovery at the border is reduced significantly because of the assurance of safe passage. These officers engage in illegal operations at great risk because federal regulations provide stiff penalties and prison terms for officers found guilty of betraying the public trust.[14] They become "corrupted gatekeepers" whose returns on their malfeasance double or triple when the illegal migrant is securely across the border into a safe house. The cash-on-delivery operations rely strictly on referrals and "reputation."

The Office of Internal Affairs has programs to curb the temptations for those disposed to those influences. There are random operations and actions that are necessary to create unpredictability in enforcement tactics. One day, operations may call for inspecting and searching all conveyances of a particular color; on other occasions, operations may call for searching conveyances with female drivers and a male passenger. Officers in all lanes must adhere to these random target operations. Lane rotations create uncertainty for would-be smugglers about which lanes will provide safe passage. Officers generally do not know beforehand which booths they will be occupying, and rotations are required during a twelve-hour work shift. The uncertainty about booth assignment reinforces the integrity of border operations. Finally, an online tracking system generates patterns of computer use.

If there is any explanation for any acts of betrayal of the public trust, it must be the generalized and trite reason: corrupt gatekeepers are motivated by personal greed because the cash-on-delivery business is lucrative. Over a span of three years, the industrious crooked officer can make more than $180,000 in nontaxable income. Each time safe passage is allowed, the successful transfer may yield upwards of seven thousand dollars per trafficked human or upwards of 25 percent of the street value of smuggled cocaine, heroin or marijuana.

The integrity of officers is critical to the mission of border security: it is the only way that the operational vision of DHS can be achieved in (1) deterring potential violators, (2) intercepting inadmissible people, conveyances and goods, (3) facilitating legitimate trade and travel and (4) ensuring consistent outcomes in all operations.

THE STATUS OF THE TRAVELER AT THE BORDER

When travelers present themselves at the border, they will attempt to call forth favorable impressions from the officers who would admit them. The traveler must present legitimate travel papers and articulate clearly, without making false claims, his or her travel purpose. This is what the traveler controls. The keen officer is aware of the traveler's departure environment and has intelligence on alerts and warnings. The encounter has four categorical status types of travelers as shown in figure 5.5; if travel documents are legitimate, and the traveler's country of departure is not known as a source city of contraband drugs, fraudulent documents and terror, then the traveler must be admissible; but secondary inspection may be warranted if the place of departure is known as a source city. The travelers with plausible explanations for incomplete travel documents must be assessed for parole.

Legitimate Travel Documents

		Yes	No
Data on Source City	Positive	Admissibles	Credible fear/Parole
	Negative	Secondary Inspections/ Targeting Rules	Inadmissibles

Figure 5.5. Status of Traveler.

The legitimate traveler wants to be assured that his or her admissibility status is not influenced by the officer's prejudgments of specific groups. So it follows that if the travel documents check out and explanations for travel are reasonable, the traveler should be admitted at primary. If the documents check out and the purpose is credible, why is the traveler sent to secondary inspections? How can we assure the legitimate traveler that the generalized rules of admissibility are applied fairly based on data and intelligence? According to Thomas Winkowski, the assistant commissioner of CBP for field operations, "The line we don't cross is that we are improperly taking into consideration individuals' race and religion and the like. To me that's the boundary, that's the line." (In the opinion of the executive director of ACLU's National Security Project, Hina Shemsi, "The difference is between routine and nonroutine questions based on identity, citizenship and legal status to determine admissibility.")[15]

At the POE, traveler status—whether positive or negative—is dependent on legitimate travel documents and intelligence reports. However, the law states that even if a traveler is admissible, he or she may be subject to other inspections. The traveler's status must not be in doubt; if he or she is "not clearly and beyond a doubt entitled to admittance, the traveler may be subjected to more inspections."[16] The fact is, legitimate travel documents are potential weapons used by violent extremists to enter our country to do harm,[17] so it is not necessarily automatic that legitimate travel documents would make a traveler admissible. It is necessary for officers to observe behavior, ask probing questions, and rely on historical information to identify inconsistencies in the stories of travelers to determine who should be admitted and who should not. Recall the statistic in chapter 1 regarding the percentage of travelers denied entry; the proportion may be small, but consider the numbers of people who may indeed be potential violent extremists or may be attempting to smuggle contraband who have been turned away at the ports.

	Traveler is legitimate	Traveler is not legitimate
Allowed	Right Decision	Wrong Decision/ False Negative
Denied	Wrong Decision/ False Positive	Right Decision

Figure 5.6. Errors in Admissibility.

In terms of the variations and distributions based on the volume of travelers, it is probable that some admissible travelers—with legitimate travel motives—may be wrongly denied entry (false positive) and some inadmissible travelers—with bad motives—may be allowed entry (false negative) as shown in figure 5.6. This is inevitable based on the fact that our human operations always involve a margin of error; sometimes these margins of error have grave consequences.

One of the terrorists in the bombing of the World Trade Center in February 1993 was a false negative; that was Ramzi Ahmed Yousef. The supervisor at secondary allowed him entry when he overruled the decision made at primary to detain him. Yousef had arrived with his coconspirator, Ahmed Mohammed Ajaj, at JFK Airport on September 1, 1992. Yousef was released with notice to appear before an immigration judge in three months.[18] About six months later, he had a hand in the deaths of six people when a bomb blast ripped through the parking garage of the North Tower of the World Trade Center; over one thousand Americans were injured in the bombing.

Our contemporary challenge at the border is (1) to facilitate immigration and global trade and (2) to maintain vigilance in screening to deter threats.[19] Beyond the authority of border operations, the challenge is to develop early warning indicators of countercultures and terror within the homeland. These are hard and complicated tasks that expand the responsibilities of the enforcement regimes of all three inspection operations. At the same time, the tasks require us to guard against any propensity to use prejudice or stereotype for identifying the threats we face.

NOTES

1. Dina Temple-Raston. 2011 (March 10). Muslim Americans question scrutiny at border. National Public Radio.

2. J. M. Glass and H. J. Scott. 1995 (August). Surgical mules: The smuggling of drugs in the gastrointestinal tract. *Journal of the Royal Society of Medicine*, *88*: 450–53. See also Mel Fabrikant. 2010 (November 13). Passenger at Newark tries to smuggle over 30 pounds of cocaine in wooden hangers and clothing. *Paramus Post*. http://www.paramuspost .com/article.php/2010111315311147. Accessed November 2010.

3. William Booth and Nick Miroff. 2010 (August 26). Cartels' cash flows across the border: U.S., Mexico intercept only a fraction of billions of drug money heading south. *Washington Post*, p. A1.

4. Ibid.

5. FoxNews. 2010 (April 15). ICE busts massive smuggling ring that stretches the length of U.S. http://www.foxnews.com/. Accessed July 2010.

6 . MSNBC. 2010 (May 27). Violence against border agents at record pace. http:// www.msnbc.msn.com. Accessed July 2010.

7. Gunmen shot and killed U.S. Border Patrol agent Robert Rosas on July 23, 2009.

8. Sergio Adrian Hernandez-Huereka and Anastasio Hernandez, two Mexicans, were killed at the U.S.-Mexican border in May/June 2010.

9. Department of Homeland Security, Office of the Inspector General. 2007. *A Review of CBP and ICE responses to recent incidents of Chinese human smuggling in maritime cargo containers*. Washington, DC: Author.

10. New Orleans CBP arrests stowaways found on vessel, May 5, 2010. http://www .cbp.gov/xp/cgov/newsroom/news_releases/archives/may_2010/05052010_12.xml. Accessed November 2010.

11. CBP and USCG intercept stowaways in Charleston. http://www.cbp.gov/xp/cgov/ newsroom/news_releases/archives/june_2010/06122010.xml. Accessed December 2010.

12. Offices partner up to apprehend stowaways using high-tech inspection equipment. http://www.cbp.gov/xp/cgov/newsroom/news_releases/archives/july_2010/07072010_2 .xml. Accessed December 2010.

13. CBP Office of Internal Affairs. http://www.cbp.gov/xp/cgov/about/organization/ assist_comm_off/internal_affairs.xml. Accessed November 2010.

14. PBS/Frontline World. 2008 (May 27). Mexico: Crimes at the border. http://www .pbs.org/frontlineworld/stories/mexico704/. Accessed July 2010.

15. Dina Temple-Raston. 2011 (March 10). Muslim Americans question scrutiny at border. National Public Radio.

16. Ruth Ellen Wasem, Jennifer Lake, Lisa Seghetti, James Monke, and Stephen Vina. 2004. *Border security: Inspections practices, policies and issues*. Washington, DC: Congressional Research Service, Library of Congress, p. 5.

17. National Commission on Terrorist Attacks upon the United States. 2004. *The 9/11 Commission report*. Washington, DC: Government Printing Office, p. 384.

18. John T. McCann. 2006. Terrorism on American soil: *A concise history of plots and perpetrators from the famous to the forgotten*. Boulder, CO: Sentient Publications, pp. 184–88.

19. CNN World. Magazine details al Qaeda cargo plane plots. http://articles.cnn .com/2010-11-21/world/. Accessed November 2010.

Chapter 6

Engagements beyond the Border

In this last chapter, we move beyond the border into the homeland where the authority of CBP ends. Within the homeland, our focus turns first to the scope of alien registration and monitoring, as a reemergent security operation. The operations of CBP's sister agencies United States Citizenship and Immigration Services (USCIS) and Immigration and Customs Enforcement (ICE) involve enforcement actions beyond the border to track and monitor aliens who are admitted into the country. Our second focus turns to the monitoring program for all citizens, who, under the new rules of engagement in the war on terror, can be tracked with a domestic network of intelligence gathering.

We also want to understand how the new war on terror is different from the wars on drugs and on crime, and how motivations differ for the three types of deviant behaviors. Finally, we must understand the evolving nature of our vulnerabilities, and how we can manage the future without letting our preventive operations overrun concerns about any threats against our community.

MONITORING THE HOMELAND

The erstwhile Immigration and Naturalization Service (now USCIS) had the statutory power to require aliens who remain in the United States for thirty days or longer to apply for registration; the agency customarily registered aliens at the POE. Aliens were required to report any change in address to the agency within ten days of moving. The current registration systems are maintained by ICE. These operations are complicated by a mobile community of travelers from all over the world. Among the provisions of the Alien

Registration Act of June 28, 1940, was the requirement that all aliens over fourteen years of age must be registered and fingerprinted. This law provided authority for removing any aliens who failed to comply with the requirement that allowed the government to track and locate aliens:

> As part of the effort to protect the nation in anticipation of World War II, Congress required aliens to register, be fingerprinted, and notify the Attorney General of each change of address, thereby providing the INS with the means to identify, track, and locate aliens while they are in the United States. According to the legislative history of the Alien Registration Act, the act was considered to be a "measure of self-defense (and) a safeguard to know something about their activities and their movements here."[1]

When this law was enacted, the INS worked together with the Post Office Department to register and fingerprint all aliens. Per the regulation, aliens were to submit an official registration form containing their demographic and address information, their occupation, immigration status and a fingerprint card. Unless they could prove that the failure to submit information was excusable, these aliens could be deported for noncompliance.

In 1950, the Alien Registration program was discontinued and replaced with the Alien Address Report program when the Internal Security Act of September 22 was passed requiring notifications of address change "within ten days of each January 1st."[2] A new division within the INS became responsible for monitoring and tracking aliens within the country. The 1940 law was the first time in our history that a government agency had been given statutory authority to gather comprehensive and detailed information on all noncitizens in the country. There were no previous laws with such provisions (see appendix A). The information was used to conduct background checks on permanent residents applying for naturalization.[3] In 1980, the last year for which there are data, there were approximately five million aliens who had reported address changes to the erstwhile INS.[4] In the latest revision in the law, the Immigration and Nationality Act amendments of December 20, 1981, eliminated the annual notification requirement, but discretionary authority was given to the attorney general for oversight. It is a law that is not widely known. For this reason, the erstwhile INS did not keep a reliable record of alien information and effective enforcement has not been done since 1970. USCIS does not widely publicize this requirement. According to assessments done by GAO, noncompliance by aliens may be because they are not aware of the requirement and have little incentive to file these address changes.

The USCIS has the mandate to compile data on aliens or immigrants who want to remain in the United States permanently and to maintain address and other information on nonimmigrants who want to remain here temporarily.

The utility of these databases is that they provide demographic and geographic information which can be used for law enforcement and national security purposes. But current operating procedures do not allow USCIS to match the arrival date stamp with the departure date stamp on Form I-94 (the arrival and departure record).

The current requirements for change of address apply to almost all noncitizens who have been in the United States for twenty-nine days or more. Form AR-11, which can be found on the website of USCIS, asks for:

- Immigrant status: whether visitor, student, permanent resident or other
- Country of citizenship
- Alien card number
- Current address and number of months at the address
- Last address
- School or employment information
- Port of entry
- Date of entry
- Date of expiration of stay

The current Form AR-11 omits one key identifier that used to be collected by INS. Under the previous address-reporting program, form I-53 asked for most of the demographic information above in addition to social security number (SSN). When the agency did away with the requirement for SSN, it became more difficult to link the records of aliens to other searchable databases (such as that for driver's license numbers).

The address change requirements were reinforced in 2002 and 2003 when a final rule for monitoring nonimmigrants was published. This rule specifically mentioned people from Afghanistan, Algeria, Bahrain, Bangladesh, Egypt, Eritrea, Indonesia, Iran, Iraq, Jordan, Kuwait, Lebanon, Libya, Morocco, North Korea, Oman, Pakistan, Qatar, Saudi Arabia, Somalia, Sudan, Syria, Tunisia, United Arab Emirates, and Yemen.[5] Before September 11, 2001, failure to file a change of address form did not lead to any enforcement actions. According to the GAO's assessment, there were no cases where aliens were placed in enforcement or removal hearings because they failed to submit change of address forms.[6]

Beyond the border, the ability to monitor is constrained by freedom of mobility. It is a difficult task that involves tracking what one researcher calls "residence tactics" of extremists within our midst.[7] The National Security Entry-Exit Registration System (NSEERS) administered by ICE is the current manifestation of the alien registration program that was first introduced in 1940. The "special registration" is described in detail on the website of ICE:

Those who fall under the nonimmigrants category must also adhere to the National Security Entry-Exit Registration System (NSEERS) also known as Special Registration, put in place after September 11, 2001, to keep track of those entering and leaving our country in order to safeguard U.S. citizens and America's borders. NSEERS was the first step taken by the Department of Justice and then by the Department of Homeland Security (DHS) in order to comply with the development of the Congressionally-mandated requirement for a comprehensive entry-exit program.

Through the Special Registration system, the U.S. government can keep track of the more than 35 million nonimmigrant visitors who enter the U.S. as well as some nonimmigrant visitors already in the United States. These individuals are required to register with immigration authorities either at a port of entry or a designated ICE office in accordance with the special registration procedures.

Nonimmigrant alien visitors subject to NSEERS registration at the port of entry:

1. Certain citizens or nationals of Iran, Iraq, Libya, Sudan and Syria, as designated by the DHS Secretary in the Federal Register.

2. Nonimmigrants who have been designated by the State Department.

3. Any other nonimmigrant, male or female regardless of nationality, identified by immigration officers at airports, seaports and land ports of entry in accordance with 8 CFR 264.1(f)(2).

These special procedures also require notification to immigration authorities of changes of address, employment, or school. Nonimmigrants must notify the DHS in writing within 10 days of any changes in address, employment or school after remaining in the U.S. for 30 days or more. Students may notify change of address through the Student Exchange Visitor Information System (SEVIS). On December 2, 2003, DHS suspended the automatic 30-day and annual re-registration requirements for NSEERS. Nonimmigrant aliens who were required to comply with NSEERS and file a petition or application with U.S. Citizenship and Immigration Services (CIS) may be required to provide proof of NSEERS registration to CIS. If the alien is unable to provide proof, then he/she will be referred by CIS to the appropriate ICE office for an NSEERS interview to determine compliance.

Nonimmigrant visitors who do not comply with special registration requirements or other terms of their admission to the U.S. during their stay will be considered out of status and may be subject to arrest, detention, fines and/or removal from the country. Any future application for an immigration benefit may also be impacted. Decisions in these instances will be made based on an individual basis and are dependent on the circumstances of each case.

The requirement to register does not apply to U.S. citizens, lawful permanent residents (green card holders), refugees, asylum applicants (depending upon whether date asylum was pending or approved), asylum grantees, and diplomats or others admitted under "A" or "G" visas. Nonimmigrants who must follow these special procedures will also have to use specially designated ports when they leave the country and report in person to an immigration officer at the designated port on their departure date.

Those who leave the United States, including visits to Mexico, Canada and adjacent islands, must appear in person on the date of departure before an inspecting officer at a designated port of departure and leave through a designated port. Failure to appear in person on the date of departure before an inspecting officer may result in denial of admission to the U.S. at a later date.

Those who are just passing through the U.S. on the way to another country and are intending to depart from a nondesignated port will leave departure information during arrival registration.

It is possible to request a waiver of all or part of the special registration requirements for up to one year. A request must be made in writing in the form of a letter sent to Customs and Border Protection (CBP). CBP will only give a ruling on requests that include relief from arrival and/or departure registration. The request letter to the director of the port of entry that the alien will be applying for admission to enter the U.S. must include a detailed description of the relief requested, your name, date-of-birth, Fingerprint Identification Number, a 1" × 1" passport-style photograph, and any documents that support your application.[8]

The current registration regime is designed to gather better information about foreign visitors and to provide more oversight about their activities in the country. The NSEERS has a database of photographs and fingerprints of registered nonimmigrants which facilitates monitoring. The requirements to stay enrolled in school, under the SEVIS program, and to attend periodic interviews are methods to track the residential movement of would-be foreign terrorists beyond the border.

For everyone else, citizen or noncitizen, there is the legal framework of the PATRIOT Act that permits surveillance beyond the border. The registration of nonimmigrants and change of address notifications are supplemented by the broad amendment to the Foreign Intelligence Surveillance Act (FISA) to make it easier to perform wiretaps and searches within the homeland.

Along the Capital Beltway Interstate 495 in Washington, DC, the overhead electronic signs flash the message "Report Suspicious Activity," asking drivers to call the number 800-492-TIPS with any information on local terrorist threats. As one drives along the beltway, these flashing messages do not seem extraordinary; they are no different from the Amber Alerts that we are used to seeing. Amber Alerts are part of the broadcast emergency response system that provides urgent bulletins to assist in the search for and safe recovery of a child. Under the PATRIOT Act, the domestic intelligence structure to collect and process information about citizens and noncitizens does not seem intrusive or over the top; there is a level of transparency about what the government wants and the domestic monitoring program seems to be channeling our collective concerns about terrorism within the homeland.

In late 2010, two *Washington Post* reporters wrote a thorough story about the new rules of engagement beyond the border. As described by Dana Priest and William M. Arkin in their report titled *Monitoring America*, "nine years after the terrorist attacks of 2001, the U.S. is assembling a vast domestic intelligence apparatus to collect information about Americans, using the FBI, local police, state homeland security offices and military criminal investigators. The system, by far the largest and most technologically sophisticated in the nation's history, collects, stores and analyzes information about thousands of U.S. citizens and residents, many of whom have not been accused of any wrongdoing."[9]

The current dispensation has birthed the Nationwide Suspicious Activity Reporting (SAR) system that is a catalogue of thousands of profiles and identities of citizens and noncitizens based on reports of suspicious activities or behaviors. These activities do not have to be criminal, but merely suspicious, such as taking pictures of certain buildings or purchasing certain materials (like fertilizer). These reports and information are analyzed and reviewed for nuggets of intelligence that might uncover some sleeper terrorist cells, or more often than not, might lead nowhere. States and local municipalities are able to use homeland security funding to map incidents and then report whatever information they have to DHS headquarters.

It is an artifact of the war on terror that the surveillance cameras mounted in neighborhoods, on streets, near bridges and near other significant infrastructure have had the consequence of reducing crime. This is because the surveillance cameras, military-grade infrared cameras, wireless scanners, biometric facial recognition technology and license plate readers are used by municipalities in their fight against localized crime and illegal drug markets.

THE THREE WARS

Tracking and monitoring activities beyond the border to secure the homeland are only as effective as our understanding of the nature and causes of criminal behavior. We want to understand the motivations of the violent extremist and how this type is different from other criminal behavior. This is what criminologists have added to their scope of research activities. The war on terror has become the third "war" in addition to the wars on drugs and crime as invoked by the political (and societal) mood.[10]

The war on drugs arguably began when the importation of opium was eventually banned in 1909. In 1970, the Comprehensive Drug Abuse Prevention and Control Act consolidated drug laws from 1914 and 1937. This new law had provisions for controlling the sale and possession of opium, cocaine and marijuana. In 1973, the Drug Enforcement Administration (DEA) was created by an executive order signed by President Nixon "to establish a single unified command to conduct an all-out global war on the drug menace."[11] In 1988, President Reagan established the Executive Office of National Drug Control Policy (ONDCP), under the provisions of the Anti-Drug Abuse Act of 1988. With the creation of ONDCP, the ongoing "war" on drug trafficking and drug use had become an official policy objective. According to the website of the ONDCP, "the creation of a drug-free America [is] a policy goal. The [role of] the Office of National Drug Control Policy (ONDCP) is to set priorities, implement a national strategy, and certify Federal drug-control budgets. The law (authorizing the agency) specified that the strategy must be comprehensive and research-based; contain long-range goals and measurable objectives; and seek to reduce drug abuse, trafficking, and their consequences."[12]

The war on crime was declared during the 1930s with the spate of bank robberies and the emergence of organized crime in the wake of the repeal of the Prohibition Act.[13] Organized crime in America consisted of the coordination and specialization in smuggling, gambling, and money laundering, availability of illegal goods and services and infiltration of legal business operations.[14] These networks of organized crime syndicates coexist with localized crimes of burglary, robbery, rape, murder and aggravated assault. The 1930s era of the war on crime was replaced in the 1960s with societal concerns about the organized financing of illegal goods and services. During the 1964 presidential elections, presidential nominee Barry Goldwater invoked the term "war" to describe societal concerns about the impact of organized crime; Presidents Johnson and Nixon also invoked the term to channel the public mood.[15] This was the backdrop to the Organized Crime Control Act of 1970 that provided for witness protection programs and other enforcement actions to deter and reduce the influence of organized crime.

Stricter regulations and expanded enforcement have been employed in the war on crime and war on drugs. For instance, under President Clinton, drug laws were stiffened to require mandatory prison time for drug offenses with the Violent Crime Control and Law Enforcement Act of 1994. When it was signed, the act became the "largest crime bill in the history of the country and provided for 100,000 new police officers, $9.7 billion in funding for prisons and $6.1 billion in funding for prevention programs. The Act also significantly expanded the government's ability to deal with problems caused by criminal aliens. The Crime Bill provided $2.6 billion in additional funding for the FBI, DEA, INS, and other Justice Department components, as well as the Federal courts and the Treasury Department."[16] In the past decade, crime rates have generally fallen,[17] but illegal drug trafficking is still a societal concern demonstrating our historic inability to prevent drugs from crossing the borders and the limits of our deterrence programs within the homeland.

In the heartsore days after the September 11, 2001, attacks, President George W. Bush declared the "war on terror" in several speeches including the one he made to a joint session of Congress on September 20. On September 29, he reported on the progress of this war in his radio address. Historical accounts note that President Reagan had made a reference to the war on terrorism in the wake of the Beirut barracks bombing in 1983. The September 11, 2001, terrorist attacks were preceded by bombings of U.S. embassies on August 7, 1998, in Nairobi, Kenya, and Dar es Salaam, Tanzania, that killed hundreds of Americans, Kenyans and Tanzanians. These terrorist attacks were followed by the bombing of the U.S. Navy destroyer *USS Cole* on October 12, 2000, which killed seventeen sailors and injured several others. The invasion of Afghanistan to bring down the Taliban government, the invasion of Iraq in search of weapons of mass destruction, the enactment of the PATRIOT Act and the creation of DHS are all outcomes of the declaration on the global war on terror.

THE MOTIVATION

What do ordinary criminals, drug traffickers and terrorists have in common, except for the fact that these behaviors are deviations from our societal values, and that we must deter and reduce their occurrence? In terms of incidence and prevalence, drug trafficking has far greater incidence and prevalence at the border than ordinary crime or terrorism, and beyond the border, ordinary crime is more prevalent than terrorism. Within the homeland, violent crimes that are localized in our neighborhoods and communities do not generally need a network of financing and facilitators, but drug traffickers and terrorists do. We know that organized crime and drug dealers are motivated by money, but some terrorists believe their actions are altruistic.[18]

Type	Declaration	Enforcement
War on drugs	Opium Exclusion Act 1909	Cross border
War on crime	Federal Bureau of Investigation 1930	Localized
War on terror	President Bush 2001	Cross border

Figure 6.1. Criminology's Three Wars.

We have to integrate three disciplines to understand the motivations behind these deviant and violent actions. Biologists who study crime have shown that the brain functioning of criminals depicts strong emotional reactions to certain conditioning.[19, 20] The biologists have also revealed that high levels of certain hormones such as endorphins (that produce the fight-or-flight response) may create violent arousals.[21] The researchers have found evidence linking high levels of testosterone to criminal behavior[22] and endocrinologists are providing more evidence of the impact of hormones on the criminal mood.[23]

But biology is one explanatory dimension of these behaviors because not all persons with the identified "deficits" or "conditioning" turn out to be criminals or socially deviant. Psychologists provide another dimension in our understanding of deviance because they have examined the influence of parenting and prevalence of abuse on the development of callous, unemotional traits during early childhood. Psychologists tell us that antisocial and violent behaviors may be due to the lack of empathy during the early years.[24] However, childhood development is not always prologue, and the arousal or excitation of feelings must be channeled by the environment. Some people are able to overcome childhood developmental problems because they possess traits that provide some kind of buffer—hardiness, for example.[25]

A final dimension is the contribution made by sociologists who have documented the impact of deprivation and how individuals in particular groups carry a certain sense of injustice. Sociologists have collected data on how individuals in a group develop perceptions of inequity based on comparisons with other group members; perceptions of inequity generate a sense of unfairness and grievance.[26, 27] The "strain" and distress caused by these perceptions—whether imagined or not—are real in their consequences. Sociologists have revealed that feelings of inequity or distress are channeled or consummated through groups that allow individuals to acquire deviant norms and behaviors; it is through these groups that socialization into criminal behavior takes form and shape.[28] The social learning that takes place is the external stimuli for biological and psychological conditioning; the arousal of feelings of envy,[29] spite,[30] hatred of the status quo,[31] equity distress, grievance and revenge[32] are the outcomes of the intersection of biology, psychology and society.[33, 34] This process is shown in figure 6.2.

By the time the individual becomes convinced of the path to take based on arousals and excitations, it is only a matter of time before he or she engages in behavior that would harm him/herself and others. There is an escalation in emotions and reactions to events or perceived events that brings about physiological changes: anger, or an emotional reaction to an action, becomes contempt or an emotional reaction directed toward the person or group perceived to be responsible for the action. Contempt is replaced by disgust, a

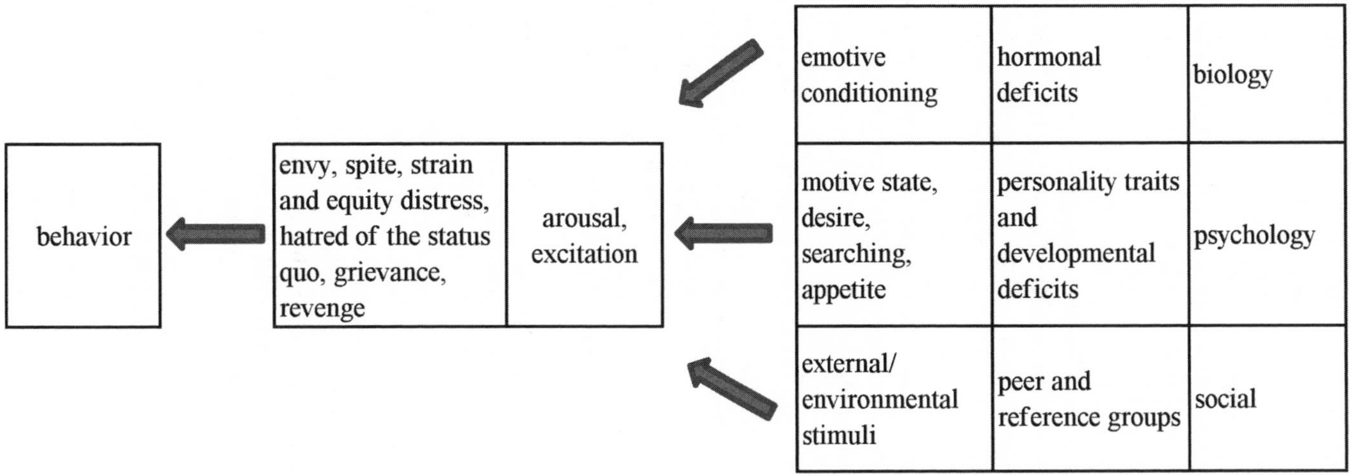

Figure 6.2. The Motivation.

moral belief or judgment and a desire to shun, avoid, dissociate from or to violently eliminate.[35, 36] The arousal and excitation that become the motivation may take many forms and will eventually lead to the deviant, criminal or violent behaviors we want to deter. "This perspective allows us to understand how groups hate, but not all hatred lead to violence or hostility. Hatred based primarily on anger and/or contempt will not be associated with violence or hostility, but hatred that involves disgust does, because disgust is the emotion of repulsion and elimination. Groups can be angry or contemptuous, but when they are also disgusted, they may become dangerous."[37]

The escalation of emotion is aided by collective storytelling. The group plays the catalyst role in transforming our feelings or emotions into criminal or violent extreme acts through routine associations based on time (a few months to one or two years), space (neighborhoods and communities, schools) and the mutual acceptance of each group member.[38]

There are nominal variations in terrorist networks and criminal organizations in terms of profiles and scope of operations, but a categorical distinction is how criminals, drug traffickers and terrorists identify themselves: "A major difference is that criminals do not look beyond their immediate group, whilst terrorists come to identify very strongly with a much larger collective."[39] Other researchers report that "terrorists often perceive themselves as altruists"[40] with political and ideological objectives. Whether it is envy, spite, some kind of strain or equity distress, hatred of the status quo, grievance or revenge, these emotions escalate into violent behavior. The escalation of emotion and the transformation of it into violent behavior make these complex interactions difficult to understand.

On the frontier of evolving threats is the nexus of organized crime, drug trafficking and terrorist networks; this is the combined and coordinated threat under the umbrella of a "transnational criminal organization." Some researchers believe this confluence is already here; the Taliban, al-Qaida and other groups are known to be involved in criminal activities such as drug distribution and trafficking. Some of the foot soldiers in the terrorist networks have criminal records and involvement in "petty crime such as fraud, thievery, small-scale drug-dealing and other offences."[41] Sustained contact between ordinary criminals and terror networks will facilitate transmission of violent methods and knowledge of smuggling pathways.

SENSE MAKING AND PREDICTING THE FUTURE

In 2004, the Massachusetts Bay Transportation Authority established a policy to randomly search bags and packages within the transit system and on commuter trains. In 2005, New York City's Metropolitan Transit Authority began random searches of bags, backpacks and luggage within their system and this has been followed by New Jersey's transit system and the Port Authority. In 2008, Amtrak expanded its program of random checks of bags and packages on all trains. These random searches were established in the wake of the deadly train bombings in Madrid, Spain, in March 2004 which killed 191 people, the bombings in London which killed fifty-six people in July 2005 and the Mumbai bombings which killed more than two hundred people in November 2008. In March 2010, the Moscow metro system was also attacked when suicide bombers killed thirty-eight people.

In December 2010, the Metro Transit system in the Washington, D.C., area began conducting random bag and package checks on buses and trains within the system. This announcement was the latest homeland security action to deter an attack on metro systems. The vulnerability of our critical infrastructure—bridges, roads, transit systems—lies at the core of homeland security concerns.[42] These preventive operations are the new status quo. Passengers who refuse to be searched may not use the system and may be questioned. Within the New York City system, police searches have so far not found any explosives, but rather have yielded illegal weapons and drugs.[43]

There is a process of sense making in our social world, where our daily experiences build on each other and our routines become taken for granted until we become victims of extreme deviations from these routines.[44, 45] The taken-for-granted reality is a superstructure of our "ordered" world where our quotidian activities are the routines of our lives. Our everyday activities are predictable and consist of formal and informal circumstances that organize the way we live. There is commonsense knowledge about what is right and what is wrong and what seems in between. We impose order and make sense of our worlds to predict the future[46] and we want to have unanimity in agreement about norms and behaviors. This is the common ground of inference we use in our interactions with our family members, colleagues at work, or at school and in other public and private spaces of our lives.

But there's always a loss function, that is, events that undermine the taken-for-granted reality. Life is not always as usual; there is trouble; things do not always go as planned as we construct our realities through our daily interactions with others in public spaces; technologies fail; structures are vulnerable; systems are not always optimal and the production of our realities is bounded by undetected patterns that are external to us.[47] Our daily routines are not anthropological case studies that require us to identify, observe, analyze, recognize and categorize our activities every time we are socially engaged; much of what we do on a daily basis are repetitious operations that accumulate. We rely on what we already know about the typical, the connected, the isolatable, the equivalent, what is uniform, what is consistent. We trust the production and construction of our realities insofar as we recognize the world around us. The ideas about probability and the theories we have developed to fashion meaning from reams of information and data are remarkable for what they can do and what they cannot do; there are many daily routines we have mastered and have "ordered," but there are other events that are not "ordered" by us. Crime, violent crime and terrorism are "ordered" only to the extent that they consistently violate and disrupt our taken-for-granted reality by breaching our trust in our shared normative expectations. To us, they are "unordered."

The declaration of war on terror signaled a crisis of legitimation[48] because extreme violence creates a deficit of trust that unorders our lives: these crises require us to be extra vigilant in our daily routines, to report any "suspicious activities" when we come upon them as encouraged by SAR. We have to be diligent when we are on mass transit systems where law enforcement has authority to conduct random searches to ensure the safety of transportation. The war on terror has taken us to Afghanistan and Iraq at significant and substantial human costs so far. Our "ordered" lives and routines have been "unordered" and we now have to manage the uncertainties wrought by the "unorder."[49]

To make sense of our social worlds, we want to have some confidence in predicting and managing the immediate future; but the unorder makes our lives "anthropologically strange"[50] where our familiar and practical activities become somewhat problematic and cannot be taken for granted any longer because of the extreme violence of terrorism. There is what we perceive as random occurrences and accidents of life that unorder our lives; this involves ordinary crime, organized crime and drug crimes. And then there's terrorism in the homeland: the motivation to violently maim or kill without discrimination for some ideological goal.[51]

The DHS is covering a lot of ground in securing the homeland and anticipating future threats at the border and beyond the border with the help of the department's Centers of Excellence research programs. These twelve centers showcase their latest findings and research at the annual National Science and Technology Summit. They include

- Center for Risk and Economic Analysis of Terrorism Events (CREATE) led by the University of Southern California.
- Center for Advancing Microbial Risk Assessment (CAMRA) led by Michigan State University and Drexel University.
- National Center for Foreign Animal and Zoonotic Disease Defense (FAZD) led by Texas A&M University.
- National Center for Food Protection and Defense (NCFPD) led by the University of Minnesota.
- National Consortium for the Study of Terrorism and Responses to Terrorism (START) led by the University of Maryland.

- National Center for the Study of Preparedness and Catastrophic Event Response (PACER) led by Johns Hopkins University.
- Center of Excellence for Awareness and Location of Explosives-Related Threats (ALERT) led by Northeastern University and the University of Rhode Island.
- National Center for Border Security and Immigration (BORDERS) led by the University of Arizona in Tucson and the University of Texas at El Paso.
- Center for Maritime, Island and Port Security led by the University of Hawaii in Honolulu and Stevens Institute of Technology.
- Center for Natural Disasters, Coastal Infrastructure, and Emergency Management led by the University of North Carolina at Chapel Hill and Jackson State University.
- National Transportation Security Center of Excellence (NTSCOE) at the Connecticut Transportation Institute of the University of Connecticut, Tougaloo College, Texas Southern University, National Transit Institute at Rutgers, the State University of New Jersey, Homeland Security Management Institute at Long Island University, Mack Blackwell National Rural Transportation Study Center at the University of Arkansas and Mineta Transportation Institute at San José State University.
- The Center of Excellence in Command, Control and Interoperability (CCI) led by Purdue University.[52]

The National Science and Technology Summits are important forums for showcasing new research for security. Under the BORDERS program, researchers are developing screening systems that would eventually be able to detect deceptions and suspicious behaviors at the POEs. The technology will be able to identify travelers who should be sent to secondary inspections based on their responses and interaction with the system.[53] The researchers have examined kinesics and facial emotions, gaze duration, linguistic content and are using natural language processing (NLP) to measure a traveler's physiological and behavioral reactions during the interview encounter with an officer at the POE. The Automated Virtual Agent for Truth Assessments in Real-Time (AVATAR) system has different "faces" and can take on attributes based on gender or ethnicity.[54]

Researchers in the PACER consortium of universities are developing urban simulation models to create evacuation strategies and emergency response planning and public health preparedness for large cities in the event of a chemical or biologic airborne catastrophe.[55] Researchers in the ALERT program are applying terahertz wave technology to security problems at the border; "the sensors using terahertz waves can penetrate packaging materials or clothing to identify the unique terahertz 'fingerprints' of hidden materials. Terahertz radiation is very low energy and poses no known health threat to humans."[56] The technology is being used to listen remotely to signals from materials because terahertz waves are naturally weakened by air and moisture. The techniques under development use sound waves or acoustics to identify potentially hazardous materials.

The consortium of universities under the NCFPD program has developed a tool to identify and protect critical assets in the food and agriculture sector. The process uses hazards analysis to help municipalities manage and communicate risks in food production and distribution.[57] The CREATE program is using risk assessment tools to evaluate the "likelihoods of specific terrorism attacks, . . . costs of terrorist attacks on critical infrastructure . . . and how to reduce threats, vulnerabilities and consequences of terrorism by cost-effective methods."[58]

Under the NTSCOE program, the Mineta Transportation Institute has conducted a comprehensive evaluation of the potential terrorist uses of highway-borne hazardous materials and has recommended the implementation of "vehicle tracking technologies, panic alarms, and immobilization capabilities for vehicles carrying large quantities of specific hazardous materials, including gasoline"[59] to safeguard surface transportation. The START program has compiled the Global Terrorism Database (GTD) containing over 87,000 terrorist incidents from 1970 to 2008. These data are valuable for examining trends in terrorist attacks, types of attacks, motivations, criminal violence and terrorism. The program "offers insights into important policy issues, including how to disrupt terrorist networks, reduce the incidence of terrorism and enhance the resilience of society in the face of terrorist threats."[60]

These and other programs sponsored by DHS are meant to help us maintain, in the production of our American realities, some levels of predictability by eliminating and minimizing the domestic and foreign terror threats we face. This is how we manage and make sense of the unorder and it is the reason for CBP and its sister agencies as they perform the dual roles of facilitating trade, travel and immigration and securing the border and the homeland against false personas and goods.

Sense making also requires us to overlay the science of securing the border (and, by extension, the homeland) with the knowledge we have about the context of our American space and human terrain—this is the science of society, which makes us appreciate the fact that an inclusive identity in this country will overrun the creep of prejudice that is associated with our immigrant past and present.

NOTES

1. General Accounting Office. 2002 (November). *INS cannot locate many aliens because it lacks reliable address information.* Washington DC: Author, p. 8.

2. *Immigration legal history: Legislation from 1941–1960*. Washington, DC: U.S. Citizenship and Immigration Services.

3. General Accounting Office. 2002 (November). *INS cannot locate many aliens because it lacks reliable address information*. Washington DC: Author, p. 37.

4. Ibid.

5. Registration of certain nonimmigrant aliens from designated countries. http://www .uscis.gov/ilink/docView/FR/HTML/FR/0-0-0-1/0-0-0-88492/0-0-0-88513/0-0-0-89789 .html. Accessed December 2010.

6. General Accounting Office. 2002 (November). *INS cannot locate many aliens because it lacks reliable address information*. Washington DC: Author, p. 17.

7. Susan Ginsburg. 2006. *Countering terrorist mobility: Shaping an operational strategy*. Washington, DC: Migration Policy Institute, p. 2.

8. Special registration. http://www.ice.gov/nseers/. Accessed December 2010.

9. Dana Priest and William M. Arkin. 2010. Monitoring America. *Washington Post*, pp. A1–A12.

10. Gary LaFree. 2009. Criminology's third war: Special issue on terrorism and responses to terrorism. *American Society of Criminology*, *8*(3): 431–44.

11. Drug Enforcement Administration: History. http://www.justice.gov/dea/history .htm. Accessed December 2010.

12. Office of National Drug Control Policy: http://www.whitehousedrugpolicy.gov/. Accessed December 2010.

13. Claire Bond Potter. 1958. *The war on crime: Bandits, G-men and the politics of mass culture*. New Brunswick, NJ: Rutgers University Press.

14. William J. Chambliss. 1988. *Exploring criminology*. New York: Macmillan.

15. Gary LaFree. 2009. Criminology's third war: Special issue on terrorism and responses to terrorism. *American Society of Criminology*, *8*(3): 431–44.

16. Violent Crime Control and Law Enforcement Act of 1994. http://www.ojp.usdoj .gov/nij/pubs-sum/000067.htm. Accessed December 2010.

17. Uniform Crime Reports. http://www.fbi.gov/about-us/cjis/ucr/ucr. Accessed December 2010.

18. Gary LaFree. 2009. Criminology's third war: Special issue on terrorism and responses to terrorism. *American Society of Criminology*, *8*(3): 431–44.

19. R. J. R. Blair. 2008. The cognitive neuroscience of pathology and implications for judgments of responsibility. *Neuroethics*, *1*: 149–57.

20. Anthony Walsh and Kevin M. Beaver. 2009. *Biosocial criminology*. New York: Routledge.

21. David C. Rowe. 2001. *Biology and crime*. Los Angeles: Roxbury.

22. Anthony Walsh and Kevin M. Beaver. 2009. *Biosocial criminology*. New York: Routledge.

23. Diana H. Fishbein. 1990. Biological perspectives in criminology. *Criminology*, *28*(1): 27–72.

24. Benjamin B. Lahey, Carol A. Van Hulle, Kate Keenan, Paul J. Rathouz, Brian M. D'Onofrio, Joseph Lee Rodgers, and Irwin D. Waldman. 2008. Temperament and parenting during first year of life predict future child conduct problems. *Journal of Abnormal Child Psychology*, *36*(8):1139–58.

25. Suzanne Kobasa. 1979. Stressful life events, personality and health: An inquiry into hardiness. *Journal of Personality and Social Psychology*, *37*(1): 1–11.

26. Robert Merton. 1968. *Social theory and social structure.* New York: Free Press.

27. Robert Agnew. 1992. Foundation for a general strain theory of crime and delinquency. *Criminology, 30*(1): 47–87.

28. Marshall B. Clinard and Robert F. Meier. 1995. *Sociology of deviant behavior.* Fort Worth: Harcourt Brace.

29. Helmut Schoeck. 1987. *Envy: A theory of social behavior.* Indianapolis: Liberty Fund.

30. Edward O. Wilson. 2000. *Sociobiology: The new synthesis.* Cambridge, MA: Harvard University Press.

31. H. Cooper. 1977. What is a terrorist? A psychological perspective. *Legal Medical Quarterly, 1:* 8–18.

32. Elaine Walster, G. William Walster, and Ellen Berscheid. 1978. *Equity.* Boston: Allyn & Bacon.

33. Adrian Raine. 1993. *The psychopathology of crime.* San Diego: Academic Press.

34. Thomas O'Connor. 2010. The neurology of crime and violence. In Laurie Fenstermacher, Larry Kuznar, Tom Rieger, and Anne Speckhard (eds.), *Protecting the homeland from international and domestic terrorism threats*, pp. 117–22. White paper: National Consortium for Study of Terrorism and Responses to Terrorism. College Park: University of Maryland.

35. Paul Ekman. 2003. *Emotions revealed.* New York: Times Books.

36. David Matsumoto. 2010. The role of emotion in escalating violent non-state actors to hostility. In Laurie Fenstermacher, Larry Kuznar, Tom Rieger, and Anne Speckhard (eds.), *Protecting the homeland from international and domestic terrorism threats*, pp. 111–16. White paper: National Consortium for Study of Terrorism and Responses to Terrorism. College Park: University of Maryland.

37. Ibid.

38. Sam Mullins and Adam Dolnik. 2010. Relations between violent non-state actors and ordinary crime. In Laurie Fenstermacher, Larry Kuznar, Tom Rieger, and Anne Speckhard (eds.), *Protecting the homeland from international and domestic terrorism threats*, pp. 219–27. White paper: National Consortium for Study of Terrorism and Responses to Terrorism. College Park: University of Maryland.

39. Ibid.

40. Gary LaFree. 2009. Criminology's third war: Special issue on terrorism and responses to terrorism. *American Society of Criminology, 8*(3): 433.

41. Sam Mullins and Adam Dolnik. 2010. Relations between violent non-state actors and ordinary crime. In Laurie Fenstermacher, Larry Kuznar, Tom Rieger, and Anne Speckhard (eds.), *Protecting the homeland from international and domestic terrorism threats*, p. 220. White paper: National Consortium for Study of Terrorism and Responses to Terrorism. College Park: University of Maryland.

42. Ann Scott Tyson and Derek Kravitz. 2010 (December 17). Metro to conduct random bag checks: Anti-terrorism teams' searches designed to prevent attacks. *Washington Post*, pp. A1–A13.

43. Ibid.

44. Ruth A. Wallace and Alison Wolf. 1995. *Contemporary sociological theory: Continuing the classical tradition.* Englewood Cliffs, NJ: Prentice-Hall, p. 246.

45. Cynthia F. Kuntz and David J. Snowden. 2003. The new dynamics of strategy: Sense-making in a complex and complicated world. *IBM Systems Journal, 42*(3): 462–83.

46. Harold Garfinkel. 1967. *Studies in ethnomethodology.* Englewood Cliffs, NJ: Prentice-Hall.

47. Nassim Nicholas Taleb. 2005. *Fooled by randomness: The hidden role of chance in life and in the markets.* New York: Random House.

48. Jürgen Habermas. 1975. *Legitimation crisis.* Boston: Beacon.

49. Gary A. Ackerman. 2006. It is hard to predict the future: The evolving nature of threats and vulnerabilities. *OIE Scientific and Technical Review, 25*(1): 353–360.

50. Harold Garfinkel. 1967. *Studies in ethnomethodology.* Englewood Cliffs, NJ: Prentice-Hall, p. 9.

51. See the definition of the term "terrorism" at Wikipedia. http://en.wikipedia.org/wiki/Terrorism. Accessed December 2010.

52. Homeland Security Centers of Excellence. http://www.dhs.gov/files/programs/editorial_0498.shtm. Accessed December 2010.

53. National Center for Border Security and Immigration: BORDERS. 2011. *AVATAR: Who is better at distinguishing truth-tellers from liars—a person or an artificial agent?* Tucson: University of Arizona.

54. Ibid.

55. National Center for the Study of Preparedness and Catastrophic Event Response: PACER. 2011. *Assessing emergency readiness for a catastrophic event.* Baltimore: Johns Hopkins University.

56. Awareness and Localization of Explosives-Related Threats: ALERT. 2011. *Terahertz enhanced acoustics.* Troy, NY, and Boston: Rensselaer Polytechnic Institute and Northeastern University.

57. National Center for Food Protection and Defense. 2011. *Defending the safety of the food system through research and education.* St. Paul: University of Minnesota.

58. National Center for Risk and Economic Analysis of Terrorism Events: CREATE: A Center of Excellence of the U.S. Department of Homeland Security. 2011. Los Angeles: University of Southern California.

59. Mineta Transportation Institute. 2010. *Potential terrorist uses of highway-borne hazardous materials.* San José, CA: San José State University.

60. National Consortium for the Study of Terrorism and Responses to Terrorism. 2009. *Research review.* College Park: University of Maryland.

Appendix A

Immigration Legislation

This listing of immigration laws was obtained from the Bureau of Citizenship and Immigration Services of the Department of Homeland Security. This is not an exhaustive list, but rather an overview of the history of some of the most important federal immigration legislation. Some of these legislations are cited throughout the book. Legislations in immigration history are provided here in chronological order and listed in five sections: 1790–1900; 1901–1940; 1940–1960; 1961–1980; and 1981–1996. The listing also includes the dates of the bills and reference numbers for statutes at large. Since 1845, the *Statutes at Large* publication has been the official source of laws and resolutions passed by Congress.

FROM 1790 TO 1900

1. Act of March 26, 1790 (1 Statutes at Large 103)
The first federal activity in an area previously under the control of the individual states, this act established a uniform rule for naturalization by setting the residence requirement at two years.

2. Act of January 29, 1795 (1 Statutes at Large 414)
Repealed the 1790 act, raised the residence requirement to five years and required a declaration of intention to seek citizenship at least three years before naturalization.

3. Naturalization Act of June 18, 1798 (1 Statutes at Large 566)
Provisions:

a. Clerks of court must furnish information about each record of naturalization to the secretary of state.
b. Registry of each alien residing in the United States at that time, as well as those arriving thereafter.
c. Raised the residence requirement for naturalization to fourteen years.

4. Aliens Act of June 25, 1798 (1 Statutes at Large 570)
Represented the first federal law pertinent to immigration rather than naturalization. Provisions:

a. Authorized the president to arrest and/or deport any alien whom he deemed dangerous to the United States.
b. Required the captain of any vessel to report the arrival of aliens on board such vessel to the collector, or other chief officer of the customs of the port.

This law expired two years after its enactment.

5. Alien Enemy Act of July 6, 1798 (1 Statutes at Large 577)
Provided that in the case of declared war or invasion the president shall have the power to restrain or remove alien enemy males of fourteen years and upwards, but with due protection of their property rights as stipulated by treaty.

6. Naturalization Act of April 14, 1802 (2 Statutes at Large 153)
Provisions:

a. Reduced the residence period for naturalization from fourteen to five years.
b. Established basic requirements for naturalization, including good moral character, allegiance to the Constitution, a formal declaration of intention, and witnesses.

7. Steerage Act of March 2, 1819 (3 Statutes at Large 488)
First significant federal law relating to immigration. Provisions:

a. Established the continuing reporting of immigration to the United States by requiring that passenger lists or manifests of all arriving vessels be delivered to the local collector of customs, copies transmitted to the secretary of state, and the information reported to Congress.
b. Set specific sustenance rules for passengers of ships leaving U.S. ports for Europe.

c. Restricted the number of passengers on all vessels either coming to or leaving the United States.

8. Act of May 26, 1824 (4 Statutes at Large 36)
Facilitated the naturalization of certain aliens who had entered the United States as minors, by setting a two-year instead of a three-year interval between declaration of intention and admission to citizenship.

9. Act of February 22, 1847 (9 Statutes at Large 127)
"Passenger Acts," provided specific regulations to safeguard passengers on merchant vessels. Subsequently amended by the Act of March 2, 1847, expanding the allowance of passenger space.

10. Passenger Act of March 3, 1855 (10 Statutes at Large 715)
Provisions:

a. Repealed the Passenger Acts (see the 1847 act) and combined their provisions in a codified form.
b. Reaffirmed the duty of the captain of any vessel to report the arrival of alien passengers.
c. Established separate reporting to the secretary of state distinguishing permanent and temporary immigration.

11. Act of February 19, 1862 (12 Statutes at Large 340)
Prohibited the transportation of Chinese on American vessels.

12. Act of July 4, 1864 (13 Statutes at Large 385)
First congressional attempt to centralize control of immigration. Provisions:

a. A commissioner of immigration was appointed by the president to serve under the authority of the secretary of state.
b. Authorized immigrant labor contracts whereby would-be immigrants would pledge their wages to pay for transportation.

On March 30, 1868, the Act of July 4, 1864, was repealed.

13. Naturalization Act of July 14, 1870 (16 Statutes at Large 254)
Provisions:

a. Established a system of controls on the naturalization process and penalties for fraudulent practices.
b. Extended the naturalization laws to aliens of African nativity and to persons of African descent.

14. Act of March 3, 1875 (18 Statutes at Large 477)—Text of this act is already provided.

15. Chinese Exclusion Act of May 6, 1882 (22 Statutes at Large 58)—Text of this act is already provided.

16. Immigration Act of August 3, 1882 (22 Statutes at Large 214)
First general immigration law, established a system of central control of immigration through state boards under the secretary of the treasury. Provisions:

a. Broadened restrictions on immigration by adding to the classes of inadmissible aliens, persons likely to become a public charge.
b. Introduced a tax of fifty cents on each passenger brought to the United States.

17. Act of February 26, 1885 (23 Statutes at Large 332)
The first "Contract Labor Law," made it unlawful to import aliens into the United States under contract for the performance of labor or services of any kind. Exceptions were for aliens temporarily in the United States engaging other foreigners as secretaries, servants or domestics; actors, artists, lecturers and domestic servants; and skilled aliens working in an industry not yet established in the United States.

18. Act of February 23, 1887 (24 Statutes at Large 414)
Amended the Contract Labor Law to render it enforceable by charging the secretary of the treasury with enforcement of the act and providing that prohibited persons be sent back on arrival.

19. Act of March 3, 1887 (24 Statutes at Large 476)
Restricted the ownership of real estate in the United States to American citizens and those who have lawfully declared their intentions to become citizens, with certain specific exceptions.

20. Act of October 19, 1888 (25 Statutes at Large 566)
First measure since the Aliens Act of 1798 to provide for expulsion of aliens—directed the return within one year after entry of any immigrant who had landed in violation of the contract labor laws (see acts of February 26, 1885, and February 23, 1887).

21. Immigration Act of March 3, 1891 (26 Statutes at Large 1084)
The first comprehensive law for national control of immigration. Provisions:

a. Established the Bureau of Immigration under the Treasury Department to administer all immigration laws (except the Chinese Exclusion Act).
b. Further restricted immigration by adding to the inadmissible classes, persons suffering from certain contagious diseases, felons, persons convicted of other crimes or misdemeanors, polygamists, and aliens assisted by others by payment of passage, and forbidding the encouragement of immigration by means of advertisement.
c. Allowed the secretary of the treasury to prescribe rules for inspection along the borders of Canada, British Columbia, and Mexico so as not to obstruct or unnecessarily delay, impede, or annoy passengers in ordinary travel between these countries and the United States.
d. Directed the deportation of any alien who entered the United States unlawfully.

22. Act of March 3, 1893 (27 Statutes at Large 570)
Provisions:

a. Added to the reporting requirements regarding alien arrivals to the United States such new information as occupation, marital status, ability to read or write, amount of money in possession, and facts regarding physical and mental health. This information was needed to determine admissibility according to the expanding list of grounds for exclusion.
b. Established boards of special inquiry to decide the admissibility of alien arrivals.

FROM 1901 TO 1940

1. Act of April 29, 1902 (32 Statutes at Large 176)
Extended the existing Chinese exclusion acts until such time as a new treaty with China was negotiated, and extended the application of the exclusion acts to insular territories of the United States, including the requirement of a certificate of residence, except in Hawaii.

2. Act of February 14, 1903 (32 Statutes at Large 825)
Transferred the Bureau of Immigration to the newly created Department of Commerce and Labor, and expanded the authority of the commissioner general of immigration in the areas of rule making and enforcement of immigration laws.

3. Immigration Act of March 3, 1903 (32 Statutes at Large 1213)
An extensive codification of existing immigration law. Provisions:

a. Added to the list of inadmissible immigrants.
b. First measure to provide for the exclusion of aliens on the grounds of proscribed opinions by excluding "anarchists, or persons who believe in, or advocate, the overthrow by force or violence the government of the United States, or of all government, or of all forms of law, or the assassination of public officials."
c. Extended to three years after entry the period during which an alien who was inadmissible at the time of entry could be deported.
d. Provided for the deportation of aliens who became public charges within two years after entry from causes existing prior to their landing.
   Reaffirmed the contract labor law.

4. Act of April 27, 1904 (33 Statutes at Large 428)
Reaffirmed and made permanent the Chinese exclusion laws. In addition, clarified the territories from which Chinese were to be excluded.

5. Naturalization Act of June 29, 1906 (34 Statutes at Large 596)
Provisions:

a. Combined the immigration and naturalization functions of the federal government, changing the Bureau of Immigration to the Bureau of Immigration and Naturalization.
b. Established fundamental procedural safeguards regarding naturalization, such as fixed fees and uniform naturalization forms.
c. Made knowledge of the English language a requirement for naturalization.

6. Immigration Act of February 20, 1907 (34 Statutes at Large 898)
Provisions:

a. Required aliens to declare intention of permanent or temporary stay in the United States and officially classified arriving aliens as immigrants and nonimmigrants, respectively.
b. Increased the head tax to $4.00 (established by the Act of August 3, 1882).
c. Added to the excludable classes imbeciles, feeble-minded persons, persons with physical or mental defects which may affect their ability to earn a living, persons afflicted with tuberculosis, children unaccompanied by their parents, persons who admitted the commission of a crime involving moral turpitude, and women coming to the United States for immoral purposes.
d. Exempted from the provisions of the contract labor law professional actors, artists, singers, ministers, professors, and domestic servants.

e. Extended from two to three years after entry authority to deport an alien who had become a public charge from causes which existed before the alien's entry.

f. Authorized the president to refuse admission to certain persons when he was satisfied that their immigration was detrimental to labor conditions in the United States.

g. Created a Joint Commission on Immigration to make an investigation of the immigration system in the United States. The findings of this commission were the basis for the comprehensive Immigration Act of 1917.

h. Reaffirmed the requirement for manifesting of aliens arriving by water and added a requirement with regard to departing aliens.

7. White Slave Traffic Act of June 25, 1910 (36 Statutes at Large 825)
The Mann Act, prohibited the importation or interstate transportation of women for immoral purposes.

8. Act of March 4, 1913 (37 Statutes at Large 737)
Divided the Department of Commerce and Labor into separate departments and transferred the Bureau of Immigration and Naturalization to the Department of Labor. It further divided the Bureau of Immigration and Naturalization into a separate Bureau of Immigration and Bureau of Naturalization, each headed by its own commissioner.

9. Immigration Act of February 5, 1917 (39 Statutes at Large 874)—Text of this act is already provided.

10. Act of May 22, 1918 (40 Statutes at Large 559)
"Entry and Departure Controls Act," authorized the president to control the departure and entry in times of war or national emergency of any alien whose presence was deemed contrary to public safety.

11. Quota Law of May 19, 1921 (42 Statutes at Large 5)
The first quantitative immigration law. Provisions:

a. Limited the number of aliens of any nationality entering the United States to 3 percent of the foreign-born persons of that nationality who lived in the United States in 1910. Approximately 350,000 such aliens were permitted to enter each year as quota immigrants, mostly from northern and western Europe.

b. Exempted from this limitation aliens who had resided continuously for at least one year immediately preceding their application in one of the independent countries of the Western Hemisphere; nonimmigrant aliens such as government officials and their households, aliens in transit through the United States, and temporary visitors for business and pleasure; and aliens whose immigration is regulated by immigration treaty.

c. Actors, artists, lecturers, singers, nurses, ministers, professors, aliens belonging to any recognized learned profession, and aliens employed as domestic servants were placed on a nonquota basis.

12. Act of May 11, 1922 (42 Statutes at Large 540)
Extended the Act of May 19, 1921, for two years, with amendments:

a. Changed from one year to five years the residency requirement in a Western Hemisphere country.
b. Authorized fines of transportation companies for transporting an inadmissible alien unless it was deemed that inadmissibility was not known to the company and could not have been discovered with reasonable diligence.

13. Immigration Act of May 26, 1924 (43 Statutes at Large 153)—Text of this act is already provided.

14. Act of May 28, 1924 (43 Statutes at Large 240)
An appropriations law, provided for the establishment of the U.S. Border Patrol.

15. Act of March 31, 1928 (45 Statutes at Large 400)
Provided more time to work out computation of the quotas established by the Immigration Act of 1924 by postponing introduction of the quotas until July 1, 1929.

16. Act of April 2, 1928 (45 Statutes at Large 401)
Provided that the Immigration Act of 1924 was not to be construed to limit the right of American Indians to cross the border, but with the proviso that the right does not extend to members of Indian tribes by adoption.

17. Registry Act of March 2, 1929 (45 Statutes at Large 1512)
Amended existing immigration law authorizing the establishment of a record of lawful admission for certain aliens not ineligible for citizenship when no record of admission for permanent residence could be found and the alien could prove entrance to the United States before July 1, 1924 (subsequently amended to June 3, 1921, by the Act of August 7, 1939—53 Statutes at Large 1243). Later incorporated into the Alien Registration Act of 1940.

18. Act of March 4, 1929 (45 Statutes at Large 1551)—Text of this act is already provided.

19. Act of February 18, 1931 (46 Statutes at Large 1171)
Provided for the deportation of any alien convicted of violation of U.S. laws concerning the importation, exportation, manufacture, or sale of heroin, opium, or coca leaves.

20. Act of March 17, 1932 (47 Statutes at Large 67)
Provisions:

a. The contract labor laws were applicable to alien instrumental musicians whether coming for permanent residence or temporarily.
b. Such aliens shall not be considered artists or professional actors under the terms of the Immigration Act of 1917, and thereby exempt from the contract labor laws, unless they are recognized to be of distinguished ability and are coming to fulfill professional engagements corresponding to such ability.
c. If the alien qualifies for exemption under the above proviso, the secretary of labor later may prescribe such conditions, including bonding, as will insure the alien's departure at the end of his engagement.

21. Act of May 2, 1932 (47 Statutes at Large 145)
Amended the Immigration Act of 1917, doubling the allocation for enforcement of the contract labor laws.

22. Act of July 1, 1932 (47 Statutes at Large 524)
Amended the Immigration Act of 1924, providing that the specified classes of nonimmigrant aliens be admitted for a prescribed period of time and under such conditions, including bonding where deemed necessary, as would ensure departure at the expiration of the prescribed time or upon failure to maintain the status under which admitted.

23. Act of July 11, 1932 (47 Statutes at Large 656)
Provided exemption from quota limits (i.e., nonquota status) the husbands of American citizens, provided that the marriage occurred prior to issuance of the visa and prior to July 1, 1932. Wives of citizens were accorded nonquota status regardless of the time of marriage.

24. Act of June 15, 1935 (49 Statutes at Large 376)
Designated as a protection for American seamen, repealed the laws giving privileges of citizenship regarding service on and protection by American

vessels to aliens having their first papers (i.e., having made declaration of intent to become American citizens).

25. Act of May 14, 1937 (50 Statutes at Large 164)
Made deportable any alien who at any time after entering the United States

a. Was found to have secured a visa through fraud by contracting a marriage which subsequent to entry into the United States had been judicially annulled retroactively to the date of the marriage; or
b. Failed or refused to fulfill his promises for a marital agreement made to procure his entry as an immigrant.

26. Act of June 14, 1940 (54 Statutes at Large 230)
Presidential Reorganization Plan, transferred the Immigration and Naturalization Service from the Department of Labor to the Department of Justice as a national security measure.

27. Alien Registration Act of June 28, 1940 (54 Statutes at Large 670)
Provisions:

a. Required registration of all aliens and fingerprinting of those over fourteen years of age.
b. Established additional deportable classes, including aliens convicted of smuggling, or assisting in the illegal entry of, other aliens.
c. Amended the Act of October 16, 1919, making past membership—in addition to present membership—in proscribed organizations and subversive classes of aliens grounds for exclusion and deportation.
d. Amended the Immigration Act of 1917, authorizing, in certain meritorious cases, voluntary departure in lieu of deportation, and suspension of deportation.

28. Act of July 1, 1940 (54 Statutes at Large 711)
Amended the Immigration Act of 1924, requiring aliens admitted as officials of foreign governments to maintain their status or depart.

FROM 1941 TO 1960

1. Nationality Act of October 14, 1940 (Effective January 13, 1941, as 54 Statutes at Large 1137)
Codified and revised the naturalization, citizenship, and expatriation laws to strengthen the national defense. The naturalization and nationality

regulations were rewritten and the forms used in naturalization proceedings were revised.

2. Public Safety Act of June 20, 1941 (55 Statutes at Large 252)

Directed a consular officer to refuse a visa to any alien seeking to enter the United States for the purpose of engaging in activities which would endanger the safety of the United States.

3. Act of June 21, 1941 (55 Statutes at Large 252)

Extended the Act of May 22, 1918—gave the president power, during a time of national emergency or war, to prevent departure from or entry into the United States.

4. Act of December 8, 1942 (56 Statutes at Large 1044)

Amended the Immigration Act of 1917, altering the reporting procedure in suspension of deportation cases to require the attorney general to report such suspensions to Congress on the first and fifteenth of each month that Congress is in session.

5. Act of April 29, 1943 (57 Statutes at Large 70)

Provided for the importation of temporary agricultural laborers to the United States from North, South, and Central America to aid agriculture during World War II. This program was later extended through 1947, then served as the legal basis of the Mexican "Bracero Program," which lasted through 1964.

6. Act of December 17, 1943 (57 Statutes at Large 600)

Amended the Alien Registration Act of 1940, adding to the classes eligible for naturalization Chinese persons or persons of Chinese descent. A quota of 105 per year was established (effectively repealing the Chinese exclusion laws—see the Act of May 6, 1882).

7. Act of February 14, 1944 (58 Statutes at Large 11)

Provided for the importation of temporary workers from countries in the Western Hemisphere pursuant to agreements with such countries for employment in industries and services essential to the war efforts. Agreements were subsequently made with British Honduras, Jamaica, Barbados, and the British West Indies.

8. War Brides Act of December 28, 1945 (59 Statutes at Large 659)

Waived visa requirements and provisions of immigration law excluding physical and mental defectives when they concerned members of the American armed forces who, during World War II, had married nationals of foreign countries.

9. G.I. Fiancees Act of June 29, 1946 (60 Statutes at Large 339)
Facilitated the admission to the United States of fiance(e)s of members of the American armed forces.

10. Act of July 2, 1946 (60 Statutes at Large 416)
Amended the Immigration Act of 1917, granting the privilege of admission to the United States as quota immigrants and eligibility for naturalization, races indigenous to India and persons of Filipino descent.

11. Act of August 9, 1946 (60 Statutes at Large 975)
Gave nonquota status to Chinese wives of American citizens.

12. Act of June 28, 1947 (61 Statutes at Large 190)
Extended by six months the attorney general's authority to admit alien fiance(e)s of veterans as temporary visitors pending marriage.

13. Act of May 25, 1948 (62 Statutes at Large 268)
Amended the Act of October 16, 1918, providing for the expulsion and exclusion of anarchists and similar classes, and gave the attorney general similar powers to exclude as the secretary of state had through the refusal of immigration visas.

14. Displaced Persons Act of June 25, 1948 (62 Statutes at Large 1009)
First expression of U.S. policy for admitting persons fleeing persecution. Permitted the admission of up to 205,000 displaced persons during the two-year period beginning July 1, 1948 (chargeable against future year's quotas). Aimed at reducing the problem created by the presence in Germany, Austria, and Italy of more than one million displaced persons.

15. Act of July 1, 1948 (62 Statutes at Large 1206)
Amended the Immigration Act of 1917. Provisions:

a. Made available suspension of deportation to aliens even though they were ineligible for naturalization by reason of race.
b. Set condition for suspension of deportation that an alien shall have proved good moral character for the preceding five years, and that the attorney general finds that deportation would result in serious economic detriment to a citizen or legal resident and closely related alien, or the alien has resided continuously in the United States for seven years or more.

16. Central Intelligence Agency Act of June 20, 1949 (63 Statutes at Large 208)

Authorized the admission of a limited number of aliens in the interest of national security. Provided that whenever the director of the Central Intelligence Agency, the attorney general, and the commissioner of immigration determine that the entry of a particular alien into the United States for permanent residence is in the interest of national security or essential to the furtherance of the national intelligence mission, such alien and his immediate family may be given entry into the United States for permanent residence without regard to their admissibility under any laws and regulations or to their failure to comply with such laws and regulations pertaining to admissibility. The number was not to exceed one hundred persons per year.

17. Agricultural Act of October 31, 1949 (63 Statutes at Large 1051)

Facilitated the entry of seasonal farm workers to meet labor shortages in the United States. Further extension of the Mexican Bracero Program.

18. Act of June 16, 1950 (64 Statutes at Large 219)

Amended the Displaced Persons Act of 1948. Provisions:

a. Extended the act to June 30, 1951, and its application to war orphans and German expellees and refugees to July 1, 1952.
b. Increased the total of persons who could be admitted under the act to 415,744.

19. Act of June 30, 1950 (64 Statutes at Large 306)

Provided relief to the sheepherding industry by authorizing that, during a one-year period, 250 special quota immigration visas be issued to skilled sheepherders chargeable to oversubscribed quotas.

20. Act of August 19, 1950 (64 Statutes at Large 464)

Made spouses and minor children of members of the American armed forces, regardless of the alien's race, eligible for immigration and nonquota status if marriage occurred before March 19, 1952.

21. Internal Security Act of September 22, 1950 (64 Statutes at Large 987)

Amended various immigration laws with a view toward strengthening security screening in cases of aliens in the United States or applying for entry. Provisions:

a. Present and former membership in the Communist Party or any other totalitarian party or its affiliates was specifically made a ground for inadmissibility.

b. Aliens in the United States who, at the time of their entry or by reason of subsequent actions, would have been inadmissible under the provisions of the Internal Security Act, were made deportable regardless of the length of their residence in the United States.
c. The discretion of the attorney general in admitting otherwise inadmissible aliens temporarily, and in some instances permanently, was curtailed or eliminated.
d. The attorney general was given authority to exclude and deport without a hearing an alien whose admission would be prejudicial to the public interest if the attorney general's finding was based on confidential information the disclosure of which would have been prejudicial to the public interest of the United States.
e. The attorney general was given authority to supervise deportable aliens pending their deportation and also was given greater latitude in selecting the country of deportation. However, deportation of an alien was prohibited to any country in which the alien would be subject to physical persecution.
f. Any alien deportable as a subversive criminal or member of the immoral classes who willfully failed to depart from the United States within six months after the issuance of the deportation order was made liable to criminal prosecution and could be imprisoned for up to ten years.
g. Every alien residing in the United States subject to alien registration was required to notify the commissioner of immigration and naturalization of his address within ten days of each January 1 in which he resided in the United States.

22. Act of March 28, 1951 (65 Statutes at Large 28)
Provisions:

a. Gave the attorney general authority to amend the record of certain aliens who were admitted only temporarily because of affiliations other than Communist.
b. Interpreted the Act of October 16, 1918, regarding exclusion and expulsion of aliens to include only voluntary membership or affiliation with a Communist organization and to exclude cases where the person in question was under sixteen years of age, or where it was for the purpose of obtaining employment, food rations, or other necessities.

23. Act of July 12, 1951 (65 Statutes at Large 119)
Amended the Agricultural Act of 1949, serving as the basic framework under which the Mexican Bracero Program operated until 1962. Provided that:

a. The U.S. government establish and operate reception centers at or near the Mexican border; provide transportation, subsistence, and medical care

from the Mexican recruiting centers to the U.S. reception centers; and guarantee performance by employers in matters relating to transportation and wages, including all forms of remuneration.
b. U.S. employers pay the prevailing wages in the area; guarantee the workers employment for three-fourths of the contract period; and provide workers with free housing and adequate meals at a reasonable cost.

24. Act of March 20, 1952 (66 Statutes at Large 26)
Provisions:

a. Amended the Immigration Act of 1917, making it a felony to bring in or willfully induce an alien unlawfully to enter or reside in the United States. However, the usual and normal practices incident to employment were not deemed to constitute harboring.
b. Defined further the powers of the Border Patrol, giving officers of the Immigration and Naturalization Service authority to have access to private lands, but not dwellings, within twenty-five miles of an external boundary for the purpose of patrolling the border to prevent the illegal entry of aliens.

25. Act of April 9, 1952 (66 Statutes at Large 50)
Added the issuance of five hundred immigration visas to sheepherders.

26. Immigration and Nationality Act of June 27, 1952 (INA) (66 Statutes at Large 163)

a. Made all races eligible for naturalization, thus eliminating race as a bar to immigration.
b. Eliminated discrimination between sexes with respect to immigration.
c. Revised the national origins quota system of the Immigration Act of 1924 by changing the national origins quota formula: set the annual quota for an area at one-sixth of 1 percent of the number of inhabitants in the continental United States in 1920 whose ancestry or national origin was attributable to that area. All countries were allowed a minimum quota of one hundred, with a ceiling of two thousand on most natives of countries in the Asia-Pacific triangle, which broadly encompassed the Asian countries.
d. Introduced a system of selected immigration by giving a quota preference to skilled aliens whose services are urgently needed in the United States and to relatives of U.S. citizens and aliens.
e. Placed a limit on the use of the governing country's quota by natives of colonies and dependent areas.
f. Provided an "escape clause" permitting the immigration of certain former voluntary members of proscribed organizations.

g. Broadened the grounds for exclusion and deportation of aliens.
h. Provided procedures for the adjustment of status of nonimmigrant aliens to that of permanent resident aliens.
i.   Modified and added significantly to the existing classes of nonimmigrant admission.
j.   Afforded greater procedural safeguards to aliens subject to deportation.
k. Introduced the alien address report system whereby all aliens in the United States (including most temporary visitors) were required annually to report their current address to the INS.
l.   Established a central index of all aliens in the United States for use by security and enforcement agencies.
m. Repealed the ban on contract labor (see Act of March 30, 1868) but added other qualitative exclusions.

27. Act of September 3, 1954 (68 Statutes at Large 1145)
Provisions:

a. Made special nonquota immigrant visas available to certain skilled sheepherders for a period of up to one year.
b. Exempted from inadmissibility to the United States aliens who had committed no more than one petty offense.

28. Act of September 3, 1954 (68 Statutes at Large 1146)
Provided for the expatriation of persons convicted of engaging in a conspiracy to overthrow or levy war against the U.S. government.

29. Act of July 24, 1957 (71 Statutes at Large 311)
Permitted enlistment of aliens into the regular army.

30. Act of August 30, 1957 (71 Statutes at Large 518)
Exempted aliens who were survivors of certain deceased members of the U.S. armed forces from provisions of the Social Security Act which prohibited the payment of benefits to aliens outside the United States.

31. Refugee-Escapee Act of September 11, 1957 (71 Statutes at Large 639)
Provisions:

a. Addressed the problem of quota oversubscription by removing the "mortgaging" of immigrant quotas imposed under the Displaced Persons Act of 1948 and other subsequent acts.

b. Provided for the granting of nonquota status to aliens qualifying under the first three preference groups on whose behalf petitions had been filed by a specified date.
c. Facilitated the admission into the United States of stepchildren, illegitimate children, and adopted children.
d. Conferred first-preference status on spouse and children of first-preference immigrants if following to join the immigrant.
e. Set an age limit of fourteen for the adoption of orphans to qualify for nonquota status and further defined which orphans were eligible under the act.
f. Gave the attorney general authority to admit certain aliens formerly excludable from the United States.

32. Act of July 25, 1958 (72 Statutes at Large 419)
Granted admission for permanent residence to Hungarian parolees of at least two years residence in the United States, on condition that the alien was admissible at time of entry and still admissible.

33. Act of August 21, 1958 (72 Statutes at Large 699)
Authorized the attorney general to adjust nonimmigrant aliens from temporary to permanent resident status subject to visa availability.

34. Act of September 22, 1959 (73 Statutes at Large 644)
Facilitated the entry of fiance(e)s and relatives of alien residents and citizens of the United States by reclassifying certain categories of relatives into preference portions of the immigration quotas. This was designed to assist in reuniting families both on a permanent basis, through the amendments to the Immigration and Nationality Act of 1952, and through temporary programs.

FROM 1961 TO 1980

1. Act of July 14, 1960 ("Fair Share Refugee Act.") (74 Statutes at Large 504)
Provisions:

a. Authorized the attorney general to parole up to five hundred alien refugee-escapees and make them eligible for permanent residence.
b. Amended the Act of September 2, 1958, to extend it to June 30, 1962.
c. Amended the Act of September 11, 1957, which provided special nonquota immigrant visas for adopted or to-be-adopted orphans under fourteen years of age, extending it to June 30, 1961.

d. Amended the Immigration and Nationality Act of 1952, adding possession of marijuana to the sections concerning excludable and deportable offenses.
e. Made alien seamen ineligible for adjustment from temporary to permanent resident status.

2. Act of August 17, 1961 (75 Statutes at Large 364)

Provided that, in peacetime, no volunteer is to be accepted into the U.S. Army or U.S. Air Force unless the person is a citizen or an alien admitted for permanent residence.

3. Act of September 26, 1961 (75 Statutes at Large 650)

Liberalized the quota provisions of the Immigration and Nationality Act of 1952:

a. Eliminated the ceiling of two thousand on the aggregate quota of the Asia-Pacific triangle.
b. Provided that whenever one or more quota areas have a change of boundaries which might lessen their aggregate quota, they were to maintain the quotas they had before the change took place.
c. Codified and made permanent the law for admission of adopted children.
d. Established a single statutory form of judicial review of orders of deportation.
e. Insured a minimum quota of one hundred for newly independent nations.
f. Called for the omission of information on race and ethnic origin from the visa application.
g. Strengthened the law against the fraudulent gaining of nonquota status by marriage.
h. Authorized the Public Health Service to determine which diseases are dangerous and contagious in constituting grounds for exclusion.

4. Act of October 24, 1962 (76 Statutes at Large 1247)

Provisions:

a. Granted nonquota immigrant visas for certain aliens eligible for fourth preference (i.e., brothers, sisters, and children of citizens) and for first preference (i.e., aliens with special occupational skills).
b. Called for a semimonthly report to Congress from the attorney general of first-preference petitions approved.
c. Created a record of lawful entry and provided for suspension of deportation for aliens who have been physically present in the United States for at least seven years in some cases and ten years in others.

5. Act of December 13, 1963 (77 Statutes at Large 363)
Extended the Mexican Bracero Program one additional year to December 31, 1964.

6. Immigration and Nationality Act Amendments of October 3, 1965 (79 Statutes at Large 911)—Text of this act is already provided.

7. Freedom of Information Act of July 4, 1966 (80 Statutes at Large 250)
Provisions:

a. Established that the record of every proceeding before the INS in an individual's case be made available to the alien or his attorney of record.
b. Required that public reading rooms be established in each central and district office of the INS, where copies of INS decisions could be made available to the public. Effective July 4, 1967.

8. Act of November 2, 1966 (80 Statutes at Large 1161)
Authorized the attorney general to adjust the status of Cuban refugees to that of permanent resident alien, chargeable to the 120,000 annual limit for the Western Hemisphere.

9. Act of November 6, 1966 (80 Statutes at Large 1322)
Provisions:

a. Extended derivative citizenship to children born on or after December 24, 1952, of civilian U.S. citizens serving abroad.
b. Provided that time spent abroad by U.S. citizens (or their dependent children) in the employ of the U.S. government or certain international organizations could be treated as physical presence in the United States for the purpose of transmitting U.S. citizenship to children born abroad.

10. Act of December 18, 1967 (81 Statutes at Large 661)
Facilitated the expeditious naturalization of certain noncitizen employees of U.S. nonprofit organizations.

11. Act of June 19, 1968 (82 Statutes at Large 197)
Omnibus crimes control and safe streets legislation, declared it illegal for aliens who are illegally in the country and for former citizens who have renounced their citizenship to receive, possess, or transport a firearm.

12. Act of October 24, 1968 (82 Statutes at Large 1343)

Amended the Immigration and Nationality Act of 1952, providing for expeditious naturalization of noncitizens who have rendered honorable services in the U.S. armed forces during the Vietnam conflict or in other periods of military hostilities.

13. Act of April 7, 1970 (84 Statutes at Large 116)

Provisions:

a. Created two new classes of nonimmigrant admission—fiance(e)s of U.S. citizens and intracompany transferees.
b. Modified the H1 temporary worker class of nonimmigrant admission (workers of distinguished merit and ability).
c. Altered the provisions of the law regarding the two-year residence requirement, making it easier for nonimmigrants who have been in the United States as exchange visitors to adjust to a different nonimmigrant status or to permanent resident status.

14. Act of August 10, 1971 (85 Statutes at Large 302)

Amended the Communications Act of 1934, providing that lawful permanent resident aliens be permitted to operate amateur radio stations in the United States and hold licenses for their stations.

15. Act of September 28, 1971 (85 Statutes at Large 348)

Amended the Selective Service Act of 1967. Provided that:

a. Registration for the selective service shall not be applicable to any alien admitted to the United States as a nonimmigrant as long as he continues to maintain a lawful nonimmigrant status in the United States.
b. No alien residing in the United States for less than one year shall be inducted for training and service into the U.S. armed forces.

16. Act of October 27, 1972 (86 Statutes at Large 1289)

Reduced restrictions concerning residence requirements for retention of U.S. citizenship acquired by birth abroad through a U.S. citizen parent and an alien parent.

17. Social Security Act Amendments of October 30, 1972 (86 Statutes at Large 1329)

Amended the Social Security Act, providing that social security numbers be assigned to aliens at the time of their lawful admission to the United States for permanent residence or temporarily to engage in lawful employment.

18. Act of October 20, 1974 (88 Statutes at Large 1387)

Repealed the legislation of 1862. Such legislation, passed to protect Chinese and Japanese aliens from exploitation caused by discriminatory treatment from immigration laws then in effect, had become virtually inoperative because most of the laws singling out Asian peoples had been repealed or modified.

19. Indochina Migration and Refugee Assistance Act of May 23, 1975 (89 Statutes at Large 87)

Established a program of domestic resettlement assistance for refugees who have fled from Cambodia and Vietnam.

20. Act of June 21, 1976 (90 Statutes at Large 691)

Made Laotians eligible for programs established by the Indochina Migration and Refugee Assistance Act of 1975.

21. Act of October 12, 1976 (90 Statutes at Large 2243)

Placed restrictions on foreign medical school graduates (both immigrants and nonimmigrants) coming to the United States for practice or training in the medical profession. Effective January 10, 1977.

22. Immigration and Nationality Act Amendments of October 20, 1976 (90 Statutes at Large 2703)

Provisions:

a. Applied the same twenty-thousand-per-country limit to the Western Hemisphere as applied to the Eastern Hemisphere.
b. Slightly modified the seven-category preference system and applied it to the Western Hemisphere.
c. Amended the 1966 act, providing that Cuban refugees who are adjusted to permanent resident status will not be charged to any numerical limitation, provided they were physically present in the United States on or before the effective date of these amendments.

23. Act of October 20, 1976 Effective January 1, 1978 (90 Statutes at Large 2706)

Denied unemployment compensation to aliens not lawfully admitted for permanent residence or otherwise permanently residing in the United States under color of law. Eased restrictions on foreign medical school graduates, for example, exempted aliens who are of national or international renown in the field of medicine, and exempted certain alien physicians already in the United States from the examination requirement. (See Act of October 12, 1976.)

24. Act of August 1, 1977 (91 Statutes at Large 394)
Eased restrictions on foreign medical school graduates, for example, exempted aliens who are of national or international renown in the field of medicine, and exempted certain alien physicians already in the United States from the examination requirement. (See Act of October 12, 1976.)

25. Act of October 28, 1977 (91 Statutes at Large 1223)
Provisions:

a. Permitted adjustment to permanent resident status for Indochinese refugees who are natives or citizens of Vietnam, Laos, or Cambodia, were physically present in the United States for at least two years, and were admitted or paroled into the United States during specified periods of time.
b. Extended the time limit during which refugee assistance may be provided to such refugees.

26. Act of October 5, 1978 (92 Statutes at Large 907)
Combined the separate ceilings for Eastern and Western Hemisphere immigration into one worldwide limit of 290,000.

27. Act of October 5, 1978 (92 Statutes at Large 917)
Provisions:

a. Made several changes pertaining to the adoption of alien children, including permission for U.S. citizens to petition for the classification of more than two alien orphans as immediate relatives.
b. Eliminated the requirement of continuous residence in the United States for two years prior to filing for naturalization.

28. Act of October 7, 1978 (92 Statutes at Large 963)
Made permanent the president's authority to regulate the entry of aliens and to require U.S. citizens to bear valid passports when entering or leaving the United States:

a. Called for unrestricted use of passports to and in any country other than a country with which the United States is at war, where armed hostilities are in progress, or where there is imminent danger to the public health or the physical safety of U.S. travelers.
b. Declared it the general policy of the United States to impose restrictions on travel within the United States by citizens of another country only when the government of that country imposes restrictions on travel of U.S. citizens within that country.

29. Act of October 14, 1978 (92 Statutes at Large 1263)
Required any alien who acquires or transfers any interest in agricultural land to submit a report to the secretary of agriculture within ninety days after acquisition or transfer.

30. Act of October 30, 1978 (92 Statutes at Large 2065)
Provided for the exclusion and expulsion of aliens who persecuted others on the basis of race, religion, national origin, or political opinion under the direction of the Nazi government of Germany or its allies.

31. Act of November 2, 1978 (92 Statutes at Large 2479)
Provided for the seizure and forfeiture of vessels, vehicles, and aircraft used in smuggling aliens or knowingly transporting aliens to the United States illegally. An exception was made where the owner or person in control did not consent to the illegal act.

32. Panama Canal Act of September 27, 1979 (93 Statutes at Large 452)
Allowed admission as permanent residents to certain aliens with employment on or before 1977 with the Panama Canal Company, the Canal Zone government, or the U.S. government in the Canal Zone, and their families.

33. Refugee Act of March 17, 1980 (94 Statutes at Large 102)
Provided the first permanent and systematic procedure for the admission and effective resettlement of refugees of special humanitarian concern to the United States:

a. Eliminated refugees as a category of the preference system.
b. Set the worldwide ceiling of immigration to the United States at 270,000, exclusive of refugees.
c. Established procedures for annual consultation with Congress on numbers and allocations of refugees to be admitted in each fiscal year, as well as procedures for responding to emergency refugee situations.
d. Defined the term "refugee" (to conform to the 1967 United Nations Protocol on Refugees) and made clear the distinction between refugee and asylee status.
e. Established a comprehensive program for domestic resettlement of refugees.
f. Provided for adjustment to permanent resident status of refugees who have been physically present in the United States for at least one year and of asylees one year after asylum is granted.

34. Refugee Education Assistance Act of October 10, 1980 (94 Statutes at Large 1799)
Established a program of formula grants to state education agencies for basic education of refugee children. Also provided for services to Cuban

and Haitian entrants identical to those for refugees under the Refugee Act of 1980.

FROM 1981 TO 1996

1. Act of June 5, 1981 (95 Statutes at Large 14)
Supplemental appropriations and rescissions bill, reduced previously appropriated funds for migration and refugee assistance, including funds provided for reception and processing of Cuban and Haitian entrants.

2. Act of August 13, 1981 (95 Statutes at Large 357)
Federal appropriations bill for fiscal year 1982, also contained items restricting the access of aliens to various publicly funded benefits. Immigration-related provisions:

a. Precluded the secretary of HUD from making financial assistance available to any alien unless that alien is a resident of the United States by virtue of admission or adjustment as a permanent resident alien, refugee or asylee, parolee, conditional entrant, or pursuant to withholding of deportation. Alien visitors, tourists, diplomats, and students were specifically excluded.
b. Severely restricted eligibility of aliens for Aid to Families with Dependent Children.

3. Immigration and Nationality Act Amendments of December 20, 1981 (95 Statutes at Large 1611)
"INS Efficiency Bill," amended the Immigration and Nationality Act of 1952 and the Act of November 2, 1978:

a. Authorized INS to seize vehicles without having to establish whether the owner was involved in the illegal activity in question.
b. Eliminated the requirement that the government bear administrative and incidental expenses where an innocent owner is involved.
c. Eliminated the requirement that the INS satisfy any valid lien or other third-party interest in a vehicle without expense to the interest holder.
d. Eliminated the required annual notification by aliens of their current address.

4. Act of September 30, 1982 (96 Statutes at Large 1157)
Allowed admission as permanent residents to certain nonimmigrant aliens residing in the Virgin Islands.

5. Act of October 2, 1982 (96 Statutes at Large 1186)
Greatly limited the categories of aliens to whom the Legal Services Corporation may provide legal assistance.

6. Act of October 22, 1982 (96 Statutes at Large 1716)
Provided that children born of U.S. citizen fathers in Korea, Vietnam, Laos, Kampuchea, or Thailand after 1950 and before enactment, may come to the United States as immediate relatives or as first- or fourth-preference immigrants.

7. Immigration Reform and Control Act of November 6, 1986 (IRCA) (100 Statutes at Large 3359)—Text of this act is already provided.

8. Immigration Marriage Fraud Amendments of November 10, 1986 (100 Statutes at Large 3537)—Text of this act is already provided.

9. Amerasian Homecoming Act of December 22, 1987 (101 Statutes at Large 1329)
An appropriations law providing for admission of children born in Vietnam between specified dates to Vietnamese mothers and American fathers, together with their immediate relatives. They are admitted as nonquota immigrants but receive refugee program benefits.

10. Act of September 28, 1988 (102 Statutes at Large 1876)
United States-Canada Free-Trade Agreement Implementation Act:

a. Facilitated temporary entry on a reciprocal basis between the United States and Canada.
b. Established procedures for the temporary entry into the United States of Canadian citizen professional businesspersons to render services for remuneration.
c. No nonimmigrant visa, prior petition, labor certification, or prior approval required, but appropriate documentation must be presented to the inspecting officer establishing Canadian citizenship and professional engagement in one of the occupations listed in the qualifying occupation schedule.

11. Act of November 15, 1988 (102 Statutes at Large 3908)
Provided for the extension of stay for certain nonimmigrant H-1 nurses.

12. Foreign Operations Act of November 21, 1989 (103 Statutes at Large 1195)
An appropriations law, provided for adjustment to permanent resident status for Soviet and Indochinese nationals who were paroled into the United States between certain dates after denial of refugee status.

13. Act of December 18, 1989 (103 Statutes at Large 2099)
The "Immigration Nursing Relief Act of 1989." Provisions:

a. Adjustment from temporary to permanent resident status, without regard to numerical limitation, of certain nonimmigrants who were employed in the United States as registered nurses for at least three years and meet established certification standards.
b. Establishment of a new nonimmigrant category for the temporary admission of qualified registered nurses.

14. Immigration Act of November 29, 1990 (104 Statutes at Large 4978)—Text of this act is already provided.

15. Armed Forces Immigration Adjustment Act of October 1, 1991 (105 Statutes at Large 555)
Provisions:

a. Granted special immigrant status to certain types of aliens who honorably served in the armed forces of the United States for at least twelve years.
b. Delayed until April 1, 1992, the implementation of provisions relating to O and P nonimmigrant visas. (See Act of November 29, 1990.)

16. Act of December 12, 1991 (105 Statutes at Large 1733)
Miscellaneous and Technical Immigration and Naturalization Amendments Act, amended certain elements of the Immigration Act of 1990. Revised provisions regarding the entrance of O and P nonimmigrants, including the repeal of numerical limits of visas for the P categories of admission, and made other technical corrections. (See Act of November 29, 1990.)

17. Chinese Student Protection Act of October 9, 1992 (106 Statutes at Large 1969)
Provided for adjustment to permanent resident status (as employment-based immigrants) by nationals of the People's Republic of China who were in the United States after June 4, 1989, and before April 11, 1990.

18. Soviet Scientists Immigration Act of October 10, 1992 (106 Statutes at Large 3316)
Provisions:

a. Conferred permanent resident status (as employment-based immigrants) on a maximum of 750 scientists from the independent states of the former

Soviet Union and the Baltic states. The limit does not include spouses and children.

b. Stipulated that employment must be in the biological, chemical, or nuclear technical field or work in conjunction with a high-technology defense project.

c. Waived the requirement that workers with expertise in these fields were needed by an employer in the United States.

19. Act of December 8, 1993 (107 Statutes at Large 2057)

North American Free-Trade Agreement Implementation Act (supersedes the United States-Canada Free-Trade Agreement Act of September 28, 1988):

a. Facilitated temporary entry on a reciprocal basis between the United States, Canada, and Mexico.

b. Established procedures for the temporary entry into the United States of Canadian and Mexican citizen professional businesspersons to render services for remuneration:

1. For Canadians, no nonimmigrant visa, prior petition, labor certification, or prior approval required, but appropriate documentation must be presented to the inspecting officer establishing Canadian citizenship and professional engagement in one of the occupations listed in the qualifying occupation schedule.

2. For Mexicans, nonimmigrant visa, prior petition by employer, and Department of Labor attestation are required in addition to proof of Mexican citizenship and professional engagement in one of the occupations listed in the qualifying occupation schedule.

3. For Canadians, nonimmigrant visas are not required of spouses and minor children who possess Canadian citizenship.

4. For Mexicans, nonimmigrant visas are required of spouses and minor children who possess Mexican citizenship.

5. For Canadians, no limit to number of admissions.

6. For Mexicans, a limit was set for a transition period of up to ten years at 5,500 initial approvals per year.

20. Violent Crime Control and Law Enforcement Act of September 13, 1994 (108 Statutes at Large 1796)

Provisions:

a. Authorized establishment of a criminal alien tracking center.

b. Established a new nonimmigrant classification for alien witness cooperation and counterterrorism information.

c. Revised deportation procedures for certain criminal aliens who are not permanent residents and expanded special deportation proceedings.
d. Provided for expeditious deportation for denied asylum applicants.
e. Provided for improved border management through increased resources.
f. Strengthened penalties for passport and visa offenses.

21. Antiterrorism and Effective Death Penalty Act of April 24, 1996 (110 Statutes at Large 1214)

Provisions:

a. Expedited procedures for removal of alien terrorists.
b. Established specific measures to exclude members and representatives of terrorist organizations:
  1. Provided for the exclusion of alien terrorists.
  2. Waived authority concerning notice of denial application for visas.
  3. Denied other forms of relief for alien terrorists.
  4. Excluded from process aliens who have not been inspected and admitted.
c. Modified asylum procedures to improve identification and processing of alien terrorists.
  1. Established mechanisms for denial of asylum to alien terrorists.
  2. Granted authority to inspection officers to both inspect and exclude asylee applicants.
  3. Improved judicial review process to expedite hearings and removal (if necessary) of alien terrorists.
d. Provided for criminal alien procedural improvements.
  1. Provided access to certain confidential immigration and naturalization files through court order.
  2. Established a criminal alien identification system.
  3. Established certain alien smuggling-related crimes as RICO-predicate offenses.
  4. Granted authority for alien smuggling investigations.
  5. Expanded criteria for deportation for crimes of moral turpitude.
  6. Established an interior repatriation program.
  7. Allowed for deportation of nonviolent offenders prior to completion of sentence of imprisonment.
  8. Authorized state and local law enforcement officials to arrest and detain certain illegal aliens.
  9. Expedited process of criminal alien removal.
  10. Limited collateral attacks on underlying deportation order.
  11. Established deportation procedures for certain criminal aliens who are not permanent residents.

22. Personal Responsibility and Work Opportunity Reconciliation Act of August 22, 1996 (110 Statutes at Large 2105)

Provisions:

a. Established restrictions on the eligibility of legal immigrants for means-tested public assistance:
   1. Barred legal immigrants (with certain exceptions) from obtaining food stamps and Supplemental Security Income (SSI) and established screening procedures for current recipients of these programs.
   2. Barred legal immigrants (with certain exceptions) entering the United States after date of enactment from most federal means-tested programs for five years.
   3. Provided states with broad flexibility in setting public benefit eligibility rules for legal immigrants by allowing states to bar current legal immigrants from both major federal programs and state programs.
   4. Increased the responsibility of the immigrants' sponsors by: making the affidavit of support legally enforceable, imposing new requirements on sponsors, and expanding sponsor-deeming requirements to more programs and lengthening the deeming period.
b. Broadened the restrictions on public benefits for illegal aliens and non-immigrants.
   1. Barred illegal, or "not qualified aliens," from most federal, state and local public benefits.
   2. Required INS to verify immigration status in order for aliens to receive most federal public benefits.

23. Illegal Immigration Reform and Immigrant Responsibility Act of September 30, 1996 (110 Statutes at Large 3009)

Provisions:

a. Established measures to control U.S. borders, protect legal workers through worksite enforcement, and remove criminal and other deportable aliens:
   1. Increased border personnel, equipment, and technology as well as enforcement personnel at land and air ports of entry.
   2. Authorized improvements in barriers along the southwest border.
   3. Increased antismuggling authority and penalties for alien smuggling.
   4. Increased penalties for illegal entry, passport and visa fraud, and failure to depart.
   5. Increased INS investigators for worksite enforcement, alien smuggling, and visa overstayers.

6. Established three voluntary pilot programs to confirm the employment eligibility of workers and reduced the number and types of documents that may be presented to employers for identity and eligibility to work.
7. Broadly reformed exclusion and deportation procedures, including consolidation into a single removal process as well as the institution of expedited removal to speed deportation and alien exclusion through more stringent grounds of admissibility.
8. Increased detention space for criminal and other deportable aliens.
9. Instituted three- and ten-year bars to admissibility for aliens seeking to reenter after having been unlawfully present in the United States.
10. Barred reentry of individuals who renounced their U.S. citizenship in order to avoid U.S. tax obligations.

b. Placed added restrictions on benefits for aliens:
1. Provided for a pilot program on limiting issuance of driver's licenses to illegal aliens.
2. Declared aliens not lawfully present ineligible for social security benefits.
3. Established procedures for requiring proof of citizenship for federal public benefits.
4. Established limitations on eligibility for preferential treatment of aliens not lawfully present on the basis of residence for higher education benefits.
5. Provided for verification of immigration status for purposes of social security and higher educational assistance.
6. Tightened the requirement for an affidavit of support for sponsored immigrants, making the affidavit a legally binding contract to provide financial support.
7. Provided authority of states and political subdivisions of states to limit assistance to aliens in providing general cash public assistance.
8. Increased maximum criminal penalties for forging or counterfeiting the seal of a federal department or agency to facilitate benefit fraud by an unlawful alien.

c. Miscellaneous provisions:
1. Recodified existing INS regulations regarding asylum.
2. Provided that the attorney general's parole authority may be exercised only on a case-by-case basis for urgent humanitarian reasons or significant public health reasons.
3. Created new limits on the ability of F-1 students to attend public schools without reimbursing those institutions.
4. Established new mandates for educational institutions to collect information on foreign students' status and nationality and provide it to INS.
5. Tightened restrictions regarding foreign physicians' ability to work in the United States.
6. Added new consular processing provisions and revised the visa waiver program.

Appendix B

Selected Immigration Statistics

Table B.1. Petitions for Naturalization Filed, Persons Naturalized, and Petitions for Naturalization Denied, Fiscal Years 1907 to 2010

Year	Petitions Filed	Persons Naturalized				Petitions Denied
		Total	Civilian	Military[a]	Not Reported	
1907[b]	21,113	7,941	7,941	NA	—	250
1908	44,032	25,975	25,975	NA	—	3,330
1909	43,141	38,374	38,374	NA	—	6,341
1910	55,750	39,448	39,448	NA	—	7,781
1911	74,740	56,683	56,683	NA	—	9,017
1912	95,661	70,310	70,310	NA	—	9,635
1913	95,380	83,561	83,561	NA	—	10,891
1914	124,475	104,145	104,145	NA	—	13,133
1915	106,399	91,848	91,848	NA	—	13,691
1916	108,767	87,831	87,831	NA	—	11,927
1917	130,865	88,104	88,104	NA	—	9,544
1918	169,507	151,449	87,456	63,993	—	12,182
1919	256,858	217,358	89,023	128,335	—	13,119
1920	218,732	177,683	125,711	51,972	—	15,586
1921	195,534	181,292	163,656	17,636	—	18,981
1922	162,638	170,447	160,979	9,468	—	29,076
1923	165,168	145,084	137,975	7,109	—	24,884
1924	177,117	150,510	140,340	10,170	—	18,324
1925	162,258	152,457	152,457	NA	—	15,613
1926	172,232	146,331	146,239	92	—	13,274
1927	240,339	199,804	195,493	4,311	—	11,946
1928	240,321	233,155	228,006	5,149	—	12,479
1929	255,519	224,728	224,197	531	—	11,848

(Continued)

151

Table B.1. Continued

Year	Petitions Filed	Persons Naturalized				Petitions Denied
		Total	Civilian	Military[a]	Not Reported	
1930	113,151	169,377	167,637	1,740	—	9,068
1931	145,474	143,495	140,271	3,224	—	7,514
1932	131,062	136,600	136,598	2	—	5,478
1933	112,629	113,363	112,368	995	—	4,703
1934	117,125	113,669	110,867	2,802	—	1,133
1935	131,378	118,945	118,945	NA	—	2,765
1936	167,127	141,265	140,784	481	—	3,124
1937	165,464	164,976	162,923	2,053	—	4,042
1938	175,413	162,078	158,142	3,936	—	4,854
1939	213,413	188,813	185,175	3,638	—	5,630
1940	278,028	235,260	232,500	2,760	—	6,549
1941	277,807	277,294	275,747	1,547	—	7,769
1942	343,487	270,364	268,762	1,602	—	8,348
1943	377,125	318,933	281,459	37,474	—	13,656
1944	325,717	441,979	392,766	49,213	—	7,297
1945	195,917	231,402	208,707	22,695	—	9,782
1946	123,864	150,062	134,849	15,213	—	6,575
1947	88,802	93,904	77,442	16,462	—	3,953
1948	68,265	70,150	69,080	1,070	—	2,887
1949	71,044	66,594	64,138	2,456	—	2,271
1950	66,038	66,346	64,279	2,067	—	2,276
1951	61,634	54,716	53,741	975	—	2,395
1952	94,086	88,655	87,070	1,585	—	2,163
1953	98,128	92,051	90,476	1,575	—	2,300
1954	130,722	117,831	104,086	13,745	—	2,084
1955	213,508	209,526	197,568	11,958	—	4,571
1956	137,701	145,885	138,681	7,204	—	3,935
1957	140,547	138,043	137,198	845	—	2,948
1958	117,344	119,866	118,950	916	—	2,688
1959	109,270	103,931	102,623	1,308	—	2,208
1960	127,543	119,442	117,848	1,594	—	2,277
1961	138,718	132,450	130,731	1,719	—	3,175
1962	129,682	127,307	124,972	2,335	—	3,557
1963	121,170	124,178	121,618	2,560	—	2,436
1964	113,218	112,234	109,629	2,605	—	2,309
1965	106,813	104,299	101,214	3,085	—	2,059
1966	104,853	103,059	100,498	2,561	—	2,029
1967	108,369	104,902	102,211	2,691	—	2,008
1968	103,085	102,726	100,288	2,438	—	1,962
1969	102,317	98,709	93,251	5,458	—	2,043
1970	114,760	110,399	99,783	10,616	—	1,979
1971	109,897	108,407	98,858	9,549	—	2,028
1972	121,883	116,215	107,740	8,475	—	1,837
1973	126,929	120,404	112,628	7,776	—	1,708

Table B.1. Continued

Year	Petitions Filed	Persons Naturalized				Petitions Denied
		Total	Civilian	Military[a]	Not Reported	
1974	136,175	131,153	124,342	6,811	—	2,210
1975	149,399	140,749	134,586	6,163	—	2,300
1976c	199,152	189,988	182,887	7,101	—	2,799
1977	186,354	159,873	154,568	5,305	—	2,845
1978	168,854	171,971	166,911	5,060	—	3,894
1979	165,434	163,107	157,305	5,802	—	3,987
1980	192,230	156,627	152,073	4,554	—	4,370
1981	171,073	164,389	160,342	4,047	—	4,316
1982	201,507	141,004	138,188	2,816	—	3,994
1983	187,719	178,415	175,159	3,182	74	3,160
1984	286,440	195,862	190,984	2,944	1,934	3,373
1985	305,981	242,451	236,202	3,237	3,012	3,610
1986	290,732	279,497	274,263	2,886	2,348	5,980
1987	232,988	223,249	220,393	2,362	494	6,771
1988	237,752	240,775	238,275	2,278	222	4,304
1989	227,692	232,655	230,088	1,947	620	5,200
1990	233,843	267,586	245,410	1,618	20,558	6,516
1991	206,668	307,394	298,741	1,802	6,851	6,268
1992	342,238	239,664	221,997	5,699	11,968	19,293
1993	521,866	313,590	302,383	7,062	4,145	39,931
1994	543,353	429,123	398,364	5,890	24,869	40,561
1995	959,963	485,720	472,518	3,855	9,347	46,067
1996	1,277,403	1,040,991	924,368	1,214	115,409	229,842
1997	1,412,712	596,010	532,871	531	62,608	130,676
1998	932,957	461,169	437,689	961	22,519	137,395
1999	765,346	837,418	740,718	711	95,989	379,993
2000	460,916	886,026	812,579	836	72,611	399,670
2001	501,643	606,259	575,030	758	30,471	218,326
2002	700,649	572,646	550,835	1,053	20,758	139,779
2003	523,370	462,435	449,123	3,865	9,447	91,599
2004	662,796	537,151	520,771	4,668	11,712	103,339
2005	602,972	604,280	589,269	4,614	10,397	108,247
2006	730,642	702,589	684,484	6,259	11,846	120,722
2007	1,382,993	660,477	648,005	3,808	8,664	89,683
2008	525,786	1,046,539	1,032,281	4,342	9,916	121,283
2009	570,442	743,715	726,043	7,100	10,572	109,813
2010	710,544	619,913	604,410	9,122	6,381	56,990

Source: U.S. Department of Homeland Security.

[a]Data on military naturalizations prior to 1918 not available. Special provisions for military naturalizations expired or suspended in 1925 and 1935.

[b]Data on naturalizations were first compiled by a single federal agency with the establishment of the Naturalization Service in 1906. The year 1907includes naturalizations from September 27, 1906, to June 30, 1907.

[c]Includes the fifteen months from July 1, 1975, to September 30, 1976, because the end date of fiscal years was changed from June 30 to September 30.

NA = not available; "—" represents zero.

Table B.2. Persons Naturalized by Region and Country of Birth, Fiscal Years 2001 to 2010

Region and Country of Birth	2001	2002	2003	2004	2005	2006	2007	2008	2009	2010
Region										
Total	606,259	572,646	462,435	537,151	604,280	702,589	660,477	1,046,539	743,715	619,913
Africa	24,255	31,489	28,529	34,531	38,830	50,397	41,652	54,420	60,383	64,023
Asia	253,275	238,965	196,972	224,072	243,514	263,516	243,783	330,361	276,375	251,598
Europe	82,451	86,540	68,902	83,916	91,692	101,068	81,756	108,618	90,149	77,951
North America	200,089	169,548	130,551	151,047	180,572	223,086	241,163	462,372	250,266	163,888
Oceania	2,585	2,348	2,889	3,551	3,898	3,657	3,342	4,781	3,928	3,646
South America	42,155	42,812	33,635	38,676	44,504	59,985	48,133	84,853	61,674	58,481
Unknown	1,449	944	957	1,358	1,270	880	648	1,134	940	326
Country										
Total	606,259	572,646	462,435	537,151	604,280	702,589	660,477	1,046,539	743,715	619,913
Afghanistan	1,938	1,424	1,235	1,323	1,464	2,018	2,013	2,650	2,588	2,230
Albania	1,032	2,450	2,284	3,324	3,830	3,964	2,786	2,972	3,483	5,088
Algeria	469	615	493	616	722	825	578	894	1,024	808
American Samoa	97	102	117	137	294	247	161	178	265	232
Angola	85	68	64	87	86	106	105	161	95	135
Anguilla	38	30	24	18	27	35	37	47	29	26
Antigua-Barbuda	477	450	325	357	371	520	416	661	456	341
Argentina	2,204	2,129	1,879	1,965	1,976	2,695	2,348	4,170	3,153	3,140
Armenia	1,968	1,814	1,673	1,793	1,737	1,605	1,495	2,195	2,021	3,168
Aruba	41	49	28	30	39	44	36	55	37	27
Australia	391	424	882	1,295	1,155	1,240	1,067	1,636	1,392	1,202
Austria	270	275	240	277	307	359	292	357	303	277
Azerbaijan	946	1,187	886	793	904	997	606	834	1,005	1,233
Bahamas	392	401	342	378	343	574	397	838	569	475
Bahrain	47	47	31	54	57	81	56	85	91	102
Bangladesh	4,416	5,626	4,345	5,148	5,503	6,683	4,746	5,345	6,644	6,979

Barbados	906	871	663	650	778	1,006	718	1,203	878	535
Belarus	2,006	2,141	1,224	1,464	1,549	1,769	1,401	1,767	1,583	1,523
Belgium	296	265	250	232	247	355	248	716	673	523
Belize	1,014	771	665	664	704	918	799	1,291	854	556
Benin	19	25	27	42	56	64	61	79	119	127
Bermuda	58	47	38	47	58	72	42	75	80	65
Bhutan	4	D	3	3	6	D	10	9	17	50
Bolivia	905	1,098	932	1,125	1,361	1,630	1,311	2,807	1,700	1,185
Bosnia-Herzegovina	2,756	4,092	4,993	8,013	8,921	9,686	8,175	8,176	4,544	4,012
Botswana	7	4	12	5	9	17	4	18	17	24
Brazil	3,925	3,885	3,091	4,074	4,583	7,028	5,745	8,808	7,960	8,867
British Virgin Islands	48	40	22	41	38	54	40	67	43	36
Brunei	8	12	9	10	13	13	20	25	14	15
Bulgaria	1,169	1,310	1,599	2,487	2,906	3,488	2,621	3,213	3,211	3,123
Burkina Faso	10	7	12	19	26	51	37	48	90	112
Burma	1,076	1,069	905	1,177	1,360	1,486	1,058	1,383	1,447	2,399
Burundi	15	28	21	59	56	71	95	76	90	145
Cambodia	3,460	3,113	3,135	3,975	4,806	4,778	4,197	5,869	4,673	3,756
Cameroon	299	461	534	575	661	771	611	967	1,098	1,519
Canada	7,528	7,581	6,399	7,682	7,815	9,607	8,473	12,387	9,753	8,539
Cape Verde	577	683	429	635	933	1,126	1,223	1,265	903	675
Cayman Islands	15	17	7	9	8	18	9	24	22	17
Central African Republic	3	10	6	5	10	14	17	19	22	27
Chad	12	3	24	27	19	18	22	22	27	39

(Continued)

Table B.2. Continued

Region and Country of Birth	2001	2002	2003	2004	2005	2006	2007	2008	2009	2010
Chile	1,200	1,148	1,073	1,142	1,183	1,549	1,346	2,851	1,585	1,249
China, People's Republic	34,353	31,987	23,991	27,309	31,708	35,387	33,134	40,017	37,130	33,969
Colombia	10,826	10,601	7,939	9,819	11,396	15,698	12,089	22,926	16,593	18,417
Congo, Democratic Republic	115	116	101	88	122	229	164	211	349	744
Congo, Republic	90	139	123	163	193	369	287	306	308	313
Costa Rica	1,138	1,000	868	970	1,161	1,402	1,227	2,376	1,517	1,114
Cote d'Ivoire	171	271	264	317	324	491	382	479	589	549
Croatia	516	620	615	1,084	1,348	1,623	1,073	1,251	718	589
Cuba	11,343	10,857	7,698	11,236	11,227	21,481	15,394	39,871	24,891	14,050
Cyprus	185	150	100	104	134	140	109	160	160	118
Czech Republic	47	64	50	69	102	122	122	192	266	367
Czechoslovakia (former)	489	453	333	434	490	614	449	629	503	372
Denmark	226	194	197	175	154	199	170	210	156	123
Djibouti	9	18	16	12	17	18	14	25	19	17
Dominica	370	456	361	441	543	741	539	975	672	543
Dominican Republic	14,958	15,562	12,607	15,464	20,831	22,165	20,645	35,251	20,778	15,451
Ecuador	6,547	6,392	5,061	5,616	7,091	8,321	7,229	11,908	7,609	5,931
Egypt	3,779	3,698	2,922	3,726	4,061	4,271	3,231	4,165	5,224	5,860
El Salvador	13,613	10,699	8,719	9,602	12,174	13,430	17,157	35,796	18,927	10,343
Equatorial Guinea	—	3	D	3	4	D	6	9	D	12
Eritrea	755	809	819	829	692	653	553	694	760	991
Estonia	105	110	102	126	104	156	132	221	209	185
Ethiopia	2,756	3,892	3,820	4,255	4,621	5,397	5,165	7,160	8,698	8,903

Fiji	1,175	1,020	1,267	1,503	1,163	1,118	1,508	998	1,140
Finland	114	140	352	431	532	359	549	385	286
France	1,742	1,718	1,802	1,963	2,449	1,979	2,765	2,464	2,203
French Polynesia	41	16	10	22	16	19	15	12	12
Gabon	5	12	12	18	23	18	24	35	43
Gambia	69	135	136	189	286	246	330	419	444
Georgia	415	444	382	443	628	514	627	864	1,107
Germany	3,200	3,424	3,836	3,811	4,556	3,617	4,708	4,564	4,001
Ghana	1,828	3,326	3,577	3,561	4,760	3,181	4,557	4,819	4,211
Greece	1,661	1,285	1,100	1,075	1,291	1,200	1,314	1,067	800
Grenada	609	607	530	649	781	511	850	683	446
Guadeloupe	14	25	21	26	36	16	39	34	38
Guatemala	6,257	5,442	5,080	6,250	6,551	8,181	17,087	8,619	5,375
Guinea	67	111	124	137	194	191	225	304	418
Guinea-Bissau	6	14	10	10	14	5	14	17	17
Guyana	7,038	7,220	4,877	5,543	7,434	5,631	8,290	6,840	4,932
Haiti	10,355	9,268	8,215	9,740	15,979	11,552	21,229	13,290	12,291
Honduras	3,248	3,496	3,455	3,953	4,949	4,669	8,794	4,858	3,056
Hong Kong	5,269	4,849	3,713	4,479	4,263	3,871	4,940	3,329	2,198
Hungary	873	827	738	720	955	788	1,089	1,142	916
Iceland	44	32	79	82	70	62	83	75	51
India	34,240	33,737	37,975	35,962	47,542	46,871	65,971	52,889	61,142
Indonesia	1,242	1,003	1,131	1,234	1,287	1,213	1,823	1,794	2,765
Iran	13,834	11,773	11,781	11,031	11,363	10,557	11,813	12,069	9,337
Iraq	3,443	3,314	3,646	3,273	3,614	2,967	5,057	4,197	3,489
Ireland	4,437	3,438	2,421	1,995	1,754	1,335	2,179	1,296	1,178
Israel	2,970	2,556	2,373	2,436	2,905	2,363	2,933	3,410	3,205

(Continued)

Table B.2. Continued

Region and Country of Birth	2001	2002	2003	2004	2005	2006	2007	2008	2009	2010
Italy	2,972	2,614	1,845	2,295	2,511	2,769	2,217	2,991	2,552	2,064
Jamaica	13,947	13,949	11,218	12,271	13,674	18,953	12,314	21,324	15,098	12,070
Japan	2,362	1,857	1,795	1,955	2,154	2,192	1,934	2,712	2,192	1,622
Jordan	2,876	2,821	1,917	2,324	2,464	2,634	2,125	2,632	2,891	2,436
Kazakhstan	429	562	455	572	726	872	725	908	917	763
Kenya	731	865	823	997	1,158	1,636	1,396	2,218	2,546	3,043
Korea, North	NA	NA	NA	NA	NA	NA	NA	NA	28	13
Korea, South[a]	17,979	17,252	15,928	17,184	19,223	17,668	17,628	22,759	17,576	11,170
Kosovo	X	X	X	X	X	X	X	89	397	590
Kuwait	766	791	606	796	846	903	755	1,031	1,152	919
Kyrgyzstan	81	128	131	159	217	246	331	361	338	380
Laos	6,469	8,363	5,841	5,678	5,261	4,114	3,787	5,553	3,081	2,743
Latvia	359	376	224	335	348	347	327	455	404	342
Lebanon	3,550	3,402	2,499	3,314	3,288	3,393	2,779	3,399	3,787	3,266
Lesotho	3	5	6	8	4	7	11	6	D	7
Liberia	778	1,047	917	1,218	1,548	2,193	1,815	2,468	2,767	3,360
Libya	171	163	112	130	173	142	136	198	249	173
Lithuania	402	489	457	738	887	964	819	969	786	843
Luxembourg	9	8	9	9	7	9	9	17	22	18
Macau	199	196	115	146	195	163	158	181	158	94
Macedonia	394	559	376	601	651	837	597	756	741	682
Madagascar	25	29	22	30	29	36	26	43	49	55
Malawi	39	44	25	52	60	67	46	64	58	80
Malaysia	1,032	1,092	983	1,019	1,221	1,264	1,217	1,705	1,178	1,211
Mali	51	72	64	66	85	118	93	124	149	200
Malta	63	85	61	80	67	86	66	71	72	46
Marshall Islands	3	D	4	9	4	14	12	12	29	21

Martinique	14	23	21	11	16	21	18	10	16	21
Mauritania	281	175	122	72	106	56	53	29	23	19
Mauritius	79	89	70	55	65	46	43	42	37	38
Mexico	67,062	111,630	231,815	122,258	83,979	77,089	63,840	55,946	76,310	102,736
Micronesia, Federated States	84	125	62	41	41	22	14	6	6	4
Moldova	1,235	1,239	1,328	1,068	988	927	711	713	919	955
Mongolia	157	137	129	53	60	41	21	17	13	9
Montenegro	167	140	32	—	X	X	X	X	X	X
Montserrat	57	59	87	51	96	78	54	64	84	86
Morocco	3,710	4,556	3,383	2,684	3,643	2,628	1,841	1,283	1,274	1,247
Mozambique	41	47	73	45	62	50	40	32	57	29
Namibia	38	27	38	22	17	18	13	13	13	15
Nepal	2,185	1,632	953	638	575	417	408	318	247	205
Netherlands	691	889	1,219	819	1,008	860	722	500	512	546
Netherlands Antilles	56	40	43	28	33	25	23	19	28	34
New Zealand	495	562	649	447	440	444	420	340	356	345
Nicaragua	4,047	7,445	17,954	8,164	9,283	5,080	3,444	3,044	3,788	3,549
Niger	89	67	73	52	46	48	46	46	110	183
Nigeria	9,126	9,298	8,597	6,582	8,652	6,894	6,470	5,691	6,412	4,349
Norway	91	128	153	105	145	136	137	93	108	126
Oman	30	32	33	15	23	16	13	16	9	8
Pakistan	11,601	12,528	11,813	9,147	10,411	9,699	8,744	7,424	8,643	8,367
Palau	71	54	62	40	36	18	19	12	9	7
Panama	1,215	1,694	2,870	1,617	1,930	1,643	1,462	1,248	1,591	1,577
Papua New Guinea	16	18	14	5	12	10	3	D	7	7

(Continued)

Table B.2. Continued

Region and Country of Birth	2001	2002	2003	2004	2005	2006	2007	2008	2009	2010
Paraguay	165	198	175	178	202	285	234	386	310	212
Peru	6,659	7,375	6,130	6,980	7,904	10,063	7,965	15,016	10,349	8,551
Philippines	35,347	30,440	29,043	31,448	36,673	40,500	38,830	58,792	38,934	35,465
Poland	11,625	12,811	9,139	10,335	9,801	10,230	9,320	14,237	10,604	8,038
Portugal	2,762	2,187	2,034	2,173	2,403	2,638	2,506	3,988	2,143	1,266
Qatar	37	48	34	48	66	59	60	85	106	115
Romania	3,512	4,014	3,267	4,388	4,602	5,484	3,986	4,515	4,388	4,385
Russia	9,395	9,841	6,669	7,586	8,297	9,412	7,660	10,778	9,490	7,566
Rwanda	60	86	77	116	123	178	91	101	161	278
Saint Kitts-Nevis	331	351	321	282	331	483	334	529	389	305
Saint Lucia	392	417	366	359	515	623	506	779	583	554
Saint Vincent and the Grenadines	439	461	374	388	491	624	450	623	513	375
Samoa	194	150	117	157	165	201	163	204	185	154
Saudi Arabia	247	309	251	354	397	511	504	615	768	739
Senegal	250	346	274	371	401	503	386	566	640	633
Serbia	X	X	X	X	X	X	—	3	15	27
Serbia and Montenegro[b]	2,076	2,302	2,012	3,159	5,857	5,555	3,382	3,582	2,597	2,653
Seychelles	18	12	15	13	8	22	5	26	19	12
Sierra Leone	516	763	777	945	1,043	1,683	1,485	2,018	1,868	1,878
Singapore	306	322	273	332	338	347	315	433	403	336
Slovakia	243	301	286	318	362	479	380	498	488	485
Slovenia	42	58	43	60	58	61	60	80	64	64
Somalia	1,167	1,789	2,235	2,714	3,238	4,242	3,594	3,816	3,818	5,728
South Africa	1,468	1,526	1,262	1,453	1,495	2,225	2,069	2,980	2,436	2,550

Soviet Union (former)	4,563	4,302	3,437	3,772	3,668	3,831	2,813	3,538	4,263	2,954
Spain	722	631	552	1,120	1,256	1,465	1,175	1,958	1,420	1,115
Sri Lanka	835	961	827	980	927	1,023	1,024	1,377	1,367	1,421
Sudan	739	1,012	839	1,104	1,551	2,587	2,785	2,893	2,855	2,885
Suriname	111	119	120	97	125	222	159	202	198	161
Swaziland	3	8	7	5	5	10	4	8	21	8
Sweden	321	819	948	1,016	980	984	786	1,207	940	774
Switzerland	516	462	430	487	541	539	501	658	529	484
Syria	2,151	2,278	1,881	2,385	2,252	2,395	1,799	2,105	2,484	2,029
Taiwan	9,052	8,599	6,742	7,889	8,295	8,819	7,486	8,711	7,606	5,621
Tajikistan	368	234	127	117	116	147	109	168	156	178
Tanzania	333	345	295	348	363	490	356	464	567	466
Thailand	4,088	4,013	3,636	3,779	4,314	4,583	4,438	6,930	4,962	4,112
Togo	57	113	153	204	291	536	473	673	1,132	1,253
Tonga	301	246	182	207	246	235	251	421	269	208
Trinidad and Tobago	4,474	4,814	3,774	3,958	4,832	6,612	4,514	7,305	5,726	4,740
Tunisia	157	165	119	192	226	315	299	390	479	407
Turkey	1,792	1,924	1,724	1,964	2,231	2,742	2,009	2,771	3,219	3,213
Turkmenistan	60	65	43	58	59	75	58	99	91	138
Turks and Caicos Islands	39	18	15	16	21	30	14	33	21	20
Uganda	296	321	279	327	340	477	344	541	489	637
Ukraine	11,819	12,106	8,236	8,069	9,343	10,184	8,594	10,992	9,123	7,345
United Arab Emirates	84	109	112	168	197	277	253	328	383	404

(Continued)

Table B.2. Continued

Region and Country of Birth	2001	2002	2003	2004	2005	2006	2007	2008	2009	2010
United Kingdom	8,038	8,194	6,717	7,785	8,087	9,104	7,752	12,095	10,060	8,401
United States	38	42	37	36	29	57	41	67	51	45
Uruguay	471	485	352	412	475	579	496	924	634	585
Uzbekistan	2,492	2,541	1,480	1,224	1,588	1,821	1,148	1,377	1,513	1,472
Venezuela	2,103	2,156	1,952	2,385	2,659	4,476	3,575	6,557	4,735	5,243
Vietnam	41,462	36,757	25,933	27,480	32,926	29,917	27,921	39,584	31,168	19,313
Yemen	807	882	589	822	814	989	734	1,080	1,243	1,186
Zambia	158	168	134	180	159	239	212	290	289	317
Zimbabwe	206	231	210	225	260	322	312	413	489	546
All other countries	37	36	32	38	43	32	40	69	56	45
Unknown	1,449	944	957	1,358	1,270	880	648	1,134	940	326

Source: U.S. Department of Homeland Security.
Note: Based on N-400 data for persons age eighteen and over.
[a]Data for South Korea prior to fiscal year 2009 include a small number of cases from North Korea.
[b]Yugoslavia (unknown republic) prior to February 7, 2003.
NA = not available; X = not applicable; D = data withheld to limit disclosure; "—" represents zero.

Table B.3. Persons Naturalized by State or Territory of Residence, Fiscal Years 2001 to 2010

State or Territory of Residence	2001	2002	2003	2004	2005	2006	2007	2008	2009	2010
Total	606,259	572,646	462,435	537,151	604,280	702,589	660,477	1,046,539	743,715	619,913
Alabama	407	1,274	1,182	734	795	1,946	1,343	1,982	1,775	2,027
Alaska	707	929	745	777	951	831	849	1,145	1,100	831
Arizona	8,239	6,064	7,218	6,500	6,785	9,707	12,091	24,055	12,377	10,340
Arkansas	132	583	715	823	990	1,133	1,214	2,330	1,648	1,275
California	202,668	149,213	135,599	145,593	170,489	152,836	181,684	297,909	179,754	129,354
Colorado	4,210	5,875	4,833	6,007	5,681	5,526	7,829	11,972	6,813	7,165
Connecticut	5,005	6,072	4,284	5,957	8,169	7,231	4,552	9,589	10,421	7,452
Delaware	697	568	707	982	945	1,187	1,094	1,425	1,545	1,829
District of Columbia	951	926	852	882	939	1,089	1,334	1,492	2,188	1,319
Florida	48,577	44,732	35,105	43,795	42,999	90,846	54,563	128,328	82,788	67,484
Georgia	3,223	11,066	11,068	6,880	7,903	19,785	14,181	20,417	15,408	18,253
Guam	282	604	599	1,052	682	873	1,057	998	654	644
Hawaii	2,875	2,881	2,287	2,050	4,663	5,276	4,521	5,205	3,744	3,190
Idaho	355	58	56	864	1,097	980	1,261	2,240	1,674	1,102
Illinois	32,256	32,585	23,401	29,432	27,739	30,156	38,735	45,224	28,112	26,180
Indiana	2,558	2,774	2,725	2,455	2,650	3,885	3,652	5,104	4,261	3,866
Iowa	1,055	1,465	1,123	1,314	234	805	2,093	3,503	2,198	1,858
Kansas	2,337	1,367	1,897	2,093	1,814	2,509	2,406	4,072	3,129	2,492
Kentucky	402	1,986	1,543	1,307	1,820	2,049	2,256	3,093	2,390	2,398
Louisiana	685	2,106	1,702	1,458	1,700	1,336	2,240	3,018	3,402	2,423
Maine	367	514	427	548	772	802	728	924	729	839
Maryland	5,405	13,217	13,836	12,295	11,503	14,465	11,613	23,342	17,099	16,220

(Continued)

Table B.3. Continued

State or Territory of Residence	2001	2002	2003	2004	2005	2006	2007	2008	2009	2010
Massachusetts	17,596	18,024	11,461	16,263	22,685	22,932	20,952	28,728	21,748	21,095
Michigan	6,109	11,113	5,191	14,615	11,418	11,675	10,678	14,634	10,703	11,162
Minnesota	5,697	5,443	6,226	7,713	7,383	9,137	9,124	9,220	9,089	9,020
Mississippi	270	506	445	557	520	495	657	944	1,170	967
Missouri	2,627	2,311	3,255	3,999	2,733	3,711	4,237	5,849	4,526	4,388
Montana	75	7	81	285	209	225	251	358	267	259
Nebraska	1,547	1,644	789	1,537	1,365	1,797	2,188	2,866	1,644	1,590
Nevada	3,321	3,779	4,095	4,622	5,901	8,202	8,363	13,150	8,470	6,791
New Hampshire	817	448	1,027	958	971	2,483	1,821	1,617	1,492	1,670
New Jersey	26,730	26,760	22,968	30,291	33,160	39,801	35,235	59,950	35,077	33,864
New Mexico	785	1,084	993	1,449	1,401	1,538	1,704	3,058	3,062	2,205
New York	98,858	94,181	63,888	66,234	84,624	103,870	73,676	90,572	88,733	67,972
North Carolina	3,866	8,348	3,577	5,084	5,862	12,592	6,606	8,509	16,294	9,988
North Dakota	200	210	146	267	203	329	415	336	273	286
Ohio	3,645	6,053	2,764	8,590	9,415	8,796	9,250	11,142	8,072	8,617
Oklahoma	1,916	1,828	1,573	1,765	1,799	2,246	1,812	3,335	2,256	2,678
Oregon	4,189	4,441	4,300	3,612	4,777	4,332	5,572	9,257	5,051	4,910
Pennsylvania	8,383	9,619	9,443	10,205	13,307	15,846	11,371	19,673	16,905	16,143
Puerto Rico	699	1,060	559	512	1,641	1,413	1,518	2,622	1,253	1,318
Rhode Island	1,058	1,158	1,620	2,185	2,604	2,266	2,088	3,721	2,458	2,078
South Carolina	694	504	1,020	1,748	916	2,940	1,499	3,488	3,506	3,081
South Dakota	202	209	177	257	354	342	460	572	415	399
Tennessee	1,255	2,441	2,011	2,613	3,578	3,334	2,927	5,560	4,938	4,229
Texas	43,287	42,767	28,638	35,417	38,553	37,835	53,032	82,129	54,024	49,699

Utah	1,828	1,789	1,682	3,110	2,874	2,740	2,777	5,394	2,823	2,908
Vermont	332	428	426	419	488	569	468	518	426	407
Virginia	7,414	10,598	9,583	13,478	17,653	20,401	14,171	29,949	24,730	17,815
Washington	8,778	9,335	11,787	12,667	14,817	12,762	14,671	18,665	19,853	16,830
West Virginia	285	302	261	237	362	390	310	505	361	550
Wisconsin	2,955	3,623	2,775	3,570	4,040	3,247	4,485	5,200	3,845	3,864
Wyoming	135	102	111	146	134	169	190	245	186	229
Other[a]	305	362	466	287	480	608	643	1,499	1,051	590
Unknown	27,008	15,310	7,193	8,661	6,733	8,313	6,030	5,907	5,805	3,770

Source: U.S. Department of Homeland Security.
Note: Based on N-400 data for persons age eighteen and over.
[a]Includes U.S. territories and armed forces posts.

Table B.4. Persons Naturalized by Core Based Statistical Area (CBSA) of Residence, Fiscal Years 2001 to 2010 (ranked by 2010 naturalizations)

Geographic Area	2001	2002	2003	2004	2005	2006	2007	2008	2009	2010
Total	606,259	572,646	462,435	537,151	604,280	702,589	660,477	1,046,539	743,715	619,913
New York-Northern New Jersey-Long Island, NY-NJ-PA	118,281	114,964	82,431	89,925	108,439	132,322	99,007	134,571	112,801	91,257
Los Angeles-Long Beach-Santa Ana, CA	96,852	69,495	62,556	66,733	78,182	65,811	78,454	138,618	84,061	51,977
Miami-Fort Lauderdale-Pompano Beach, FL	33,503	31,113	23,995	28,848	24,110	63,621	36,159	89,440	54,202	42,220
Chicago-Naperville-Joliet, IL-IN-WI	30,492	31,323	22,787	28,264	27,054	29,047	37,736	43,548	26,676	25,053
Washington-Arlington-Alexandria, DC-VA-MD-WV	9,982	18,214	16,981	19,711	22,473	26,463	19,367	40,731	32,690	24,861
San Francisco-Oakland-Fremont, CA	32,375	22,393	23,744	22,931	25,490	24,038	25,873	37,852	20,956	21,281
Houston-Sugar Land-Baytown, TX	22,221	16,743	10,362	12,816	13,401	13,893	18,398	28,275	18,380	18,344
Boston-Cambridge-Quincy, MA-NH	14,246	14,850	9,198	13,177	18,273	18,585	16,954	22,859	17,429	17,027
Dallas-Fort Worth-Arlington, TX	10,193	13,413	7,586	11,248	12,748	12,111	18,069	25,172	17,423	16,572

Atlanta-Sandy Springs-Marietta, GA	2,636	9,395	9,327	5,634	6,647	16,823	11,720	16,812	12,651	15,519
San Jose-Sunnyvale-Santa Clara, CA	16,316	15,320	10,174	15,408	15,494	14,129	12,347	24,142	14,201	13,455
Philadelphia-Camden-Wilmington, PA-NJ-DE-MD	6,838	6,540	6,773	7,623	10,526	13,252	9,272	16,720	14,285	13,453
Seattle-Tacoma-Bellevue, WA	6,949	7,144	9,058	9,586	11,318	9,407	10,066	12,534	15,061	12,774
San Diego-Carlsbad-San Marcos, CA	14,239	9,667	8,757	11,184	12,265	12,682	17,924	21,154	12,978	11,473
Riverside-San Bernardino-Ontario, CA	10,489	7,264	9,522	8,368	13,417	11,311	12,253	23,627	19,422	8,724
Detroit-Warren-Livonia, MI	4,440	8,331	3,709	10,811	8,271	8,724	7,868	10,731	7,494	8,084
Minneapolis-St. Paul-Bloomington, MN-WI	5,075	4,836	5,455	6,776	6,388	7,932	7,839	7,834	7,969	7,917
Phoenix-Mesa-Scottsdale, AZ	5,828	4,010	4,772	4,250	4,467	7,016	8,344	17,594	8,653	7,527
Orlando-Kissimmee, FL	4,355	3,970	1,965	2,382	5,326	9,247	3,622	11,914	7,181	6,744
Sacramento-Arden-Arcade-Roseville, CA	7,082	4,930	5,903	5,913	7,556	6,424	8,968	11,347	6,372	6,099

(Continued)

Table B.4. Continued

Geographic Area	2001	2002	2003	2004	2005	2006	2007	2008	2009	2010
Tampa-St. Petersburg-Clearwater, FL	4,550	4,489	3,939	4,650	4,754	5,394	4,721	9,623	7,587	5,786
Las Vegas-Paradise, NV	2,753	2,945	3,188	3,905	4,833	6,986	6,829	11,058	7,357	5,724
Baltimore-Towson, MD	1,470	3,581	3,946	3,452	3,391	4,310	3,490	6,920	5,296	5,150
Denver-Aurora-Broomfield, CO	2,869	4,072	3,364	4,221	3,987	3,688	5,414	8,047	4,497	4,751
Portland-Vancouver-Beaverton, OR-WA	3,789	3,941	4,024	3,586	4,425	4,044	5,037	7,779	4,821	4,611
Columbus, OH	1,300	837	478	2,529	3,624	3,090	3,141	4,014	2,742	3,075
Austin-Round Rock, TX	2,008	2,449	2,110	1,935	2,043	2,120	3,004	4,707	2,829	2,953
Jacksonville, FL	1,079	644	1,079	1,860	2,491	2,278	2,626	3,208	2,305	2,859
Providence-New Bedford-Fall River, RI-MA	1,939	1,632	2,456	3,024	3,746	3,390	3,202	5,536	3,470	2,819
Bridgeport-Stamford-Norwalk, CT	1,931	2,486	1,526	2,291	3,319	2,441	1,625	3,534	3,930	2,732
Charlotte-Gastonia-Concord, NC-SC	1,051	2,293	797	1,195	1,455	3,277	1,850	2,620	4,243	2,650
Raleigh-Cary, NC	783	1,725	700	997	1,150	2,778	1,399	1,556	4,121	2,560
Honolulu, HI	2,385	2,250	1,915	1,854	4,326	4,207	3,585	4,083	2,950	2,551
Saint Louis, MO-IL	1,502	1,379	1,943	2,471	1,656	2,119	2,711	3,532	2,549	2,531

Hartford-West Hartford-East Hartford, CT	1,651	1,955	1,485	1,874	2,561	2,496	1,510	3,142	3,323	2,466
San Antonio, TX	1,788	2,355	1,944	1,714	2,069	1,758	2,568	5,387	2,594	2,457
Worcester, MA	1,413	1,704	986	1,494	2,128	2,149	1,883	2,572	2,038	2,273
Kansas City, MO-KS	1,598	1,167	1,612	1,724	1,485	1,770	2,016	3,250	2,439	2,199
Fresno, CA	2,859	3,482	1,579	1,483	1,579	1,812	3,070	5,133	2,396	2,152
Cleveland-Elyria-Mentor, OH	537	2,580	941	3,014	2,568	2,583	2,599	2,975	2,173	2,122
Nashville-Davidson-Murfreesboro-Franklin, TN	636	1,041	954	932	1,835	1,661	1,422	2,619	2,290	2,112
Virginia Beach-Norfolk-Newport News, VA-NC	977	1,419	1,705	1,705	2,176	2,156	1,547	2,826	2,028	2,065
El Paso, TX	1,173	1,493	1,368	1,975	2,056	1,239	2,314	4,436	3,512	1,980
Stockton, CA	2,507	1,562	1,974	1,848	2,218	2,102	3,157	4,196	2,044	1,845
Indianapolis-Carmel, IN	859	966	1,181	883	873	1,617	1,421	2,058	1,766	1,834
Oxnard-Thousand Oaks-Ventura, CA	3,001	2,357	1,991	2,087	3,387	2,743	3,221	5,235	3,371	1,823
Salt Lake City, UT	1,240	1,267	1,179	2,082	1,962	1,835	1,717	3,230	1,727	1,781
Cincinnati-Middletown, OH-KY-IN	946	956	577	1,012	1,371	1,297	1,568	2,037	1,354	1,693
Richmond, VA	715	694	903	969	1,237	1,386	1,276	2,376	1,633	1,689
New Haven-Milford, CT	974	1,151	888	1,276	1,649	1,642	999	2,088	2,162	1,656

(Continued)

Table B.4. Continued

Geographic Area	2001	2002	2003	2004	2005	2006	2007	2008	2009	2010
Other CBSAs	69,934	77,964	63,716	78,047	84,695	104,989	106,890	165,752	124,232	107,081
Other metropolitan areas	61,045	68,134	55,508	68,135	74,231	90,952	93,349	144,937	107,390	93,435
Other micropolitan areas	8,889	9,830	8,208	9,912	10,464	14,037	13,541	20,815	16,842	13,646
Non-CBSA	4,641	4,583	3,740	4,813	4,651	5,927	6,401	9,636	7,251	5,803
Unknown	27,009	15,312	7,192	8,661	6,735	8,467	6,024	5,899	5,800	3,769

Source: U.S. Department of Homeland Security.
Note: Based on N-400 data for persons age eighteen and over.

Table B.5. Refugee Arrivals by Region and Country of Nationality, Fiscal Years 2001 to 2010

Region and Country of Nationality	2001	2002	2003	2004	2005	2006	2007	2008	2009	2010
Region										
Total	68,925	26,785	28,286	52,840	53,738	41,094	48,218	60,107	74,602	73,293
Africa	19,070	2,551	10,719	29,108	20,746	18,129	17,486	8,943	9,678	13,325
Asia	16,985	7,723	6,731	12,276	15,769	10,086	23,563	44,819	58,309	52,695
Europe	29,897	14,579	10,381	7,879	10,524	9,615	4,193	2,059	1,693	1,238
North America	2,968	1,924	306	2,998	6,368	3,145	2,922	4,177	4,800	4,856
Oceania	—	—	—	—	—	—	—	—	—	—
South America	5	8	149	579	331	119	54	100	57	126
Unknown	—	—	—	—	—	—	—	9	65	1,053
Country										
Total	68,925	26,785	28,286	52,840	53,738	41,094	48,218	60,107	74,602	73,293
Afghanistan	2,930	1,683	1,453	959	902	651	441	576	349	515
Algeria	31	—	4	D	D	D	—	—	—	D
Angola	34	16	21	20	21	13	4	—	8	—
Armenia	27	30	63	88	86	87	29	9	4	D
Azerbaijan	449	114	406	407	299	77	78	30	38	18
Belarus	971	680	702	659	445	350	219	111	146	103
Bhutan	—	—	—	—	—	3	—	5,320	13,452	12,363
Bosnia-Herzegovina	14,593	3,481	506	244	61	16	D			
Burma	543	128	203	1,056	1,447	1,612	13,896	18,139	18,202	16,693
Burundi	109	62	16	276	214	466	4,545	2,889	762	530
Cambodia	23	4	7	3	9	9	15	8	15	9
Cameroon	5	6	6	D	6	29	5	D	4	6
Central African Republic	D	—	D	24	—	23	15	56	59	45
Chad	D	D	D	4	—	4	10	23	6	28

(*Continued*)

Table B.5. Continued

Region and Country of Nationality	2001	2002	2003	2004	2005	2006	2007	2008	2009	2010
China, People's Republic	12	9	9	3	13	21	27	50	54	72
Colombia	—	8	149	577	323	115	54	94	57	123
Congo, Democratic Republic	260	107	251	569	424	405	848	727	1,135	3,174
Congo, Republic	6	5	41	73	43	66	206	197	293	154
Cote d'Ivoire	D	3	4	—	5	23	11	30	9	4
Croatia	1,020	109	144	92	39	D	—	—	—	—
Cuba	2,944	1,919	306	2,980	6,360	3,143	2,922	4,177	4,800	4,818
Djibouti	12	D	D	6	—	D	3	5	3	—
Egypt	8	—	—	3	25	11	3	—	7	15
Equatorial Guinea	—	—	3	—	—	D	14	—	9	9
Eritrea	109	13	23	128	327	538	963	251	1,571	2,570
Estonia	57	38	28	27	17	7	6	6	D	—
Ethiopia	1,429	330	1,702	2,689	1,663	1,271	1,028	299	321	668
Gambia	5	—	9	3	—	6	13	6	10	10
Georgia	49	14	53	33	11	4	7	20	4	4
Haiti	24	5	—	17	8	—	—	—	—	18
Honduras	—	—	17	—	—	—	—	—	—	20
Indonesia	5	18	17	5	6	10	—	—	—	—
Iran	6,590	1,535	2,471	1,786	1,856	2,792	5,481	5,270	5,381	3,543
Iraq	2,473	466	298	66	198	202	1,608	13,822	18,838	18,016
Kazakhstan	291	222	118	312	80	124	45	62	52	46
Kenya	13	24	3	—	D	5	5	D	D	—
Korea, North	—	—	—	—	—	9	22	37	25	8
Kuwait	—	6	—	14	—	—	24	D	7	40
Kyrgyzstan	116	69	46	100	38	15	17	25	46	27

Laos	22	18	13	6,005	8,517	830	117	59	14	36
Latvia	125	57	49	52	25	21	17	6	D	—
Liberia	3,429	560	2,957	7,140	4,289	2,346	1,606	992	385	244
Lithuania	40	D	21	13	9	D	4	—	—	4
Macedonia	D	4	13	—	—	D	—	—	—	—
Mauritania	202	6	—	—	3	88	62	26	16	74
Moldova	1,168	1,022	616	1,711	1,016	721	565	487	445	356
Nigeria	85	28	57	34	11	15	20	76	3	D
Pakistan	3	—	18	11	9	20	30	104	67	59
Russia	4,454	2,105	1,394	1,446	5,982	6,003	1,773	426	495	326
Rwanda	94	47	47	176	183	112	202	108	111	230
Serbia and Montenegro	X	X	X	151	40	11	X	X	X	X
Sierra Leone	2,004	176	1,378	1,084	829	439	166	99	51	54
Somalia	4,951	237	1,994	13,331	10,405	10,357	6,969	2,523	4,189	4,884
Soviet Union, former	133	—	—	D	—	—	D	D	—	—
Sri Lanka	D	5	7	D	—	6	D	D	33	118
Sudan	5,959	897	2,139	3,500	2,205	1,848	705	375	683	558
Syria	8	4	3	—	7	27	17	24	25	25
Tajikistan	9	4	13	D	6	4	—	D	—	3
Togo	280	16	47	35	72	18	40	204	14	9
Tunisia	10	D	D	—	—	—	—	—	—	D
Uganda	12	D	D	8	10	20	38	42	8	30
Ukraine	7,172	5,217	5,065	3,482	2,889	2,483	1,605	1,022	601	449
Uzbekistan	681	394	166	426	271	527	190	134	152	185
Vietnam	2,730	2,988	1,354	979	2,009	3,039	1,500	1,112	1,486	873
Yemen		—	D	8	D	11	6	—	47	15
Yugoslavia, former	153	1,860	1,839	X	X	X	X	X	X	X

(Continued)

Table B.5. Continued

Region and Country of Nationality	2001	2002	2003	2004	2005	2006	2007	2008	2009	2010
Zimbabwe	6	—	—	D	D	13	D	3	10	7
All other countries	49	31	29	18	20	23	25	31	30	46
Unknown[a]	—	—	—	—	—	—	—	9	65	1,053

Source: U.S. Department of State, Bureau of Population, Refugees, and Migration, Worldwide Refugee Admissions Processing System (WRAPS), Fiscal Years 2001 to 2010.

Note: Excludes Amerasian immigrants.

[a]Includes admissions from Palestinian Territory.

"—" represents zero; D = data withheld to limit disclosure; X = not applicable.

Table B.6. Individuals Granted Asylum Affirmatively by Region and Country of Nationality, Fiscal Years 2001 to 2010

Region and Country of Nationality	2001	2002	2003	2004	2005	2006	2007	2008	2009	2010
Region										
Total	29,160	25,946	15,357	14,325	13,471	12,942	12,343	12,075	11,904	11,244
Africa	6,471	5,896	4,020	3,835	2,670	2,030	2,491	2,639	2,807	2,643
Asia	12,714	11,772	5,227	3,043	3,851	3,327	4,420	4,842	5,534	5,429
Europe	1,938	1,432	1,062	855	675	548	675	753	813	730
North America	1,720	1,397	1,508	2,207	2,911	3,596	2,238	1,747	1,479	1,441
Oceania	344	178	60	64	23	18	27	23	17	8
South America	5,856	5,164	3,420	4,264	3,305	3,382	2,439	1,978	1,125	940
Unknown	117	107	60	57	36	41	53	93	129	53
Country										
Total	29,160	25,946	15,357	14,325	13,471	12,942	12,343	12,075	11,904	11,244
Afghanistan	339	183	29	35	14	9	43	45	81	114
Albania	539	379	251	178	91	44	33	31	33	26
Algeria	40	22	15	10	6	6	3	8	5	9
Angola	52	28	19	6	5	3	5	4	3	3
Armenia	1,447	976	466	250	160	155	202	105	86	85
Azerbaijan	366	254	75	88	34	28	16	10	23	21
Bangladesh	76	103	64	41	37	36	29	32	46	35
Belarus	80	73	106	145	113	100	86	78	113	65
Bhutan	15	9	6	D	D	8	13	4	8	—
Bolivia	4	D	12	5	3	D	3	8	10	15
Bosnia-Herzegovina	32	31	10	13	25	17	13	9	5	7
Brazil	27	35	28	24	28	36	43	38	51	46
Bulgaria	59	67	49	44	43	34	37	48	25	18
Burkina Faso	4	3	7	7	9	13	31	17	21	41
Burma	1,309	324	191	189	97	93	124	152	168	160

(Continued)

Table B.6. Continued

Region and Country of Nationality	2001	2002	2003	2004	2005	2006	2007	2008	2009	2010
Burundi	50	62	26	25	17	29	25	28	21	21
Cambodia	21	42	27	42	23	12	11	D	D	8
Cameroon	324	709	813	598	387	224	295	282	219	182
Central African Republic	5	23	22	7	17	5	6	12	15	13
Chad	11	13	24	20	13	19	31	35	38	18
China, People's Republic	4,938	5,785	2,409	930	2,233	1,550	1,825	2,038	2,700	2,888
Colombia	5,659	4,940	2,966	2,899	2,211	2,177	1,490	1,113	637	357
Congo, Democratic Republic	149	198	76	69	52	46	35	38	31	29
Congo, Republic	248	256	119	92	56	51	72	53	43	60
Cote d'Ivoire	44	24	126	86	94	71	49	43	38	36
Croatia	11	7	D	D	3	D	4	3	D	D
Cuba	77	53	35	26	71	50	43	64	27	24
Djibouti	3	D					D	D	7	16
Ecuador	13	29	D	9	D	10	14	11	7	9
Egypt	474	490	242	143	142	175	193	234	308	320
El Salvador	160	76	91	120	183	499	417	313	202	158
Eritrea	143	167	124	132	142	112	152	180	234	180
Estonia	11	16	11	10	10		D	D	5	
Ethiopia	1,171	1,050	574	755	464	439	499	586	700	686
Fiji	343	176	60	64	23	18	27	23	16	8
Gambia	31	21	29	31	28	37	43	50	49	53
Georgia	118	66	49	57	37	14	13	20	21	16
Ghana	14	7	D	10	D	5	8	6	8	6
Guatemala	151	187	158	206	249	471	541	378	347	299
Guinea	160	184	123	156	127	94	123	117	119	126

Country										
Guinea-Bissau	D	D	D	11	D	—	—	—	3	—
Haiti	1,231	1,000	1,166	1,781	2,282	2,423	1,058	727	594	665
Honduras	17	25	9	5	16	26	19	22	38	53
India	860	1,058	274	146	70	51	75	103	148	109
Indonesia	610	472	206	100	97	429	567	383	176	71
Iran	882	695	325	205	145	139	170	328	257	402
Iraq	645	563	325	161	192	179	392	586	544	276
Israel	15	14	12	4	7	4	10	13	17	7
Jamaica	—	—	4	D	9	7	12	19	42	49
Jordan	55	57	24	19	28	17	25	23	19	7
Kazakhstan	25	25	19	24	10	15	23	18	26	34
Kenya	127	251	239	191	131	84	182	215	234	176
Kosovo	X	X	X	X	X	X	X	—	5	23
Kyrgyzstan	17	22	22	18	13	9	22	26	36	51
Laos	10	11	13	26	12	13	33	15	13	16
Latvia	8	11	15	14	8	4	5	D	D	—
Lebanon	50	38	37	30	25	11	50	44	37	22
Liberia	770	607	354	315	123	65	50	61	44	36
Libya	5	4	D	3	—	3	—	3	D	11
Lithuania	10	17	12	8	8	3	D	D	D	4
Macedonia	32	36	7	7	D	8	—	D	4	4
Madagascar	—	D	D	—	—	—	—	D	—	11
Malaysia	19	26	16	11	6	D	5	7	6	D
Mali	3	9	9	18	25	28	51	35	53	76
Mauritania	98	92	60	58	44	14	11	5	13	34
Mexico	52	36	35	53	85	84	103	176	191	143

(Continued)

Table B.6. Continued

Region and Country of Nationality	2001	2002	2003	2004	2005	2006	2007	2008	2009	2010
Moldova	23	14	11	11	14	12	35	49	114	80
Mongolia	6	4	21	60	73	56	103	77	49	105
Morocco	8	15	3	5	6	3	D	D	4	D
Nepal	21	69	142	163	228	211	282	347	496	410
Nicaragua	20	12	D	D	8	20	20	28	20	20
Niger	39	19	30	22	8	8	4	11	4	8
Nigeria	33	26	18	31	31	23	28	36	38	31
Pakistan	429	502	273	182	122	92	132	162	196	201
Peru	98	73	74	108	92	59	44	44	18	22
Philippines	3	21	13	24	12	8	20	16	16	12
Romania	94	135	126	55	18	15	26	10	6	3
Russia	552	393	287	233	236	229	287	372	366	389
Rwanda	61	39	33	32	51	64	70	75	59	96
Saudi Arabia	10	14	D	4	5	7	D	8	7	16
Senegal	15	18	15	18	9	7	11	9	23	10
Serbia and Montenegro	X	X	X	58	26	30	65	52	37	18
Sierra Leone	304	173	44	62	44	22	24	20	34	22
Singapore	11	D	D	3	D	D	—	D	D	D
Somalia	1,279	434	142	151	74	52	71	69	93	60
South Africa	D	13	10	4	11	5	4	4	5	3
Sri Lanka	97	83	16	18	16	16	34	39	126	107
Sudan	520	446	110	84	56	52	84	86	73	72
Syria	28	46	10	26	19	12	8	23	8	12
Tajikistan	D	5	6	7	—	—	3	10	14	24
Tanzania	17	16	4	11	19	4	6	8	6	7

Togo	85	198	326	349	199	82	58	38	34	14
Turkey	74	71	33	24	16	9	16	34	25	48
Turkmenistan	18	17	13	20	21	26	15	13	7	11
Uganda	120	155	71	59	45	31	78	55	55	87
Ukraine	104	101	62	49	61	40	64	65	73	69
United Arab Emirates	D	11	4	D	—	—	—	D	D	D
Uzbekistan	125	134	82	112	74	87	108	106	100	78
Venezuela	41	71	315	1,198	952	1,080	836	756	393	479
Vietnam	7	14	8	6	8	15	11	21	35	22
Yemen	42	36	D	5	D	7	26	18	25	43
Yugoslavia, former	362	123	87	X	X	X	X	X	X	X
Zambia	8	14	7	14	13	D	9	9	D	6
Zimbabwe	42	94	191	238	202	141	160	194	153	61
All other countries	81	86	67	84	63	55	80	75	82	99
Unknown	117	107	60	57	36	41	53	93	129	53

Source: U.S. Department of Homeland Security, U.S. Citizenship and Immigration Service (USCIS), Refugee, Asylum, and Parole System (RAPS).
"—" represents zero; D = data withheld to limit disclosure; X = not applicable.

Table B.7. Individuals Granted Asylum Defensively by Region and Country of Nationality, Fiscal Years 2001 to 2010

Region and Country of Nationality	2001	2002	2003	2004	2005	2006	2007	2008	2009	2010
Region										
Total	10,001	10,977	13,376	13,022	11,757	13,300	12,836	10,757	10,186	9,869
Africa	1,957	1,908	2,264	2,413	2,276	2,827	2,513	2,034	2,313	2,225
Asia	5,164	5,745	6,558	6,073	5,286	6,668	6,700	5,454	5,362	5,515
Europe	1,395	1,321	1,706	1,696	1,621	1,441	1,316	1,169	917	884
North America	767	728	917	937	1,016	1,008	1,068	1,050	840	643
Oceania	119	90	97	95	36	45	25	36	32	20
South America	583	1,162	1,802	1,748	1,448	1,224	1,130	948	633	486
Unknown	16	23	32	60	74	87	84	66	89	96
Country										
Total	10,001	10,977	13,376	13,022	11,757	13,300	12,836	10,757	10,186	9,869
Afghanistan	134	74	70	58	33	25	22	28	7	6
Albania	513	515	717	724	610	497	420	324	211	148
Algeria	26	15	15	13	23	13	6	D	6	D
Angola	9	4	D	9	6	16	7	8	6	D
Argentina	3	13	10	18	10	9	15	14	10	8
Armenia	203	323	412	305	268	289	179	141	196	206
Azerbaijan	33	38	46	31	30	27	23	12	13	9
Bangladesh	121	104	107	149	120	113	100	81	47	48
Belarus	22	18	47	56	89	106	76	80	73	67
Bolivia	11	D	6	7	4	D	D	6	D	8
Bosnia-Herzegovina	5	23	8	6	8	7	18	6	17	4
Brazil	9	9	19	33	24	33	33	31	22	17
Bulgaria	64	47	47	43	77	72	66	48	42	20
Burkina Faso	6	D	4	D	5	13	20	23	39	49
Burma	124	126	118	138	166	157	129	125	108	80
Burundi	11	9	19	12	11	13	13	12	15	7

Country										
Cambodia	21	9	28	31	29	20	13	12	12	13
Cameroon	135	116	186	273	263	357	204	161	203	196
Canada	—	4	4	5	4	9	9	3	11	5
Central African Republic	3	D	9	D	18	10	12	13	16	10
Chad	4	D	D	5	10	16	21	24	40	28
Chile	11	D	3	6	D	D	D	D	6	D
China, People's Republic	2,677	3,113	3,601	3,419	3,014	4,048	4,545	3,424	3,418	3,795
Colombia	396	1,019	1,590	1,473	1,151	780	682	533	356	234
Congo, Democratic Republic	37	36	38	24	38	24	23	24	11	12
Congo, Republic	129	129	125	129	76	94	78	71	56	60
Cote d'Ivoire	10	13	38	77	111	159	135	91	96	66
Cuba	77	23	37	33	21	26	25	21	15	9
Dominican Republic	4	4	D	3	D	D	5	D	3	11
Ecuador	5	D	13	D	11	11	10	13	6	7
Egypt	194	228	277	268	194	239	232	182	173	216
El Salvador	89	41	30	42	65	95	139	172	117	146
Eritrea	59	42	66	61	68	96	119	120	196	179
Estonia	12	4	8	8	6	D	13	3	8	D
Ethiopia	218	232	239	260	266	341	352	314	409	407
Fiji	119	89	97	95	35	45	24	24	29	18
Gambia	17	18	30	16	30	46	59	53	49	42
Georgia	55	66	58	66	64	59	27	26	24	32
Germany	9	D	6	4	5	9	4	5	D	11
Ghana	18	8	10	5	4	6	8	12	8	8
Greece	—	D	D	3	8	3	12	—	—	D

(Continued)

Table B.7. Continued

Region and Country of Nationality	2001	2002	2003	2004	2005	2006	2007	2008	2009	2010
Guatemala	140	113	162	177	140	161	134	162	155	166
Guinea	64	94	155	258	257	356	325	238	193	186
Guyana	9	D	6	32	30	16	15	D	—	3
Haiti	369	479	566	535	653	569	586	510	406	167
Honduras	22	16	34	46	67	66	86	73	46	65
India	506	494	595	452	311	450	358	269	260	241
Indonesia	181	283	366	427	375	314	210	195	155	116
Iran	232	210	212	203	143	117	108	71	91	83
Iraq	188	280	197	115	94	192	279	408	364	149
Israel	7	6	11	9	17	25	18	16	17	10
Jordan	18	14	33	28	21	27	16	19	20	19
Kazakhstan	21	28	39	28	13	25	31	14	20	17
Kenya	42	32	47	62	54	60	50	60	94	90
Kyrgyzstan	8	3	13	16	12	20	7	6	7	10
Laos	11	12	10	5	19	11	6	4	13	7
Latvia	6	6	12	17	4	12	6	D	D	—
Lebanon	57	53	38	42	23	26	29	20	9	26
Liberia	132	141	146	91	70	59	53	31	31	25
Lithuania	4	D	11	9	5	18	4	D	D	D
Macedonia	15	18	22	14	21	20	27	11	15	10
Malaysia	4	3	11	4	5	4	4	D	D	8
Mali	7	6	3	10	18	62	60	28	71	74
Mauritania	90	118	181	220	193	218	173	94	94	59
Mexico	46	37	64	68	34	49	49	72	62	49
Moldova	10	8	14	13	D	D	7	16	22	46
Mongolia	D	—	7	13	25	39	49	42	28	50
Morocco	D	4	10	D	4	8	4	23	4	D

Nepal	31	37	57	93	85	165	131	148	171	230
Nicaragua	9	4	7	7	16	15	23	20	19	15
Niger	4	3	13	6	3	10	10	8	14	4
Nigeria	74	42	50	50	33	30	39	28	29	35
Niue	—	D	—	—	—	—	D	11	3	D
Pakistan	155	180	227	164	140	178	140	142	99	113
Peru	129	88	118	111	59	88	54	51	39	25
Philippines	37	22	26	29	26	17	9	15	13	5
Poland	7	8	10	5	6	D	7	7	5	D
Romania	58	49	79	61	18	43	31	55	30	27
Russia	351	312	381	320	251	203	209	198	127	159
Rwanda	24	17	23	28	19	26	22	19	24	25
Saudi Arabia	3	D	D	5	6	13	5	5	3	3
Senegal	10	4	13	17	26	15	30	18	24	18
Serbia and Montenegro	X	X	X	207	225	175	152	151	148	108
Seychelles	9	X	D	6	4	D	D	—	—	D
Sierra Leone	91	15	117	122	82	79	48	47	29	27
Somalia	354	236	149	89	88	116	109	100	167	208
South Africa	6	16	7	5	5	20	8	D	3	D
Soviet Union, former	4	D	D	86	169	188	191	172	153	176
Sri Lanka	218	140	55	63	74	85	89	87	112	111
Sudan	78	86	96	68	55	45	19	30	40	35
Syria	17	10	25	10	11	20	23	11	15	13
Tanzania	4	5	6	3	7	17	16	5	6	3
Togo	30	43	62	66	102	145	81	63	39	45
Turkey	18	23	36	27	12	34	23	11	17	12

(Continued)

Table B.7. Continued

Region and Country of Nationality	2001	2002	2003	2004	2005	2006	2007	2008	2009	2010
Turkmenistan	5	5	7	16	13	23	12	15	14	7
Uganda	51	40	53	50	53	36	50	34	28	26
Ukraine	86	96	106	90	69	45	40	59	26	62
United Kingdom	13	14	10	7	7	D	3	3	5	D
Uzbekistan	30	45	91	76	95	95	74	67	64	54
Venezuela	5	24	35	59	153	279	316	294	191	181
Vietnam	15	10	10	5	8	10	10	7	10	9
Yemen	19	9	26	9	10	10	8	8	7	7
Yugoslavia, former	189	177	181	X	X	X	X	X	X	X
Zambia	D	4	6	5	9	8	7	5	5	7
Zimbabwe	D	21	54	71	58	56	97	67	69	52
All Other Countries	64	64	74	113	93	100	88	91	92	93
Unknown	16	23	32	60	74	87	84	66	89	96

Source: U.S. Department of Justice (DOJ), Executive Office for Immigration Review (EOIR).
"—" represents zero; D = data withheld to limit disclosure; X = not applicable.

Table B.8. Deportable Aliens Located by Region and Country of Nationality, Fiscal Year 2010

Region and Country of Nationality	Number	Region and Country of Nationality	Number
Region		Cameroon	97
Total	516,992	Canada	808
Africa	2,848	Cape Verde	31
Asia	8,548	Cayman Islands	7
Europe	2,579	Central African Republic	7
North America	495,209	Chad	3
Oceania	168	Chile	106
South America	7,542	China, People's Republic	1,970
Unknown	98	Cocos (Keeling) Islands	D
Country		Colombia	1,160
Total	516,992	Congo, Democratic	
Afghanistan	50	Republic	14
Albania	243	Congo, Republic	36
Algeria	34	Costa Rica	275
Angola	10	Cote d'Ivoire	62
Antigua-Barbuda	18	Croatia	17
Argentina	171	Cuba	1,187
Armenia	61	Cyprus	D
Australia	18	Czech Republic	48
Austria	6	Czechoslovakia, former	17
Azerbaijan	13	Denmark	9
Bahamas	57	Djibouti	D
Bahrain	4	Dominica	21
Bangladesh	274	Dominican Republic	2,076
Barbados	21	Ecuador	2,363
Belarus	17	Egypt	164
Belgium	5	El Salvador	18,520
Belize	109	Equatorial Guinea	5
Benin	5	Eritrea	176
Bermuda	D	Estonia	8
Bhutan	D	Ethiopia	127
Bolivia	125	Fiji	41
Bosnia-Herzegovina	80	Finland	3
Botswana	3	France	53
Brazil	2,232	French Guiana	D
British Virgin Islands	3	French Polynesia	7
Brunei	D	Gabon	11
Bulgaria	52	Gambia	58
Burkina Faso	16	Georgia	42
Burma	22	Germany	65
Burundi	9	Ghana	192
Cambodia	86	Greece	18

(Continued)

Table B.8. Continued

Region and Country of Nationality	Number	Region and Country of Nationality	Number
Grenada	21	Micronesia, Federated	
Guadeloupe	19	States	17
Guam	22	Moldova	75
Guatemala	23,068	Monaco	D
Guinea	58	Mongolia	36
Guinea-Bissau	4	Montenegro	D
Guyana	116	Montserrat	3
Haiti	680	Morocco	133
Honduras	17,899	Mozambique	32
Hong Kong	25	Namibia	D
Hungary	36	Nauru	D
India	1,672	Nepal	182
Indonesia	404	Netherlands	24
Iran	101	Netherlands Antilles	D
Iraq	94	New Zealand	15
Ireland	28	Nicaragua	1,347
Israel	153	Niger	49
Italy	44	Nigeria	222
Ivory Coast	11	Norway	8
Jamaica	787	Oman	D
Japan	30	Pakistan	384
Jordan	218	Palau	D
Kazakhstan	87	Panama	75
Kenya	488	Papua New Guinea	D
Korea[a]	224	Paraguay	19
Kosovo	9	Peru	812
Kuwait	30	Philippines	465
Kyrgyzstan	44	Poland	248
Laos	200	Portugal	59
Latvia	13	Qatar	D
Lebanon	110	Romania	492
Lesotho	D	Russia	261
Liberia	72	Rwanda	5
Libya	9	Saint Kitts-Nevis	5
Lithuania	29	Saint Lucia	30
Macau	4	Saint Vincent and the	
Macedonia	20	Grenadines	16
Malawi	10	Samoa	7
Malaysia	41	Saudi Arabia	126
Mali	93	Senegal	76
Marshall Islands	6	Serbia	7
Mauritania	59	Serbia and Montenegro[b]	113
Mauritius	5	Seychelles	D
Mexico	427,940	Sierra Leone	59

Table B.8. Continued

Region and Country of Nationality	Number	Region and Country of Nationality	Number
Singapore	5	Tonga	28
Slovakia	31	Trinidad and Tobago	207
Slovenia	D	Tunisia	41
Solomon Islands	D	Turkey	254
Somalia	79	Turkmenistan	16
South Africa	79	Turks and Caicos Islands	7
Soviet Union, former	78	Uganda	31
Spain	31	Ukraine	135
Sri Lanka	238	United Arab Emirates	17
Sudan	45	United Kingdom	163
Suriname	10	Uruguay	79
Swaziland	D	Uzbekistan	143
Sweden	13	Vanuatu	D
Switzerland	17	Venezuela	348
Syria	66	Vietnam	290
Taiwan	16	Western Sahara	D
Tajikistan	59	Yemen	77
Tanzania	36	Zambia	28
Thailand	208	Zimbabwe	36
Togo	20	Unknown	98

Source: U.S. Department of Homeland Security, Customs and Border Protection (CBP) Office of Border Patrol (OBP), Immigration and Customs Enforcement (ICE) Homeland Security Investigations (HSI), and the Office of Enforcement and Removal Operations (ERO).

Note: CBP Border Patrol data are current as of December 2010. ICE Enforcement and Removal Operations (ERO) data are current as of February 2011. ICE Homeland Security Investigations (HSI) data are current as of January 2011.

[a]Korea includes both North and South Korea.
[b]Yugoslavia (unknown republic) prior to February 7, 2003.
D = data withheld to limit disclosure.

Table B.9. Aliens Returned by Region and Country of Nationality, Fiscal Year 2010

Region and Country of Nationality	Number	Region and Country of Nationality	Number
Region		Cambodia	28
Total	476,405	Cameroon	56
Africa	3,442	Canada	29,146
Asia	57,949	Cape Verde	43
Caribbean	2,705	Cayman Islands	11
Central America	4,987	Central African Republic	6
Europe	19,155	Chad	9
North America	384,128	Chile	133
Oceania	820	China, People's Republic	16,454
South America	3,085	Colombia	760
Unknown	134	Congo, Democratic	
Country		Republic	6
Total	476,405	Congo, Republic	47
Afghanistan	85	Costa Rica	121
Albania	48	Cote d'Ivoire	119
Algeria	131	Croatia	193
Andorra	D	Cuba	106
Angola	9	Cyprus	10
Anguilla	D	Czech Republic	128
Antigua-Barbuda	19	Czechoslovakia, former	72
Argentina	98	Denmark	102
Armenia	15	Djibouti	4
Australia	448	Dominica	29
Austria	83	Dominican Republic	753
Azerbaijan	32	Ecuador	323
Bahamas, The	473	Egypt	519
Bahrain	11	El Salvador	909
Bangladesh	282	Equatorial Guinea	D
Barbados	45	Eritrea	9
Belarus	51	Estonia	68
Belgium	128	Ethiopia	74
Belize	52	Fiji	109
Benin	60	Finland	50
Bermuda	88	France	1,051
Bhutan	3	French Polynesia	5
Bolivia	54	Gabon	4
Bosnia-Herzegovina	25	Gambia, The	10
Botswana	7	Georgia	308
Brazil	748	Germany	749
British Virgin Islands	5	Ghana	160
Brunei	D	Gibraltar	D
Bulgaria	269	Greece	374
Burkina Faso	17	Grenada	39
Burma	3,951	Guatemala	2,292
Burundi	19	Guinea	17

Table B.9. Continued

Region and Country of Nationality	Number	Region and Country of Nationality	Number
Guyana	182	Moldova	55
Haiti	304	Mongolia	41
Honduras	1,366	Montserrat	4
Hong Kong	106	Morocco	212
Hungary	171	Namibia	4
Iceland	14	Nepal	41
India	4,736	Netherlands	427
Indonesia	1,898	Netherlands Antilles	14
Iran	434	New Caledonia	D
Iraq	94	New Zealand	144
Ireland	253	Nicaragua	169
Israel	434	Niger	28
Italy	883	Nigeria	463
Jamaica	508	Norway	124
Japan	505	Oman	D
Jordan	167	Pakistan	640
Kazakhstan	38	Palau	23
Kenya	126	Panama	78
Kiribati	37	Papua New Guinea	3
Korea[a]	1,615	Paraguay	20
Kosovo	D	Peru	452
Kuwait	27	Philippines	21,421
Kyrgyzstan	18	Poland	865
Laos	11	Portugal	237
Latvia	235	Qatar	7
Lebanon	192	Romania	1,011
Liberia	16	Russia	3,191
Libya	51	Rwanda	15
Liechtenstein	D	Saint Kitts-Nevis	13
Lithuania	653	Saint Lucia	29
Luxembourg	D	Saint Vincent and the Grenadines	53
Macau	3		
Macedonia	29	Samoa	19
Madagascar	10	San Marino	D
Malawi	D	Saudi Arabia	225
Malaysia	231	Senegal	127
Maldives	61	Serbia and Montenegro[b]	119
Mali	28	Seychelles	D
Malta	7	Sierra Leone	16
Marshall Islands	6	Singapore	71
Martinique	3	Slovakia	102
Mauritania	9	Slovenia	30
Mauritius	270	Solomon Islands	3
Mexico	354,982	Somalia	25
Micronesia, Federated States	12	South Africa	160

(Continued)

Table B.9. Continued

Region and Country of Nationality	Number	Region and Country of Nationality	Number
Soviet Union, former	150	Tunisia	56
Spain	546	Turkey	1,811
Sri Lanka	252	Turkmenistan	5
Sudan	22	Turks and Caicos Islands	11
Suriname	8	Uganda	21
Swaziland	D	Ukraine	4,417
Sweden	178	United Arab Emirates	20
Switzerland	117	United Kingdom	1,942
Syria	88	Uruguay	33
Taiwan	296	Uzbekistan	46
Tajikistan	15	Venezuela	274
Tanzania	319	Vietnam	723
Thailand	470	Yemen	24
Togo	75	Zambia	14
Tonga	10	Zimbabwe	41
Trinidad and Tobago	197	Unknown	134

Source: U.S. Department of Homeland Security. ENFORCE Alien Removal Module (EARM), January 2011, Enforcement Integrated Database (EID), December 2010.
[a]Korea includes both North and South Korea.
[b]Yugoslavia (unknown republic) prior to February 7, 2003.
D = data withheld to limit disclosure.

Table B.10a. Aliens Removed by Criminal Status and Region and Country of Nationality, Fiscal Years 2001 to 2003

Region and Country of Nationality	2001			2002			2003		
	Total	Criminal[a]	Noncriminal	Total	Criminal[a]	Noncriminal	Total	Criminal[a]	Noncriminal
Region									
Total	189,026	73,298	115,728	165,168	73,429	91,739	211,098	83,731	127,367
Africa	1,532	570	962	2,110	687	1,423	2,706	854	1,852
Asia	3,853	1,012	2,841	5,287	1,211	4,076	6,865	1,442	5,423
Caribbean	7,341	4,233	3,108	7,111	4,340	2,771	7,637	4,685	2,952
Central America	14,452	5,078	9,374	15,593	5,144	10,449	23,144	6,487	16,657
Europe	2,569	885	1,684	3,256	938	2,318	3,535	1,058	2,477
North America	151,996	59,202	92,794	123,133	58,471	64,662	156,813	66,551	90,262
Oceania	308	133	175	418	133	285	371	133	238
South America	6,946	2,181	4,765	8,218	2,503	5,715	9,990	2,513	7,477
Unknown	29	4	25	42	2	40	37	8	29
Country									
Total	189,026	73,298	115,728	165,168	73,429	91,739	211,098	83,731	127,367
Afghanistan	13	3	10	13	5	8	74	29	45
Albania	115	14	101	100	10	90	208	18	190
Algeria	23	8	15	40	8	32	61	18	43
Angola	13	4	9	16	D	D	15	D	D
Antigua-Barbuda	35	24	11	40	35	5	44	33	11
Argentina	264	53	211	513	64	449	552	92	460
Armenia	37	9	28	65	4	61	143	21	122
Australia	92	17	75	164	21	143	114	16	98
Austria	16	4	12	23	5	18	17	3	14
Azerbaijan	D	—	D	6	D	D	D	D	D
Bahamas	112	91	21	134	99	35	164	123	41
Bangladesh	87	15	72	121	11	110	149	23	126
Barbados	48	34	14	56	49	7	61	49	12
Belarus	4	D	D	8	D	D	12	D	D
Belgium	12	5	7	24	8	16	27	14	13

Table B.10a. Continued

Region and Country of Nationality	2001			2002			2003		
	Total	Criminal[a]	Noncriminal	Total	Criminal[a]	Noncriminal	Total	Criminal[a]	Noncriminal
Belize	185	104	81	178	114	64	179	117	62
Benin	D	D	—	D	D	D	D	D	D
Bermuda	—	—	—	—	—	—	—	—	—
Bolivia	243	16	227	240	24	216	271	40	231
Bosnia-Herzegovina	9	5	4	10	5	5	25	17	8
Brazil	1,693	83	1,610	2,623	131	2,492	4,046	219	3,827
Bulgaria	46	14	32	60	15	45	75	13	62
Burkina Faso	3	D	D	7	—	7	9	D	D
Burma	4	D	D	D	D	D	7	D	D
Cambodia	18	D	D	24	18	6	66	51	15
Cameroon	15	6	9	28	7	21	48	4	44
Canada	1,234	627	607	1,075	545	530	1,001	449	552
Cape Verde	46	36	10	48	37	11	44	32	12
Chile	201	62	139	168	44	124	247	69	178
China, People's Republic	661	120	541	679	126	553	998	138	860
Colombia	2,252	1,443	809	2,306	1,473	833	2,386	1,346	1,040
Congo, Democratic Republic	8	3	5	23	7	16	12	5	7
Congo, Republic	13	—	13	23	D	D	28	D	D
Costa Rica	392	63	329	376	56	320	514	64	450
Cote d'Ivoire	28	10	18	37	8	29	46	13	33
Croatia	12	D	D	12	3	9	17	7	10
Cuba	93	80	13	76	60	16	76	40	36
Czech Republic	18	3	15	26	5	21	15	D	D

Czechoslovakia, former	130	25	105	226	26	200	179	25	154
Denmark	11	4	7	16	D	D	21	4	17
Dominica	18	12	6	32	26	6	23	17	6
Dominican Republic	4,033	2,113	1,920	3,563	1,985	1,578	3,472	2,137	1,335
Ecuador	960	164	796	729	166	563	722	195	527
Egypt	95	16	79	290	67	223	322	46	276
El Salvador	3,928	1,895	2,033	4,066	1,771	2,295	5,561	2,115	3,446
Eritrea	5	—	5	12	D	D	18	4	14
Estonia	16	D	D	28	D	D	15	D	D
Ethiopia	22	13	9	31	12	19	77	25	52
Fiji	39	16	23	36	18	18	58	19	39
Finland	6	D	D	8	3	5	7	3	4
France	114	37	77	187	47	140	173	49	124
Gambia	42	16	26	43	15	28	90	25	65
Georgia	29	9	20	30	6	24	67	16	51
Germany	141	60	81	162	66	96	195	66	129
Ghana	227	47	180	213	41	172	306	60	246
Greece	38	20	18	47	19	28	54	24	30
Grenada	24	13	11	27	18	9	25	17	8
Guatemala	4,716	1,223	3,493	5,396	1,344	4,052	7,726	1,731	5,995
Guinea	60	10	50	56	13	43	73	18	55
Guyana	134	43	91	321	237	84	356	182	174
Haiti	492	359	133	513	300	213	1,154	517	637
Honduras	4,548	1,436	3,112	4,946	1,502	3,444	8,182	2,036	6,146
Hong Kong	15	7	8	14	7	7	18	6	12

(Continued)

Table B.10a. Continued

Region and Country of Nationality	2001			2002			2003		
	Total	Criminal[a]	Noncriminal	Total	Criminal[a]	Noncriminal	Total	Criminal[a]	Noncriminal
Hungary	86	16	70	125	14	111	107	20	87
India	511	71	440	590	89	501	877	105	772
Indonesia	242	14	228	207	18	189	325	14	311
Iran	45	21	24	64	22	42	89	18	71
Iraq	9	D	D	13	3	10	28	D	D
Ireland	57	19	38	69	16	53	80	19	61
Israel	140	38	102	179	41	138	182	42	140
Italy	130	68	62	133	57	76	142	65	77
Jamaica	2,046	1,276	770	2,172	1,517	655	2,086	1,467	619
Japan	117	53	64	104	30	74	119	28	91
Jordan	86	44	42	222	77	145	295	104	191
Kazakhstan	D	D	D	21	3	18	17	3	14
Kenya	50	20	30	90	35	55	118	46	72
Korea[b]	274	108	166	333	123	210	383	93	290
Kosovo	X	X	X	X	X	X	X	X	X
Kuwait	13	5	8	15	5	10	27	10	17
Kyrgyzstan	D	D	D	5	—	5	6	D	D
Laos	10	5	5	6	—	6	15	D	D
Latvia	18	D	D	15	D	D	23	D	D
Lebanon	56	18	38	130	37	93	168	45	123
Liberia	46	29	17	39	27	12	41	22	19
Lithuania	38	7	31	64	9	55	82	12	70
Macedonia	23	D	D	23	6	17	37	3	34
Malawi	D	D	—	5	—	5	4	—	4
Malaysia	91	14	77	104	16	88	80	20	60
Mali	44	D	D	46	D	D	33	4	29

Marshall Islands	4	4	—	4	D	D	6	6	—
Mauritania	6	D	D	16	D	D	32	D	D
Mexico	150,762	58,575	92,187	122,058	57,926	64,132	155,812	66,102	89,710
Micronesia, Federated States	37	31	6	33	30	3	29	D	D
Moldova	4	—	4	8	D	D	10	3	7
Mongolia	7	D	D	20	D	D	44	D	D
Morocco	35	17	18	118	35	83	131	52	79
Nepal	12	D	D	23	D	D	38	3	35
Netherlands	83	43	40	101	50	51	119	71	48
New Zealand	64	12	52	113	18	95	90	14	76
Nicaragua	526	251	275	468	248	220	820	323	497
Niger	23	9	14	28	15	13	42	12	30
Nigeria	421	238	183	471	233	238	640	328	312
Norway	11	5	6	8	—	8	14	6	8
Pakistan	412	53	359	912	127	785	977	151	826
Palau	8	D	D	6	6	—	7	7	—
Panama	157	106	51	163	109	54	162	101	61
Paraguay	14	D	D	22	—	22	35	4	31
Peru	829	169	660	917	215	702	893	205	688
Philippines	497	274	223	760	299	461	920	354	566
Poland	364	82	282	374	88	286	335	70	265
Portugal	108	82	26	123	70	53	108	72	36
Romania	92	23	69	110	36	74	154	34	120
Russia	100	42	58	167	38	129	212	58	154
Rwanda	—	—	—	4	D	D	5	—	5

(Continued)

Table B.10a. Continued

Region and Country of Nationality	2001			2002			2003		
	Total	Criminal[a]	Noncriminal	Total	Criminal[a]	Noncriminal	Total	Criminal[a]	Noncriminal
Saint Kitts-Nevis	20	D	D	26	23	3	27	22	5
Saint Lucia	23	13	10	30	19	11	36	24	12
Saint Vincent and the Grenadines	35	18	17	39	26	13	24	17	7
Samoa	10	D	D	24	15	9	20	12	8
Saudi Arabia	16	7	9	40	10	30	55	13	42
Senegal	72	14	58	99	18	81	110	12	98
Serbia and Montenegro	82	31	51	69	16	53	106	25	81
Sierra Leone	38	9	29	44	19	25	57	30	27
Singapore	30	9	21	33	3	30	24	9	15
Slovakia	22	3	19	40	8	32	46	D	D
Slovenia	10	D	D	D	D	D	7	D	D
Somalia	40	7	33	45	25	20	27	7	20
South Africa	37	15	22	54	13	41	74	25	49
Soviet Union, former	6	3	3	12	8	4	14	5	9
Spain	64	24	40	82	27	55	97	46	51
Sri Lanka	107	7	100	78	7	71	102	12	90
Sudan	13	3	10	24	D	D	42	9	33
Suriname	5	D	D	7	4	3	18	5	13
Sweden	29	6	23	34	D	D	43	10	33
Switzerland	13	3	10	27	6	21	19	6	13
Syria	35	8	27	65	20	45	72	17	55
Taiwan	48	26	22	60	19	41	83	23	60
Tajikistan	D	—	D	—	D	D	D	D	—
Tanzania	11	5	6	14	D	D	35	12	23

Thailand	74	31	43	74	24	50	98	30	68
Togo	9	4	5	14	D	D	17	3	14
Tonga	51	37	14	38	22	16	47	32	15
Trinidad and Tobago	362	181	181	403	183	220	445	222	223
Tunisia	14	3	11	53	9	44	55	13	42
Turkey	76	10	66	135	28	107	156	22	134
Turks and Caicos Islands	—	—	—	—	—	—	—	—	—
Uganda	18	8	10	21	10	11	28	6	22
Ukraine	126	16	110	181	15	166	198	26	172
United Arab Emirates	D	D	D	5	D	D	8	D	D
United Kingdom	411	209	202	549	252	297	540	254	286
Uruguay	49	11	38	85	15	70	161	27	134
Uzbekistan	32	4	28	48	5	43	44	D	D
Venezuela	302	135	167	287	130	157	303	129	174
Vietnam	11	7	4	19	6	13	28	10	18
Yemen	20	7	13	55	13	42	67	15	52
Zambia	10	D	D	12	4	8	19	5	14
Zimbabwe	19	3	16	25	9	16	17	6	11
Unknown	29	4	25	42	2	40	37	8	29
All other countries	37	14	23	33	8	25	39	9	30

Source: U.S. Department of Homeland Security, ENFORCE Alien Removal Module (EARM), January 2011, Enforcement Integrated Database (EID), December 2010.

Note: Beginning in 2008, excludes criminals removed by Customs and Border Protection (CBP); CBP ENFORCE does not identify if aliens removed were criminals.

aRefers to persons removed who have a criminal conviction.

bKorea includes both North and South Korea.

cYugoslavia (unknown republic) prior to February 7, 2003.

"—" represents zero; D = data withheld to limit disclosure; X = not applicable.

Table B.10b. Aliens Removed by Criminal Status and Region and Country of Nationality, Fiscal Years 2004 to 2006

Region and Country of Nationality	2004			2005			2006		
	Total	Criminal[a]	Noncriminal	Total	Criminal[a]	Noncriminal	Total	Criminal[a]	Noncriminal
Region									
Total	240,665	92,380	148,285	246,431	92,221	154,210	280,974	98,490	182,484
Africa	2,662	838	1,824	2,372	761	1,611	2,103	704	1,399
Asia	6,827	1,518	5,309	6,414	1,445	4,969	6,366	1,206	5,160
Caribbean	8,544	4,936	3,608	8,067	5,039	3,028	6,515	4,242	2,273
Central America	27,686	8,241	19,445	40,773	8,352	32,421	62,298	14,370	47,928
Europe	3,574	1,198	2,376	3,345	1,107	2,238	3,155	1,054	2,101
North America	177,362	72,090	105,272	170,592	71,241	99,351	188,139	73,594	114,545
Oceania	300	152	148	247	123	124	219	113	106
South America	13,618	3,400	10,218	14,535	4,152	10,383	12,103	3,199	8,904
Unknown	92	7	85	86	1	85	76	8	68
Country									
Total	240,665	92,380	148,285	246,431	92,221	154,210	280,974	98,490	182,484
Afghanistan	38	14	24	37	21	16	20	12	8
Albania	209	26	183	236	32	204	252	32	220
Algeria	54	12	42	39	9	30	41	18	23
Angola	13	3	10	13	—	13	16	D	D
Antigua-Barbuda	36	25	11	34	26	8	40	33	7
Argentina	648	71	577	574	95	479	457	88	369
Armenia	144	38	106	120	32	88	97	27	70
Australia	62	12	50	39	11	28	54	20	34
Austria	16	8	8	11	D	D	10	D	D
Azerbaijan	9	D	D	10	D	D	6	D	D
Bahamas	132	95	37	153	120	33	91	68	23
Bangladesh	131	21	110	145	21	124	151	22	129
Barbados	75	68	7	65	55	10	46	41	5

Belarus	20	11	9	25	6	19	24	7	17
Belgium	38	10	28	19	7	12	14	4	10
Belize	202	119	83	219	118	101	211	112	99
Benin	3	—	3	D	D	D	11	4	7
Bermuda	3	—	3	—	—	—	D	—	D
Bolivia	336	51	285	303	62	241	352	61	291
Bosnia-Herzegovina	26	21	5	23	14	9	42	28	14
Brazil	6,390	761	5,629	7,097	1,431	5,666	4,217	563	3,654
Bulgaria	84	12	72	82	15	67	64	10	54
Burkina Faso	10	D	D	11	3	8	17	3	14
Burma	15	3	12	12	5	7	14	—	14
Cambodia	70	42	28	51	28	23	27	11	16
Cameroon	80	17	63	61	8	53	60	11	49
Canada	1,497	520	977	1,561	462	1,099	1,413	423	990
Cape Verde	42	31	11	47	38	9	37	30	7
Chile	227	73	154	225	61	164	245	60	185
China, People's Republic	1,225	144	1,081	1,252	147	1,105	1,362	132	1,230
Colombia	2,725	1,456	1,269	2,594	1,367	1,227	2,788	1,307	1,481
Congo, Democratic Republic	22	D	D	18	D	D	23	7	16
Congo, Republic	24	7	17	30	3	27	26	3	23
Costa Rica	599	74	525	676	82	594	795	100	695
Cote d'Ivoire	35	8	27	34	6	28	41	8	33
Croatia	19	7	12	11	4	7	15	5	10
Cuba	465	67	398	730	44	686	124	39	85
Czech Republic	34	5	29	30	D	D	34	D	D
Czechoslovakia, former	185	19	166	107	10	97	68	16	52

(Continued)

Table B.10b. Continued

Region and Country of Nationality	2004			2005			2006		
	Total	Criminal[a]	Noncriminal	Total	Criminal[a]	Noncriminal	Total	Criminal[a]	Noncriminal
Denmark	14	3	11	14	6	8	8	D	D
Dominica	47	16	31	28	17	11	28	14	14
Dominican Republic	3,760	2,479	1,281	3,210	2,308	902	3,107	2,206	901
Ecuador	1,116	307	809	1,490	393	1,097	1,750	470	1,280
Egypt	256	59	197	233	47	186	172	30	142
El Salvador	7,269	2,805	4,464	8,305	2,827	5,478	11,050	3,850	7,200
Eritrea	13	D	D	12	D	D	10	3	7
Estonia	14	4	10	22	4	18	23	4	19
Ethiopia	78	15	63	94	19	75	105	48	57
Fiji	65	27	38	74	18	56	47	19	28
Finland	4	D	D	8	—	8	6	D	D
France	121	36	85	136	45	91	123	35	88
Gambia	72	16	56	61	16	45	43	7	36
Georgia	65	18	47	35	18	17	42	7	35
Germany	171	100	71	169	79	90	158	61	97
Ghana	299	53	246	218	76	142	187	69	118
Greece	36	22	14	50	24	26	35	19	16
Grenada	28	19	9	38	27	11	27	20	7
Guatemala	9,729	2,176	7,553	14,522	2,143	12,379	20,527	3,850	16,677
Guinea	92	22	70	92	24	68	78	18	60
Guyana	388	230	158	396	255	141	289	174	115
Haiti	878	222	656	1,204	591	613	907	290	617
Honduras	8,752	2,544	6,208	15,572	2,704	12,868	27,060	5,752	21,308
Hong Kong	22	5	17	20	7	13	15	8	7

Hungary	99	9	90	110	12	98	75	14	61
India	928	131	797	867	139	728	1,048	150	898
Indonesia	361	21	340	375	17	358	388	22	366
Iran	64	23	41	52	17	35	59	16	43
Iraq	26	3	23	24	8	16	21	4	17
Ireland	77	25	52	72	13	59	54	11	43
Israel	240	63	177	284	84	200	197	53	144
Italy	161	100	61	144	73	71	144	78	66
Jamaica	2,541	1,614	927	2,023	1,475	548	1,662	1,234	428
Japan	93	38	55	46	12	34	53	10	43
Jordan	207	74	133	223	81	142	190	75	115
Kazakhstan	17	—	17	18	3	15	15	3	12
Kenya	129	47	82	117	36	81	97	36	61
Korea[b]	434	156	278	401	113	288	451	115	336
Kosovo	X	X	X	X	X	X	X	X	X
Kuwait	13	4	9	13	5	8	6	D	D
Kyrgyzstan	4	—	4	D	D	D	D	D	D
Laos	14	D	D	12	4	8	12	D	D
Latvia	23	5	18	28	7	21	19	4	15
Lebanon	172	32	140	149	38	111	154	36	118
Liberia	67	40	27	98	70	28	64	39	25
Lithuania	74	9	65	66	16	50	63	15	48
Macedonia	30	8	22	33		D	38	7	31
Malawi	7	3	4	10	4	6	D	—	D
Malaysia	108	15	93	89	13	76	66	8	58
Mali	47	6	41	34	4	30	24	3	21
Marshall Islands	10	D	D	7	D	D	D	D	—
Mauritania	44	6	38	32	—	32	46	3	43
Mexico	175,865	71,570	104,295	169,031	70,779	98,252	186,726	73,171	113,555

(Continued)

Table B.10b. Continued

Region and Country of Nationality	2004			2005			2006		
	Total	Criminal[a]	Noncriminal	Total	Criminal[a]	Noncriminal	Total	Criminal[a]	Noncriminal
Micronesia, Federated States	37	D	D	24	21	3	30	23	7
Moldova	12	4	8	12	4	8	12	6	6
Mongolia	42	4	38	27	D	D	48	4	44
Morocco	128	42	86	108	35	73	90	26	64
Nepal	49	4	45	38	8	30	30	8	22
Netherlands	88	53	35	103	65	38	89	47	42
New Zealand	38	9	29	35	13	22	32	11	21
Nicaragua	947	401	546	1,292	356	936	2,446	592	1,854
Niger	48	12	36	34	8	26	30	8	22
Nigeria	557	279	278	480	232	248	418	202	216
Norway	19	6	13	8	3	5	15	5	10
Pakistan	650	119	531	655	104	551	567	94	473
Palau	7	7	—	6	6	—	11	11	—
Panama	188	122	66	187	122	65	209	114	95
Paraguay	62	D	D	57	11	46	59	6	53
Peru	1,121	306	815	1,220	304	916	1,338	314	1,024
Philippines	936	364	572	755	357	398	658	260	398
Poland	426	107	319	449	135	314	450	116	334
Portugal	120	77	43	123	78	45	146	93	53
Romania	144	34	110	133	27	106	188	53	135
Russia	223	67	156	189	54	135	169	44	125
Rwanda	7	—	7	15	D	D	3	D	D
Saint Kitts-Nevis	26	15	11	24	21	3	25	22	3
Saint Lucia	50	18	32	50	18	32	35	13	22

Country									
Saint Vincent and the Grenadines	44	32	12	44	30	14	21	14	7
Samoa	27	14	13	21	15	6	7	3	4
Saudi Arabia	23	3	20	20	5	15	23	4	19
Senegal	121	23	98	91	22	69	124	23	101
Serbia and Montenegro[c]	117	22	95	145	35	110	105	29	76
Sierra Leone	62	22	40	60	16	44	35	15	20
Singapore	30	10	20	30	12	18	16	3	13
Slovakia	47	7	40	37	5	32	35	5	30
Slovenia	14	—	14	8	3	5	3	D	D
Somalia	30	D	D	40	5	35	39	5	34
South Africa	72	30	42	73	23	50	69	24	45
Soviet Union, former	17	9	8	22	14	8	8	5	3
Spain	109	56	53	66	29	37	59	25	34
Sri Lanka	94	8	86	85	4	81	82	6	76
Sudan	28	11	17	17	4	13	22	5	17
Suriname	24	7	17	24	6	18	21	7	14
Sweden	29	9	20	34	13	21	25	8	17
Switzerland	13	3	10	17	5	12	15	10	5
Syria	72	25	47	59	15	44	70	21	49
Taiwan	101	31	70	68	18	50	86	9	77
Tajikistan	6	—	6	4	D	D	D	—	D
Tanzania	27	9	18	18	5	13	20	5	15
Thailand	96	30	66	75	31	44	73	16	57
Togo	41	10	31	27	4	23	23	7	16
Tonga	50	38	12	41	34	7	32	23	9

(Continued)

Table B.10b. Continued

Region and Country of Nationality	2004			2005			2006		
	Total	Criminal[a]	Noncriminal	Total	Criminal[a]	Noncriminal	Total	Criminal[a]	Noncriminal
Trinidad and Tobago	457	266	191	455	307	148	398	248	150
Tunisia	39	12	27	39	12	27	33	8	25
Turkey	149	24	125	184	26	158	158	25	133
Turks and Caicos Islands	D	—	D	3	—	3	—	—	—
Uganda	30	8	22	24	5	19	26	7	19
Ukraine	245	47	198	168	47	121	174	48	126
United Arab Emirates	D	D	D	D	—	D	10	—	10
United Kingdom	490	254	236	431	218	213	385	195	190
Uruguay	146	17	129	157	23	134	142	19	123
Uzbekistan	73	10	63	56	8	48	48	5	43
Venezuela	435	119	316	398	144	254	444	130	314
Vietnam	33	18	15	27	11	16	41	19	22
Yemen	52	12	40	76	23	53	47	16	31
Zambia	22	8	14	16	6	10	14	7	7
Zimbabwe	23	11	12	34	5	29	26	12	14
Unknown	92	7	85	86	1	85	76	8	68
All other countries	68	16	52	65	14	51	60	13	47

Source: U.S. Department of Homeland Security, ENFORCE Alien Removal Module (EARM), January 2011, Enforcement Integrated Database (EID), December 2010.
[a]Refers to persons removed who have a criminal conviction.
[b]Korea includes both North and South Korea.
[c]Yugoslavia (unknown republic) prior to February 7, 2003.
"—" represents zero; D = data withheld to limit disclosure; X = not applicable.

Table B.10c. Aliens Removed by Criminal Status and Region and Country of Nationality, Fiscal Years 2007 to 2009

Region and Country of Nationality	2007			2008			2009		
	Total	Criminal[a]	Noncriminal	Total	Criminal[a]	Noncriminal	Total	Criminal[a]	Noncriminal
Region									
Total	319,382	102,394	216,988	359,795	105,266	254,529	395,165	131,840	263,325
Africa	2,112	805	1,307	2,064	647	1,417	2,047	718	1,329
Asia	5,745	1,217	4,528	5,799	1,339	4,460	6,276	1,334	4,942
Caribbean	6,763	4,207	2,556	7,329	4,216	3,113	7,064	4,543	2,521
Central America	79,060	14,913	64,147	79,814	17,045	62,769	81,122	20,839	60,283
Europe	3,164	953	2,211	3,928	1,076	2,852	4,624	1,078	3,546
North America	210,259	77,378	132,881	248,565	77,878	170,687	281,548	100,037	181,511
Oceania	248	143	105	305	165	140	317	160	157
South America	11,988	2,774	9,214	11,831	2,890	8,941	12,094	3,118	8,976
Unknown	43	4	39	160	10	150	73	13	60
Country									
Total	319,382	102,394	216,988	359,795	105,266	254,529	395,165	131,840	263,325
Afghanistan	27	11	16	31	11	20	18	6	12
Albania	246	23	223	331	34	297	296	42	254
Algeria	27	6	21	21	4	17	27	3	24
Angola	17	3	14	17	D	D	20	D	D
Antigua-Barbuda	45	37	8	28	23	5	43	28	15
Argentina	395	76	319	390	84	306	448	106	342
Armenia	74	34	40	86	43	43	96	29	67
Australia	52	21	31	47	14	33	83	19	64
Austria	13	8	5	18	3	15	21	D	D
Azerbaijan	8	D	D	9	D	D	7	D	D
Bahamas	97	72	25	105	82	23	143	99	44
Bangladesh	138	25	113	115	17	98	104	17	87
Barbados	40	33	7	44	39	5	48	36	12

(Continued)

Table B.10c. Continued

Region and Country of Nationality	2007			2008			2009		
	Total	Criminal[a]	Noncriminal	Total	Criminal[a]	Noncriminal	Total	Criminal[a]	Noncriminal
Belarus	21	4	17	25	9	16	36	11	25
Belgium	17	4	13	21	D	D	27	3	24
Belize	233	116	117	213	109	104	244	126	118
Benin	7	3	4	14	3	11	9	4	5
Bermuda	D	—	D	9	3	6	15	9	6
Bolivia	382	37	345	276	54	222	282	54	228
Bosnia-Herzegovina	42	29	13	45	31	14	57	49	8
Brazil	4,210	352	3,858	3,836	368	3,468	3,727	388	3,339
Bulgaria	80	23	57	77	11	66	82	14	68
Burkina Faso	13	4	9	18	6	12	11	5	6
Burma	22	D	D	10	D	D	5	D	D
Cambodia	29	17	12	40	22	18	46	28	18
Cameroon	63	10	53	66	12	54	55	10	45
Canada	1,263	411	852	1,302	347	955	1,329	418	911
Cape Verde	61	50	11	35	26	9	49	42	7
Chile	237	73	164	211	68	143	205	70	135
China, People's Republic	864	97	767	877	188	689	970	135	835
Colombia	2,993	1,191	1,802	2,590	1,081	1,509	2,721	1,124	1,597
Congo, Democratic Republic	17	4	13	32	5	27	17	6	11
Congo, Republic	17	5	12	22	5	17	21	4	17
Costa Rica	655	88	567	692	132	560	699	123	576
Cote d'Ivoire	30	4	26	43	10	33	24	4	20
Croatia	13	6	7	24	9	15	23	7	16
Cuba	76	26	50	65	32	33	130	86	44

Czech Republic	41	8	33	52	13	39	66	17	49
Czechoslovakia, former	52	12	40	55	12	43	48	5	43
Denmark	14	3	11	17	D	D	31	5	26
Dominica	49	29	20	35	22	13	35	18	17
Dominican Republic	2,990	2,044	946	3,232	2,046	1,186	3,583	2,207	1,376
Ecuador	1,564	392	1,172	2,330	532	1,798	2,383	602	1,781
Egypt	145	29	116	166	37	129	157	36	121
El Salvador	20,045	4,949	15,096	20,050	5,558	14,492	20,849	6,344	14,505
Eritrea	11	6	5	10	4	6	D	D	D
Estonia	21	8	13	25	5	20	26	8	18
Ethiopia	150	78	72	87	32	55	77	18	59
Fiji	45	21	24	71	26	45	54	24	30
Finland	D	—	D	11	4	7	10	—	10
France	100	22	78	152	29	123	235	24	211
Gambia	35	10	25	26	7	19	28	7	21
Georgia	53	17	36	55	15	40	72	23	49
Germany	165	60	105	178	63	115	204	53	151
Ghana	231	88	143	202	61	141	231	60	171
Greece	30	13	17	50	23	27	48	18	30
Grenada	28	19	9	28	17	11	29	21	8
Guatemala	25,898	3,917	21,981	27,527	5,138	22,389	29,661	6,547	23,114
Guinea	66	20	46	74	16	58	62	14	48
Guyana	293	191	102	284	188	96	305	216	89
Haiti	1,492	519	973	1,584	416	1,168	766	473	293
Honduras	29,737	5,236	24,501	28,885	5,476	23,409	27,293	6,998	20,295

(Continued)

Table B.10c. Continued

Region and Country of Nationality	2007			2008			2009		
	Total	Criminal[a]	Noncriminal	Total	Criminal[a]	Noncriminal	Total	Criminal[a]	Noncriminal
Hong Kong	28	4	24	23	6	17	25	9	16
Hungary	85	10	75	95	19	76	131	19	112
India	832	125	707	932	164	768	1,055	186	869
Indonesia	434	39	395	489	68	421	431	42	389
Iran	48	9	39	40	11	29	55	15	40
Iraq	27	3	24	37	7	30	34	16	18
Ireland	57	20	37	79	19	60	129	19	110
Israel	246	53	193	258	41	217	419	50	369
Italy	158	69	89	215	74	141	244	61	183
Jamaica	1,490	1,139	351	1,628	1,214	414	1,667	1,246	421
Japan	38	11	27	88	17	71	87	12	75
Jordan	212	65	147	161	45	116	214	66	148
Kazakhstan	19	D	D	25	7	18	34	9	25
Kenya	126	43	83	140	44	96	175	70	105
Korea[b]	417	123	294	419	116	303	395	129	266
Kosovo	X	X	X	—	—	—	14	4	10
Kuwait	7	—	7	10	—	10	14	D	D
Kyrgyzstan	4	D	D	10	3	7	11	D	D
Laos	19	D	D	20	5	15	21	D	D
Latvia	19	3	16	23	7	16	30	4	26
Lebanon	128	33	95	108	24	84	144	35	109
Liberia	69	43	26	26	10	16	51	22	29
Lithuania	77	14	63	69	13	56	72	14	58
Macedonia	34	8	26	60	8	52	49	11	38
Malawi	7	D	D	9	D	D	5	D	D
Malaysia	65	21	44	52	11	41	59	15	44

Mali	35	4	31	33	7	26	24	3	21
Marshall Islands	10	10	—	15	11	4	11	D	D
Mauritania	21	4	17	24	D	D	18	D	D
Mexico	208,996	76,967	132,029	247,263	77,531	169,732	280,219	99,619	180,600
Micronesia, Federated States	43	35	8	64	56	8	66	52	14
Moldova	16	6	10	45	9	36	44	14	30
Mongolia	46	6	40	50	10	40	48	9	39
Morocco	88	27	61	61	31	30	95	48	47
Nepal	43	5	38	46	8	38	55	11	44
Netherlands	75	36	39	93	29	64	129	29	100
New Zealand	35	13	22	39	13	26	35	6	29
Nicaragua	2,307	508	1,799	2,257	533	1,724	2,176	620	1,556
Niger	40	20	20	39	7	32	31	9	22
Nigeria	435	241	194	435	209	226	429	222	207
Norway	9	4	5	20	4	16	30	D	D
Pakistan	545	112	433	383	74	309	362	73	289
Palau	6	6	—	10	6	4	14	10	4
Panama	185	99	86	190	99	91	200	81	119
Paraguay	49	6	43	40	5	35	47	4	43
Peru	1,208	295	913	1,275	337	938	1,286	365	921
Philippines	697	278	419	689	280	409	749	269	480
Poland	410	112	298	498	115	383	601	135	466
Portugal	124	80	44	158	87	71	206	92	114
Romania	200	39	161	216	50	166	153	34	119
Russia	188	49	139	238	68	170	263	61	202

(Continued)

Table B.10c. Continued

Region and Country of Nationality	2007			2008			2009		
	Total	Criminal[a]	Noncriminal	Total	Criminal[a]	Noncriminal	Total	Criminal[a]	Noncriminal
Rwanda	6	D	D	7	3	4	10	D	D
Saint Kitts-Nevis	14	D	D	14	8	6	12	8	4
Saint Lucia	46	27	19	30	16	14	37	20	17
Saint Vincent and the Grenadines	26	15	11	23	12	11	33	16	17
Samoa	23	12	11	20	12	8	19	13	6
Saudi Arabia	31	5	26	32	11	21	18	6	12
Senegal	79	15	64	87	20	67	88	24	64
Serbia and Montenegro[c]	137	32	105	165	30	135	101	24	77
Sierra Leone	51	16	35	27	7	20	17	4	13
Singapore	16	5	11	21	3	18	23	8	15
Slovakia	44	6	38	35	6	29	42	7	35
Slovenia	9	D	D	4	—	4	7	D	D
Somalia	19	3	16	23	D	D	32	6	26
South Africa	45	13	32	59	18	41	53	15	38
Soviet Union, former	5	D	D	14	6	8	5	D	D
Spain	65	25	40	94	27	67	156	21	135
Sri Lanka	60	6	54	113	9	104	100	4	96
Sudan	13	5	8	15	4	11	21	10	11
Suriname	12	6	6	14	4	10	17	7	10
Sweden	35	10	25	38	7	31	65	8	57
Switzerland	16	4	12	20	5	15	22	D	D
Syria	40	7	33	46	9	37	34	12	22
Taiwan	126	15	111	81	24	57	86	14	72

Tajikistan	D	—	D	10	3	7	14	D	D
Tanzania	23	8	15	41	12	29	42	15	27
Thailand	91	13	78	102	20	82	108	25	83
Togo	23	7	16	30	4	26	28	14	14
Tonga	32	23	9	38	27	11	31	23	8
Trinidad and Tobago	363	234	129	478	273	205	489	258	231
Tunisia	23	5	18	38	9	29	15	3	12
Turkey	155	35	120	183	33	150	149	18	131
Turks and Caicos Islands	3	—	3	10	5	5	11	4	7
Uganda	31	7	24	28	10	18	31	13	18
Ukraine	162	36	126	182	62	120	193	55	138
United Arab Emirates	5	—	5	5	—	5	D	—	D
United Kingdom	378	162	216	479	179	300	720	201	519
Uruguay	163	31	132	173	49	124	171	52	119
Uzbekistan	46	7	39	56	9	47	89	5	84
Venezuela	482	124	358	412	120	292	502	130	372
Vietnam	27	9	18	30	8	22	53	29	24
Yemen	64	17	47	44	10	34	53	14	39
Zambia	25	13	12	20	7	13	16	7	9
Zimbabwe	29	D	D	43	3	40	28	3	25
Unknown	43	4	39	160	10	150	73	13	60
All other countries	56	13	43	83	24	59	100	35	65

Source: U.S. Department of Homeland Security, ENFORCE Alien Removal Module (EARM), January 2011, Enforcement Integrated Database (EID), December 2010.
aRefers to persons removed who have a criminal conviction.
bKorea includes both North and South Korea.
cYugoslavia (unknown republic) prior to February 7, 2003.
"—" represents zero; D = data withheld to limit disclosure; X = not applicable.

Table B.10d. Aliens Removed by Criminal Status and Region and Country of Nationality, Fiscal Year 2010

Region and Country of Nationality	Total	Criminal[a]	Noncriminal
Region			
Total	387,242	168,532	218,710
Africa	1,695	641	1,054
Asia	5,165	1,483	3,682
Caribbean	6,000	4,081	1,919
Central America	76,603	29,257	47,346
Europe	3,765	1,227	2,538
North America	283,304	128,173	155,131
Oceania	304	202	102
South America	10,348	3,450	6,898
Unknown	58	18	40
Country			
Total	387,242	168,532	218,710
Afghanistan	14	5	9
Albania	218	50	168
Algeria	14	D	D
Angola	8	D	D
Antigua-Barbuda	24	18	6
Argentina	340	119	221
Armenia	75	30	45
Australia	63	30	33
Austria	18	7	11
Azerbaijan	3	D	D
Bahamas	111	89	22
Bangladesh	84	24	60
Barbados	41	33	8
Belarus	21	9	12
Belgium	27	7	20
Belize	253	157	96
Benin	7	4	3
Bermuda	13	8	5
Bolivia	207	65	142
Bosnia-Herzegovina	58	48	10
Brazil	3,190	481	2,709
Bulgaria	65	17	48
Burkina Faso	8	3	5
Burma	13	D	D
Cambodia	39	25	14
Cameroon	65	19	46
Canada	1,301	445	856
Cape Verde	46	36	10
Chile	176	91	85
China, People's Republic	745	158	587
Colombia	2,267	1,223	1,044

Table B.10d. Continued

Region and Country of Nationality	Total	Criminal[a]	Noncriminal
Congo, Democratic Republic	10	4	6
Congo, Republic	23	D	D
Costa Rica	522	152	370
Cote d'Ivoire	28	4	24
Croatia	20	7	13
Cuba	95	64	31
Czech Republic	75	19	56
Czechoslovakia, former	25	5	20
Denmark	26	4	22
Dominica	36	23	13
Dominican Republic	3,309	2,215	1,094
Ecuador	2,321	686	1,635
Egypt	112	39	73
El Salvador	19,809	8,315	11,494
Eritrea	5	—	5
Estonia	24	3	21
Ethiopia	65	30	35
Fiji	60	28	32
Finland	15	D	D
France	189	40	149
Gambia	25	8	17
Georgia	52	21	31
Germany	187	80	107
Ghana	177	62	115
Greece	39	21	18
Grenada	48	29	19
Guatemala	29,378	9,359	20,019
Guinea	24	6	18
Guyana	219	166	53
Haiti	375	125	250
Honduras	24,611	10,358	14,253
Hong Kong	29	12	17
Hungary	88	10	78
India	869	172	697
Indonesia	306	43	263
Iran	55	10	45
Iraq	54	32	22
Ireland	103	20	83
Israel	309	51	258
Italy	197	62	135
Jamaica	1,475	1,161	314
Japan	46	16	30
Jordan	121	56	65
Kazakhstan	32	6	26

(Continued)

Table B.10d. Continued

Region and Country of Nationality	Total	Criminal[a]	Noncriminal
Kenya	140	54	86
Korea[b]	326	142	184
Kosovo	22	8	14
Kuwait	6	—	6
Kyrgyzstan	12	4	8
Laos	10	D	D
Latvia	32	5	27
Lebanon	145	56	89
Liberia	48	26	22
Lithuania	60	16	44
Macedonia	40	12	28
Malawi	5	—	5
Malaysia	51	18	33
Mali	30	4	26
Marshall Islands	16	16	—
Mauritania	13	—	13
Mexico	282,003	127,728	154,275
Micronesia, Federated States	64	60	4
Moldova	41	8	33
Mongolia	46	16	30
Morocco	67	37	30
Nepal	43	7	36
Netherlands	90	27	63
New Zealand	35	17	18
Nicaragua	1,847	794	1,053
Niger	18	4	14
Nigeria	348	179	169
Norway	13	4	9
Pakistan	295	74	221
Palau	11	11	—
Panama	183	122	61
Paraguay	39	8	31
Peru	1,047	409	638
Philippines	707	322	385
Poland	508	162	346
Portugal	179	81	98
Romania	155	56	99
Russia	209	86	123
Rwanda	5	D	D
Saint Kitts-Nevis	15	7	8
Saint Lucia	33	13	20
Saint Vincent and the Grenadines	25	18	7
Samoa	14	D	D
Saudi Arabia	35	10	25
Senegal	62	12	50
Serbia and Montenegro[c]	102	26	76

Table B.10d. Continued

Region and Country of Nationality	Total	Criminal[a]	Noncriminal
Sierra Leone	33	10	23
Singapore	15	8	7
Slovakia	61	18	43
Slovenia	10	3	7
Somalia	29	6	23
South Africa	56	12	44
Soviet Union, former	4	D	D
Spain	136	30	106
Sri Lanka	81	11	70
Sudan	21	15	6
Suriname	9	5	4
Sweden	47	8	39
Switzerland	12	D	D
Syria	48	16	32
Taiwan	56	17	39
Tajikistan	13	D	D
Tanzania	28	14	14
Thailand	104	24	80
Togo	16	6	10
Tonga	33	22	11
Trinidad and Tobago	368	261	107
Tunisia	27	10	17
Turkey	161	47	114
Turks and Caicos Islands	11	6	5
Uganda	26	10	16
Ukraine	160	58	102
United Arab Emirates	4	D	D
United Kingdom	481	201	280
Uruguay	164	64	100
Uzbekistan	76	17	59
Venezuela	369	133	236
Vietnam	35	8	27
Yemen	36	10	26
Zambia	22	5	17
Zimbabwe	29	5	24
Unknown	58	18	40
All other countries	106	39	67

Source: U.S. Department of Homeland Security, ENFORCE Alien Removal Module (EARM), January 2011, Enforcement Integrated Database (EID), December 2010.
[a]Refers to persons removed who have a criminal conviction.
[b]Korea includes both North and South Korea.
[c]Yugoslavia (unknown republic) prior to February 7, 2003.
"—" represents zero; D = data withheld to limit disclosure.

Index